90 Days to Success as a Small Business Owner

Barry Thomsen

Course Technology PTR

A part of Cengage Learning

Australia, Brazil, Japan, Korea, Mexico, Singapore, Spain, United Kingdom, United States

COURSE TECHNOLOGY
CENGAGE Learning™

90 Days to Success as a Small Business Owner

Barry Thomsen

Publisher and General Manager, Course Technology PTR:
Stacy L. Hiquet

Associate Director of Marketing: Sarah Panella

Manager of Editorial Services:
Heather Talbot

Marketing Manager:
Mark Hughes

Senior Acquisitions Editor:
Mitzi Koontz

Project Editor/Copy Editor:
Cathleen D. Small

Interior Layout Tech:
Judy Littlefield

Cover Designer: Mike Tanamachi

Indexer: Kelly Talbot Editing Services

Proofreader: Sandi Wilson

For product information and technology assistance, contact us at **Cengage Learning Customer & Sales Support, 1-800-354-9706**

For permission to use material from this text or product, submit all requests online at **cengage.com/permissions**. Further permissions questions can be e-mailed to **permissionrequest@cengage.com**.

All trademarks are the property of their respective owners.

All images © Cengage Learning unless otherwise noted.

Library of Congress Control Number: 2011922400

ISBN-13: 978-1-4354-5926-7

ISBN-10: 1-4354-5926-1

Course Technology, a part of Cengage Learning
20 Channel Center Street
Boston, MA 02210
USA

Cengage Learning is a leading provider of customized learning solutions with office locations around the globe, including Singapore, the United Kingdom, Australia, Mexico, Brazil, and Japan. Locate your local office at: **international.cengage.com/region**.

Cengage Learning products are represented in Canada by Nelson Education, Ltd.

For your lifelong learning solutions, visit **courseptr.com**.

Visit our corporate Web site at **cengage.com**.

Printed in the United States of America
1 2 3 4 5 6 7 13 12 11

This book is dedicated to all the hard-working, risk-taking, street-smart, and dedicated small-business people who make the business world successful. Never give up your dream!

About the Author

Barry Thomsen started his entrepreneurial career when he was only five years old. He decided that he wasn't going to sit for hours in front of his house and try to sell lemonade. Instead, he loaded two pitchers in his wagon, took them to nearby construction sites, and sold out in 15 minutes. When he got back home, his friends' pitchers were still almost full. At age 10, he was given the worst paper route because he was the youngest delivery boy, but he tripled the number of subscribers within a year.

Growing up on the south side of Chicago automatically meant Barry had to be street smart if he wanted a chance at prosperity. To make extra money when he first got married, he sold Amway and Avon products and a family-portrait program door to door. By working on his own, he learned firsthand the importance of great customer service. Then, working on commission at a computer-placement service, he became the number-two producer out of 40 people. To learn other types of businesses, he also worked part-time as a bartender at a bowling center, delivered pizzas, and rose to assistant manager at a chain pizza parlor. Next, he worked evenings and weekends at a family-owned Italian restaurant, where he learned food service and how to handle slow and busy periods.

By then Barry was ready to take the plunge and try his hand at a business of his own...well, almost. Along with another associate from the placement service, Barry opened an employment agency. But after a year or so, Barry wanted more, so he started a computer-supply distributorship at the same time. After building extensive mailing lists for both companies, he sold these to other non-competitors and did very well with three businesses going at the same time. Long hours and extra work have never bothered him.

As time went on and Barry's interests changed, he became an expert in old collector cookie jars—the rare ones worth hundreds of dollars each. He started buying and selling them nationwide by direct mail. (There was no eBay then.) Next, he started a business-forms company in the mid-1980s, which grew to more than $3 million in sales after 14 years. During those years, he also became a collector and seller of rare casino chips and authentic hand-signed Norman Rockwell lithographs. He bought and sold enough of these to purchase a second home in Colorado, where he now lives.

As more years passed and Barry gained more knowledge, he became a partner in a retail ice cream store and sold decorative Asian items at an antique mall. Then he started his current business, which sells plastic cards, scratch cards, and promotional items.

In his years in business, Barry has advised and helped many other small-business people to grow their startups. Barry found that he got a lot of personal satisfaction from helping others, so he started a monthly newsletter called the Idea-Letter, which has subscribers nationwide. He also started writing small-business articles, many of which have been published in magazines, in newspapers, and on the AMA website.

Barry decided to write several books to share all the good and bad experiences he has encountered along the way. He now enjoys traveling around the country and the world, speaking to groups about his many successes and what he has learned from his failures.

Barry knows firsthand that the life of a small-business person is not all fun and profits—it sometimes includes problems and even disasters. He loves small business, though, and although the road has been rocky at times, Barry wouldn't have it any other way.

Barry's other books include:

- *When the Sh*t Hits the Fan!: How to Keep Your Business Afloat for More Than a Year* (Career Press, 2007)
- *The Jelly Bean Principle: 105 Ways to Stand Out from the Competition* (Oak Tree Books, 2009)
- *Save Your Business: 25 Common Business Threats and How to Avoid Them* (Crimson Publishing, 2009)
- *23 Reasons Why Businesses Fail and What You Can Do about It* (Jaico Publishing)
- *The Smart Guide to Business Startups* (Smart Guide Publishing, 2011)
- *Small Business: A Love Story* (Expected publication late 2011)

Contents

Introduction. xiii

Chapter 1: In the Beginning 1
Getting Creative Ideas...3
What Are You Waiting For? 5
What Does It Take?..6
The Goals of Marketing 7
The Commandments of Business Marketing 8
Join Up 10
Common Business Mistakes...12
Action Plan..13

Chapter 2: Smart Guide to Startup 15
Home Business Setup...17
Small Office Startup...18
Your New Retail Store Location 20
Mission Statement...23
What's Your Marketing Plan? 24
Naming a New Business 26
Merchant Services for Credit Cards..27
Startup Blues: Nothing Will Happen without Marketing 29
Jump-Starting Your New Business before It Opens 30
Making a Wish List 34
Making a Bigger Impression 35
Working with Suppliers 36
Finding New Suppliers...37
Pursuing New Customers...38
Action Plan..39

Chapter 3: Franchises 41
What Franchise Should You Choose? 43
Where Do You Find a Franchise? 44
Questions about Buying a Franchise...45
The Franchise Agreement...48
The Franchise Manual 51
The Training Period..51
Big Brother Is Watching 52
Is There Any Risk?...53
Action Plan..53

Chapter 4: Advertising. 55

Setting an Advertising Budget...56
Advertising to Four Levels 57
Print Ad Copy Questions 58
Headlines...59
Hot Words 60
Where's My Ad?..61
Is It an Ad? 62
Competitors' Advertising 63
An Advertising Agency..63
Where's Your Business Card?..64
Sign of the Times..65
Do It Outdoors...66
Your Moving Billboard...68
TV Direct Response..69
Let's Try an Infomercial 70
Message on Hold...71
Piggyback—Cheap!...72
Co-Op Advertising 73
A Final Thought on Advertising 74
Action Plan..74

Chapter 5: Publicity 75

Publicity versus Advertising..76
Press the Press 77
Tips for Getting Publicity...79
If a Reporter Calls 80
On-the-Air Publicity...81
Publicity by Speaking 83
Publicity by Writing..84
Do Something Outrageous! 84
Action Plan..86

Chapter 6: Direct Mail 87

Mail Your Customers 89
Effective Direct Mail 90
Mailing Lists 92
Consumer Targets..93
Consumer Direct Mail 94
Business Direct Mail..96
Layout and Design 98
Evaluate Your Response...99
Direct Mail Timing...100
Co-Op Direct Mail..101
Action Plan..102

Chapter 7: Business Promotions 103

Coupons versus Rebates 104
Show Off Your Logo..105
Collaborate with Your Strip Mall Neighbors.......................................107
Special Discount Days and Nights 109

Fast-Food Delivery Convenience..110
Stick with Magnets..111
Sponsor a Nonprofit 113
Nonprofit Your Way to Profits...113
Cross-Promotions 114
Have a Contest 115
Don't Be Unoccupied...117
Celebrate Your Anniversary...118
A Weekend at the Mall..119
Some Other Fun, Profitable, and Outrageous Promotions 120
Action Plan..122

Chapter 8: The Website **123**
Purpose of Your Website..125
Some Design Ideas 126
Website Don'ts..127
Promoting Your Site...129
Lure Visitors Back with Interesting Bait 130
Order Follow-Up...131
Getting Attention 131
Don't Let Your Site Get Stale 132
Be Charitable 133
Social Media...133
Blogs 135
Don't Quit Your Day Job 136
Asking Permission First 136
Action Plan..137

Chapter 9: Pricing Strategies **139**
Pricing Headaches...140
Higher Prices!..142
Raising Prices 143
Lowering Prices 145
Pricing Strategies...147
Offer Platinum, Gold, and Silver Levels 149
Being the High-Priced Brand...149
Loss Leaders 150
Customer Quotes 151
Price and Quality 152
Prices on Window Items? 153
Action Plan..153

Chapter 10: Face-to-Face Selling **155**
What Is a Sales Professional? 156
The Decision Maker 159
Ears before Mouth 160
Some Good Things to Know 161
Don't Ignore the Advisors 162
Closing Signals 163
Make Lunch Pay Off...164
The Honeymoon Is Over? 166

Should You Take the Small Order? 166
Ready to Buy? 168
Your Personal Billboard 169
Break the Ice! 170
Play Your Cards Right 171
Dress for a Sale 172
Qualify the Buyer 172
Sales Rejection 173
I'm Still Waiting… 174
Ace in the Hole 174
Don't Lose More Than the Sale 175
No Ceiling on Sales Commission..176
Reduce Your Sales Staff 177
Be a Yankee Peddler 178
Action Plan...178

Chapter 11: Retail Sales 179
Why Should Customers Shop at a Small Store?........................181
Finding Retail Employees...183
Hiring Part-Time Employees 184
Entice Customers to Visit the Store 186
Be Customer Friendly 187
Customer Satisfaction 188
So You Want to Have a Sale 191
Overstocks, Deals, and Consignments 193
When Goliath Moves into Town...194
Why Offer a Discount? 196
Use Gift Cards...198
Offer a Big Selection 199
Senior Sales 199
The Unfriendly Customer...201
The Indecisive Customer 201
Impulse Buyers 202
Slow-Day Marketing Ideas...202
Hey, I've Got a Coupon! 203
Get Visitors' Business 204
Retail Payment Choices 204
Let Their Fingers Do the Walking 205
Store within a Store...206
Keep It Clean..206
Free Displays and Signs..207
Action Plan...208

Chapter 12: Business-to-Business Sales 209
Finding New Business 211
Respond Quickly..212
You Score Better in Your Ballpark 213
You Must Follow Up...215
The Lowest Bidder? 215
Be Their Associate Buyer 216
Reorder Reminders..217

All Your Eggs in One Basket 218
Taking the Order and Billing 219
Late Deliveries and Problems..220
Coupons, Bells, and Whistles 222
Host a Seminar..222
Letters of Recommendation 223
Problem Customers...224
Action Plan..225

Chapter 13: Tradeshows 227
Finding the Right Shows...229
Reasons for Exhibiting 231
Tradeshow Expenses 232
Selecting a Space...235
Getting Your Exhibit/Display...236
Generate Tradeshow Traffic 237
Working Your Booth..238
Lead a Seminar 240
After the Show...241
Getting the Most out of Attending a Tradeshow.....................242
Action Plan..243

Chapter 14: Telemarketing 245
Inbound Telemarketing...246
Outbound Telemarketing..248
Hiring Telemarketing Employees..250
Planning and Making the Call 252
Telesales Lead Finders 254
Cold-Call Fears 255
Voicemail Smarts...255
Is Telemarketing Paying Off? 256
Check the Laws 257
Some Final Telemarketing Don'ts..257
Action Plan..258

Chapter 15: Customer Loyalty 259
Get Close to Your Customers...261
Ways to Create Loyalty 264
Ways to Destroy Loyalty..265
Your Business Personality..266
What's Your Brand? 267
Customer Cards and Tracking...268
Loyalty Breeds Referrals 270
Tell How or Tell Who 270
A Doctor's Loyalty 271
Action Plan..271

Chapter 16: Customer Service. 273
Keep Your Customers..276
Wear Your Customers' Shoes...279
The Customer Is Angry 281

Customer Service Don'ts..282
Look Down to See the Profits..284
Rally the Troops...285
Reward Great Service 286
Employee of the Month 287
Don't Lock 'Em Out 288
Pay Attention...288
One-Hundred Percent Satisfaction 289
Transaction Time..291
The Good, the Bad, and the Real...291
Action Plan...295

Chapter 17: Financial Crisis. 297
Financial Crisis Planning 298
Know What You Need...300
Unemployment Numbers and You 300
Banks and Small Business 301
Hold Your Prices 303
Defer Debt..304
Reduce Fixed Expenses..305
Sell Off Anything..307
Keep Marketing 308
Network, Network, Network 309
Contingency Plans..311
Action Plan..312

Chapter 18: In the End. 313
Know Your Competitors..314
Cultivate Your Ideas...318
Risk Taking 319
Small-Business Networking..319
Cornucopia of Information 322
Buy Your Umbrella When the Sun Is Shining...........................324
Why Businesses Fail...326
Strength in Numbers..329
A Final Thought..331

Appendix A: Myths of Small Business 333

Appendix B: Additional Resources 337

Index 339

Introduction

Business success for many is the American Dream, and it is the goal of most entrepreneurs. But what is the American Dream, anyway? Is it having a loving spouse, a big house, a luxury car, and healthy, well-educated children, or is it having your own business? It's probably all of these and more. But they don't come easily; you have to work continually at improving yourself and your situation. In business—especially in small business—the more you know, observe, and are aware of, the better chance you have to be successful in today's competitive marketplace. Knowledge is power, and money will usually follow power. Knowledge will give you an edge as you strive to achieve success.

A million-dollar business and/or sales of a million dollars have long been benchmark goals for most small-business owners. But once you've attained that goal, you automatically create the desire for two million, three million, or much more. The first million is always the hardest to reach. After that, everything starts to fall in place, and the uphill climb is steadier and less stressful. Set your own goals and plan your road to get there. The lessons you learn while reaching this goal will carry you on to even greater achievements.

There's an old saying that money can't buy happiness, and that is true as it's worded. But money can buy things that make you happy. It can buy luxuries and the best healthcare available, and that makes many people happy. It can also let you support your place of worship and assist those less fortunate than you, and that, too, makes many people happy. When are you the happiest? Small-business owners should have their money goals near the top of their list, after family, health, and spiritual goals.

So why do people start small businesses in the first place? A small business can bring a constant stream of headaches, employee problems, money problems, customer problems, lost sales, and long hours. Who would knowingly put himself in a position like this? Do you wake up one morning and say to yourself, "I think I'll start a life of constant aggravation today." I may be exaggerating a bit, but every small-business owner (except the fraction who hit it big the first day and never looked back) has run into roadblocks along the way. But how you handle the roadblocks, detours, and dark tunnels determines the short-term and long-term outcome of your efforts. The lessons you learn along the way will stay with you forever. And small failures along the way are just valuable lessons learned that you can put to use in the future.

Successful business owners know that you have to put much effort and initiative into your business to get the desired results. Stay aware of what's going on around you all the time. You need to be working on your business physically or mentally 24/7/365. Even on vacation (if you're lucky enough to get one), you need to be open to new ideas you observe or encounter. Bring them back with you and find a way to apply them to your business. Learning from seeing and doing is the best teacher you'll ever have. Remember that Bill Gates and Sam Walton were once small-business owners just like you.

Much of what you need to know to be successful in a small business cannot be found in college textbooks. Textbooks are usually two years or so behind, and many teachers and professors never had to tough it out in the real business world. Observation and trial and error will give you the insight and ability to deal with many unplanned situations that come up when you're running your own business.

Don't think that because your business is successful and growing today, you can sit back, put your feet up, and just count the money. Being complacent in today's fast-changing business world is a mistake that you don't want to make. I can assure you that you're not the only one who knows about your business success; competitors and would-be competitors are working today to steal your customers and market share. If you just ignore them, you'll be playing catch-up later (or maybe sooner than you think). This doesn't mean you should run scared; it means you must always be trying to improve your products and services to keep a step ahead of the competition. And getting close to your customers to keep them coming back builds your business and helps you survive the tough times. Remember, if you aren't talking to your customers, someone else is.

Many years ago, when I was starting out in business, I thought I knew everything, as many young people do. I read a couple of books and watched the movie *How to Succeed in Business without Really Trying,* and I figured I was ready for the big time. Just open a business checking account, hire a receptionist, get an accountant, and sit back and watch the money roll in. Well, I quickly learned there's a lot more to it if you want to be a real success. You have to learn something every day and try new things regularly. Luckily, I struggled through and made it, but with a lot more effort and stress than I had originally planned. I was missing some of the basics that would have made the early journey easier. I was chasing success without really knowing which direction I was going. I was able to recover, but many others do not and never make it past the first year.

But what if you're already on top in your market, not just starting out? The same rules and principles still apply to find new and better ways of pleasing customers, creating value, and being innovative. So whether your business is just starting, growing, or maturing, a constant inflow of new ideas is essential to create and sustain success and growth. New ideas become old, and you always need more new ideas to keep traveling on the long road to success, because the road never ends. Success is a journey, not a destination, so keep your idea suitcases packed at all times.

The Perks

Being your own boss and owning a business allows you many perks you usually don't get when you work for someone else—especially if that someone is a large corporation. You can lease or buy any type of automobile your business can afford. You can locate your physical store or office anywhere you want to and move anytime. And even working at home is an option for many types of businesses. You can travel on business wherever you think you'll find orders and customers. You can hire the people you need to grow and promote them as you see fit. You can set your own work hours and even leave early when business is slow. You can earn a great income when profits are high, plus bonuses.

What more could you ask for? But don't forget all the hard work it takes to get there. The perks only come with success, which is never as easy to achieve as it sounds.

You'll be smarter, sharper, and more profitable if you don't take too many things for granted. Every industry changes constantly (look at computers and cell phones), so be ready. Your competitors will always be waiting to steal your customers; don't make it easy for them. Be mentally on the job all the time. It's been said that a nice thing about owning your own business is that you only have to work a half day—and you get to choose which 12 hours. But don't be afraid of long hours, because you will reap the benefits of them.

This book was written for hard-working, risk-taking business-people to review some of the basics and create new ideas. It's not to supply you with the forms and legal procedures to start and run a business; there are plenty of other books (and websites) that cover that information. This is a guidebook to help you develop your own unique plan of action to market your small and growing business. Without marketing and ideas to acquire and keep customers, you won't have a business. But your perseverance, tenacity, and drive will make success possible.

Most small-business owners spend the majority of their time running their business rather than growing it. The following pages contain hundreds of ideas that you can introduce into your daily routine today to keep your valued customers and attract new ones. There are a lot of ideas in list format so you can quickly and easily refer back to them. Mark the ones that will assist your type of business and refer back to them often. Focus on your goals, always watch your back, and build your business into something you're proud of. It's all waiting for you, and there's no better time to begin than today!

"When you see an entrepreneur with a new idea, join up or get out of the way!"

—BT

Chapter 1

In the Beginning

- Getting Creative Ideas
- What Are You Waiting For?
- What Does It Take?
- The Goals of Marketing
- The Commandments of Business Marketing
- Join Up
- Common Business Mistakes

Why do we do it? Why go through all the trouble of starting, buying, or inheriting a small business instead of having a comfortable position at a big corporation? Why worry about making your payroll instead of just being on someone else's? What is it that makes people want to own their own business so badly? Could it be the independence or the need to prove that you can go it alone? What happens after you prove all these things to yourself? Do you give up and go back to work for the big corporation? Or do you just keep going because you're too embarrassed to close your business and look like a failure? You keep working your 12-hour days doing all the little things that you should delegate and are miserable most of the time—but you can't let anyone know. Well, get street smart and be a real success. Owning your own business is supposed to be fun and fulfilling, not a depressing situation. You're supposed to love going to work every day, not hate it.

Is your business really worth what you're paying for it—the financial investment, your time, your effort, and all of the problems? Are you getting the return you expected? (And that doesn't mean just money.) If your business is not adding to your life, then it's taking away from it. You need to find a way to make your business work for you, not vice versa. You should spend more of your time growing and managing your business than working in it.

It's been said that a franchise company looks for new franchisees who have absolutely *no* experience in their industry so that they will manage and grow the franchise rather than work in it. If you're not going to manage your business, then who is? Will you have time to make decisions, perform training, and plan your overall growth strategy if you're waiting on customers all day? If not you, then who will do the marketing to bring in the customers you need to survive and grow? Who will keep track of your progress?

People often have the wrong impression about owning their own business. You may be an excellent car mechanic, baker, or tool and die maker, but are you also a good businessperson? Can you plan your marketing strategy to get new sales, repeat business, and long-term customers? Do you even have a marketing strategy? You may be the best carpenter in town, but if you don't promote your business constantly, how will anyone know about it? Just putting an ad in the yellow pages or online isn't enough; you need to use a marketing mix of promotions. Some will work and some won't— there is some trial and error involved. But in the end, you need to get new and repeat business today, tomorrow, and next year.

Getting Creative Ideas

Sure, marketing will take some of your time, but if you ignore it, your business won't prosper and grow. You need to be using, or at least trying, all of your creative ideas to make your business unique in your marketplace. But what are those creative ideas and where do they come from? Creative ideas will come to you when you least expect them. Always be ready and write them down. Here are some ways to make sure that you get those new creative ideas flowing:

- Be aware of things going on around you 24/7/365.

- Regularly read or scan all the business publications, trade magazines, and newspapers you can. Some offer free subscriptions, or you can check them at the library.

- Monitor your competitors. Check out their stores, websites, ads, and promotions.

- Attend at least 50 percent of the trade shows that pertain to your company and industry. *Find* the time to seek out new products and suppliers.

- Watch for changing market trends in your industry and in related areas.

- Observe big companies in your industry for changes and new ideas.

- Join trade associations and regularly read their publications, newsletters, and bulletins.

- Ask your customers what new products or services they want and find a way to provide these products or services profitably.

- In retail, watch demographic changes in your area and new businesses.

- Read business books and listen to self-help CDs and tapes.

- Ask your employees for their opinions and suggestions—they will have them.

- Ask suppliers what's new and coming or what's phasing out.

- Watch TV commercials (oh no!) and see whether you can get ideas for your business.

- Read the direct mail you receive for ideas you can use in your business.

- Listen instead of talking! Absorb all you can, all the time.

- Network with other businesspeople and exchange ideas.

Creative ideas can come to you anytime and anywhere. Have pen and paper or a recorder available wherever you go and on your nightstand. Once an idea is gone, you may not be able to recall it.

Here's a little exercise you can do to select your best ideas and decide which to try first. Take a piece of copy paper or a legal pad and draw a line down the middle vertically. On the left side, write down at least 10 new products or services you would like to add to your company. Ten should not be difficult—just think of what your competitors or related businesses are doing that you are not. Now, circle two ideas that would be the most appealing to your customers and that might sell right away. These are the ones you will want to try first.

On the right side of the paper, write down as many conditions as you can think of to bring these new ideas to market. These might be things such as cost of materials, new equipment, whether you can make it yourself or buy it wholesale, whether you need to hire more staff, how long it will be before it's ready to sell, what literature you need to print, what ads you need to place, what guarantees are necessary, mailings announcing availability, and so on.

Commit to trying new ideas for products and services at least twice a year.

Circle the conditions that are necessary for the two ideas you selected on the left side of the paper. Now you need to select the best idea to try first. Once you have made a commitment, stick with it until you see some results. Even the best new ideas take a little time to catch on. If you are convinced that you can't make a profit, then stop and go to the next idea, but don't give up too early. Make it a goal to try new ideas for products and services at least twice a year. Some will work quickly and some will not, but don't stop testing.

Your ideas could also be a way to enhance or improve current products or to find new ways of offering them. Regardless of how you look at it, you want the ideas to be working for your business. Don't just think about them—get them out of your mind and start using them. Use them before competitors come up with something similar and beat you to the market. If your competitors beat you to the punch, you'll be the follower instead of the leader, and the leader always gets the biggest share of the business.

Smaller businesses can use new ideas much faster than bigger corporations can; cash in on that advantage and make it work for you. Smaller businesses don't have to go through all the meetings and red tape to get an idea approved. They can test their ideas right away, and if an idea works, they can put it into the mainstream operations of their business right away.

There are customers out there right now waiting to buy your new ideas!

What Are You Waiting For?

I've started many small businesses and assisted in starting several others. If you're thinking and planning and thinking and planning, the one thing I can tell you is to get started. If you're going to do it, do it now! See where that first step takes you. You'll need to adjust as you grow, but if you have the basic concept, product, and plan ready, what are you waiting for? Don't tell everyone you know about your idea and plan and then sit back and let someone else beat you to it. Make the commitment and do it! If you don't get started now, you never will. Remember that the rewards in business don't come to you; you have to go get them. Chasing success is the only way.

It's up to you to go get the rewards in business! If you are dedicated and focused on your goals, they will happen automatically.

Many entrepreneurs start a second business using the location, office equipment, and resources of a first business. This works great and allows you to test the waters without diving in completely. I've done this many times, and it's easy to get out if the business isn't working the way you had planned. If you're starting a second or third venture, you can make it part of the original business or another independent business altogether. Just because you're using the office or store of the first business doesn't mean it has to be part of the same company. You're simply investing all the resources you already have and taking some of the burden off the new venture.

I've always believed that when you start additional businesses while owning and running another business, the new business should be a separate company as soon as possible. Within six months of the business's birth, I always open a separate checking account for the business at a different bank. This is important because it allows you to sell or terminate one business without affecting the financial resources of your other businesses. Speaking from experience, it's smart to know when to get into a new business, but it's even more important to know when to get out.

My words of advice are that if you're procrastinating about starting a business or adding a second business, stop wasting time and get started *today*. If you're young enough and you stay healthy, you can open and prosper in perhaps 10 or more businesses in your lifetime. Unless you're going to live to age 150, you'd better not wait any longer. Get those ideas to work and start reaping the rewards and the satisfaction.

What Does It Take?

Focus, passion, and dedication will give you the drive you need to succeed. Believe in yourself first and then in your business ideas. Then dedicate your skills to making it happen.

Not everyone can be an entrepreneur or a small business owner; some people just don't have the characteristics or qualities necessary. If you study or talk to successful business builders, you'll see many similar qualities among them. Without the majority of these qualities, success will be harder to achieve, if not impossible. Some characteristics you are born with and some you can learn, but desire alone is not enough.

Here are nine unique qualities that will serve you well in starting your small business:

- **Ability to sell your ideas.** You need to be able to get others to jump on the wagon to success and follow you because they believe in you and your pursuits.

- **Ability to accept risks.** Risk taking is a part of every entrepreneur's life. But being able to recognize a manageable risk that will still offer above-average results is necessary.

- **Persistence.** You need that keep-going attitude when the process is difficult, tedious, and boring. You must be able to see the light at the end of the tunnel and not give up.

- **Willingness to do what's necessary.** You must be willing to sacrifice your personal time and activities to complete business tasks. If you can't afford to hire someone, you have to be willing to do it yourself.

- **Ability to understand reports.** You must be able to use a logical approach to analyze the profit or loss numbers in your business. You'll have to read and use all financial information regularly. You should barely be able to wait to see your successes down on paper!

- **Ability to learn from experience.** You must be willing to admit that you don't know everything and continually seek and absorb knowledge. You have to be open to new information wherever you find it. Realize that even failure is a learning experience.

- **Ability to delegate and train.** You can't do everything yourself and be a big success. You must be able to educate others and trust them to grow with the business.

- **Strong curiosity.** You must look for new ideas that will be useful and profitable in the marketplace. You should want to know everything that's going on in your chosen field.

- **Willingness to face facts.** It's important to know when it's time to abandon a project and go in another direction. Don't throw money and resources at a losing venture. Instead, reorganize and try again.

Enhance the qualities you already have and pursue the ones you lack. If there are characteristics you just won't ever possess, you can always partner with someone who *does* have those qualities. Either way, successful businesses are built by people, not products.

The Goals of Marketing

If you want to increase sales (and profits) or market share, you will need to increase one or more of the four segments of your marketing. If one or more of these increases, sales totals will increase. Figure out which one(s) are easiest and best for your industry and then act on what you find.

- **More products.** Regardless of whether you have 10 or 10,000 things you can sell to your customers, find even more related items. If you manufacture a product, what else can you make with the same equipment you already have? Check with suppliers to find out about other products available for your retail store. Increase the products or services you offer by 10 to 20 percent, and sales will obviously go up, too. Ask customers what new products they want and find a way to offer those products.

- **More people.** Get more and new customers to buy your product or service. Everyone wants more customers and clients, but sometimes business owners fail to look at other groups than those to which they're currently selling. Take off the blinders and look beyond your current customer base to other prospects who can purchase from you. Research at the library or on the Internet can help you find new customer groups and market segments.

- **More often.** Advertising, dated coupons, promotions, or specials can entice people to purchase more often. A restaurant could offer a twice-a-week special, for example—the second time you visit in the same week, you receive a free dessert. An auto-service shop could offer a free tire-pressure check to get customers to stop in more often. Think of an idea for your business that will keep customers active and contacting you more often.

- **More money.** Oh no! Not raising prices! If your costs increase 6 percent, you can raise prices 10 percent or more to make more money. If you don't do it too often, there shouldn't be a lot of resistance, but you should be ready to explain your price increase when asked. You don't have to say how much your costs went up; you can just say it was for material, labor, or distribution costs. Most customers expect prices to increase occasionally and will accept an increase if it is done correctly.

Decide which of these four factors you can increase in your business and then plan your strategy. If you can increase two or more factors, your sales and cash flow will be that much more. Don't hesitate—do it today, and you'll see the positive results tomorrow.

The Commandments of Business Marketing

This section contains 13 commandments for your business marketing. However, don't just read these commandments only once. Set a specific time each quarter to review them with your senior staff. Decide which ones are in place and which need more work, and then take the necessary steps to follow up.

- **Thou shall know thy target customer.** You'll spend your advertising and direct-mail dollars wisely if you know exactly who you're going after and you use the correct media. Be constantly searching for new ways to reach your target market.

- **Thou shall provide excellent purchase follow-up.** Whether they're in your store, at a sales call, or on the phone, make your customers feel like the important people they really are. Make sure customers are pleased with their purchase and resolve any problems promptly.

- **Thou shall know what thy competitors are doing.** Shop their stores, surf their websites, watch their ads, and get on their direct-mail list, and you won't be surprised later. Find a way to provide better products or services than they are.

- **Thou shall go after free publicity often.** You can always think of something new or different to send a press release for—do it monthly. Write articles for or give speeches to your target market.

- **Thou shall deliver more than thou promises.** Surprise your customers and prospects by giving something extra—faster delivery, free refills, faster quotes, free upgrades, a small gift, and so on. It breeds loyalty, repeat business, referrals, and long-term customers.

- **Thou shall use a website and email.** If you're not a computer whiz, learn the basics so you can communicate in today's Internet world. Computers are here to stay, so get with it and get a website that promotes your business.

- **Thou shall reward customer loyalty.** Your repeat customers will keep you in business and make you grow. Show them you care and that you need them with rewards and discounts. Compile a preferred customer list so you know who these customers are by name.

- **Thou shall use advertising and direct mail religiously.** People won't remember your ad or mailings from three months ago; you need to remind them again and again. Spend the majority of your budget with prospects where you get the best results or the most responses.

- **Thou shall test, test, test.** The ad or direct-mail pieces you used last time may need to be changed, and your mailing list needs to be refined. Always monitor responses, and change your copy often so it doesn't get stale or boring.

- **Thou shall always look for new products and new markets.** Expand your prospect base and sell more products to your existing customers. Keep looking; they're out there! Check the Thomas Register and computer directories and search by category. Attend industry tradeshows regularly to see new products when they are first available.

- **Thou shall ask for referrals.** If you don't ask, you probably won't get them. Your current customers are great sources of new business. Ask for written testimonials you can use with other prospects and name-drop often.

- **Thou shall provide outstanding customer service.** Develop a relationship with your customers—know their names, their likes, and their dislikes. Demand excellent service from your employees and survey your customers to make sure they're satisfied.

- **Thou shall review the previous 12 commandments.** Review these commandments monthly or weekly to remind yourself how to build your business. Many of these rules are forgotten or overlooked if they are not visible all the time. Make a list on your computer, print it out, frame it, and hang it in your office and break room.

You can probably think of several more commandments that pertain to your specific business. Have brainstorming meetings with your employees to come up with methods to provide new products and better ways to serve your customers. Discuss them with your associates and your accountant. Goals are difficult to reach without a plan that works in your business. Make a list of goals, frame them, and hang them where you and your employees can see them.

Join Up

Join relevant associations to help network your small business.

As a business owner, you can become a member of a multitude of associations and organizations. They will all want you to join to get your "dues and views," but you can't possibly join them all—there are thousands of them. Many will find you and send you information via direct mail, or you can search the web for others. Just use the main word that describes your business and put "association" after it (for example, travel association, widget association, pizza association, and so on). A long list of results will come up; you can view their websites and send an email to the ones about which you want further information. Another source in your local library's reference department is *Gale's Dictionary of Associations*, which has more than 100,000 associations listed by category. When in doubt, ask the reference librarian for assistance in finding the type of association that will benefit you.

If you sell locally, the Chamber of Commerce tops the list, along with the Better Business Bureau. There may also be other businesses or retail organizations with members just like you. These organizations will have up-to-date information on local events that you may want to co-sponsor or participate in. Select two or three associations in your industry where you can exchange information on what's happening and what's coming up. There are also weekly breakfast or lunch lead groups where non-competitors exchange information about possible customers. Just search the Internet for "business meetings, your city," and several will come up. The Monday edition of your local paper should also list many of them in the business section.

Where else can you find what your competitors and their suppliers are doing? Most associations will want you to contribute information as well as attend their meetings and/or conventions. Be sure you have the time available or send a senior associate to make your investment worthwhile. You also need to consider whether the benefits of joining are equal to the cost and time invested. If you can't come out ahead or at least break even, then keep looking.

Another possible perk that comes with joining an association may be when and where they have their conventions. Are they business only, or do they tie in the convention with a vacation resort where spouses are welcome? You'll get reduced airfare and hotel rates and a possible tax deduction—but what you save will probably go to pay the attendance fees.

Pick your favorite and most useful association and try to attend some of their shorter interim meetings. Don't just go for social contact; you're there for business. Most organizations should let you attend at least one meeting before joining to see whether it's a good fit for you. It's probably a good idea to keep the number of associations you join to five or six, because as a small-business person, you have a limited budget and limited time available.

Another advantage of joining an association is that most will give you a personalized membership card and a plaque or certificate that you can hang near your business entrance. In many cases, you can also use their logo on your letterhead and product literature. If you find an association you really like, you can join a committee or even consider running for an officer position. You've heard the old saying that birds of a feather flock together—indeed, it's better than flying solo.

In the wide world of associations, lead-generating groups, networking clubs, and Internet forums, there's no reason to go it alone. Exchanging ideas, attending seminars, joining group discussions, and meeting new businesspeople can only benefit you and your business.

Common Business Mistakes

- **Trying to outsmart the market.** The market for your products and services will buy when and if it wants to. You can't force buying decisions; you can only persuade or influence. Don't attempt to make customers change their buying habits too quickly—it usually backfires every time. A classic mistake is thinking that you know what's best for your customers.

- **Loss of focus.** This is a failure to look at your customers' objectives, rather than your own goals. Your goals will be achieved when you first satisfy customers' wants and needs. Regardless of whether you're starting out, growing, or just trying to survive, don't underestimate the lifetime value of a customer.

- **Lack of marketing.** When things are going great and your business is growing, you must still focus on marketing. Markets, buyers, consumers, and the economy are constantly changing. What's great today may need rethinking tomorrow, so have a plan and work it.

- **Underestimating repeat business.** A growing business thrives on a customer's repeat purchases and orders. Do what's necessary to keep all of your best customers and to eliminate those who are holding you back. Repeat business costs you little more than great products, customer service, and a smile.

- **Poor customer service.** You may have the greatest product or service around, but if customers are not treated with honesty, promptness, and respect, they'll look elsewhere. Remind employees that without regular customers, their job isn't necessary. Customers will remember poor customer service longer than anything else.

- **Failure to test.** Most small businesses have limited funds for advertising and direct mail. Finding what works best before investing a substantial part of your budget will help you get the most out of your advertising dollars. Do tests on everything and monitor your results and responses. When you find something that works well, make the bigger commitment quickly.

- **Giving up on publicity.** If your publicity efforts have not been rewarded, find new ways or turn the job over to a PR firm. Free publicity is available if the approach and timing are correct. But you won't get any if you give up too soon or you don't try at all.

- **Failure to observe competitors.** Your competitors are looking to increase sales and profits, just like you are. If you ignore them and the changes they make, you'll be playing catch-up later. Be alert to all your competition and adjust accordingly.

- **Failure to change with the market.** What worked last year may need a face-lift this year. Don't get stuck in a rut and let your competition pass you by. The market will change with or without you, so jump on!

- **Not being street smart.** If you can't learn from your failures and your successes, you won't achieve the marketing savvy you need to really compete in your market. Street-smart lessons are learned by doing every day. Always figure out why something worked or didn't work and make a mental note of it.

Making mistakes and learning from failures is the best way to become street smart. But lack of common sense and making the same mistakes over and over will harm your business. So be aware of your errors and omissions and act accordingly.

So, why do we start a small business? Because we love it. The challenges, the successes, and, yes, even the failures. We love the control we have to use our own ideas and watch them grow. And we love the feeling we get from providing our employees with a source of income and accomplishment. You won't find these feelings in a position with a large corporation. Only your own business can give you the personal success and satisfaction many of us crave.

Action Plan

✓ Write down all your creative ideas.

✓ Determine whether you have what it takes to be an entrepreneur.

✓ Avoid the most common business mistakes.

"Your ideas and imagination are your best marketing tools."

—BT

Chapter 2

Smart Guide to Startup

- Home Business Setup
- Small Office Startup
- Your New Retail Store Location
- Mission Statement
- What's Your Marketing Plan?
- Naming a New Business
- Merchant Services for Credit Cards
- Startup Blues: Nothing Will Happen without Marketing
- Jump-Starting Your New Business before It Opens
- Making a Wish List
- Making a Bigger Impression
- Working with Suppliers
- Finding New Suppliers
- Pursuing New Customers

You finally made the decision, and there's no turning back now—you're finally going to start your own business. You'll be successful, make a lot of money, and travel all over the world. Why did you wait so long? This is going to be great! Your family and friends will love it, your employees will respect you, and your banker will have coffee waiting every time you come into the bank. Customers will be loyal and will stand in line waiting for you to open your doors every day. Could life be any better?

When you're finished dreaming, let's get back to reality and find out how you're really going to accomplish this. It's going to take a lot of hard work, long hours, aggravation, indecision, stress, and probably more money than you thought it would. But don't let me discourage you. When it works—and it will, if you do it right—it's the best feeling of accomplishment you'll ever have. And if you're not street smart before you start, you will be in a year or two.

So let's get started. If you want your best chance to succeed, you must make the total mental commitment to accomplish what you set out to do. If your attitude is "I'll try opening my own business," forget it. You have a better chance of success by putting all your money on one hand of blackjack in Las Vegas. *Trying* won't make it; *street-smart* dedication will. But when you see the dream in your mind and are willing to do what's necessary to achieve it, then you will accomplish it. So what do you do first to get you closer to your dream?

The first decision you need to make is whether to start as a home-based business or to rent office/retail space. Renting takes a real commitment because you'll sign a multiyear lease, and you may be asked to personally guarantee it. Even if you sell your business before the lease term is over, you'll still be the guarantor on the balance of the term. Many service-type business owners start from home until their business grows large enough to support paying rent or buying a building, so let's start with a home-based business. You must approach whichever plan you choose for your business's infancy in a very professional manner.

Home Business Setup

When starting or growing your home-based business, you will need your work area clearly defined and separate from your living and family areas. Find a room or build one in the basement, backyard, or garage that you can dedicate to your business and nothing else. The area must be separate (mentally and physically) from your personal living space. Let your kids know this area is off limits to them 24/7. If you're going to have a successful business, you need a professional business location. And if you use this area *only* for business purposes, you may even get a tax deduction. Check with your accountant for the current guidelines.

Separate your work area completely from your living area. If you're serious about your business, you need a place that's all business, where everyday day personal situations don't interfere.

Here are some important things to consider so you can make your home-based business a success:

- Close off your work/business area in some way from the rest of the house.

- Lock the office door when you're out or during non-business hours.

- Keep children and family members *out* of your business area.

- Use a modern phone system with multiple lines and voicemail for when you're busy or out of your office.

- Forward calls to your cell phone if you feel comfortable taking them when you aren't in the office.

- Get dedicated lines for your fax and Internet. (Your fax line shouldn't be busy just because you're using the Internet.)

- If you will accept credit cards, connect your merchant machine through your fax machine.

- An inexpensive air purifier will refresh musty and dirty air from a closed-in room.

- Install a closed-circuit TV system to watch your children, if applicable.

- Paint walls a light, neutral color. It can help avoid fatigue.

- Hang motivational posters or pictures on free wall space.

- Mount a dry erase or blackboard to keep schedules and appointments in view.

- Have a smoke alarm and a fire extinguisher *in the room*.

- Use a large wastebasket that doesn't need to be emptied daily.

With Internet websites being the base for many businesses, the business's physical location is less important. If you're going to start and operate a home-based business, you should put a lot of energy into creating an attractive and functional website. You need to generate a positive image for that all-important first impression.

- If you have space, get a water cooler so you don't have to keep leaving your office to refill your water glass.

- Use a radio or stereo for soft background music, but do *not* use a television.

- Buy a comfortable chair that swivels and rolls.

- Use locking file cabinets for records (and keep them locked during non-business hours).

- If you have room, a small refrigerator for drinks and snacks is a nice addition.

- Get an offsite mailbox with a street address. These are usually available from the UPS Store or Postal Annex.

If you have a vehicle with your business name, phone number, and slogan on it, don't just park it in the garage. Find a high-traffic area to park it, and you'll get free advertising. It's essentially your billboard with free name recognition, so keep it clean. Get a package deal at a local carwash or do it yourself regularly. A dirty van or truck doesn't show that you care much about how your business looks, and it's especially off-putting if your business has anything to do with food.

Never let a caller hear children crying or yelling in the background (unless your business is daycare)—that's an immediate turnoff. If you can't control it or you have a sudden emergency, just let your voicemail take the call. You can return the call as soon as things settle down. Your customers need to know they are working with a professional who puts their needs first. And if you need to take your child to the doctor or dentist during working hours, just say you have another appointment and don't explain further.

Clean and organize your home office regularly during non-business hours. You don't want to spend valuable customer-contact time looking for things that have been misplaced. Good office organization is key to quick and effective work habits. If you plan correctly, customers and clients won't realize that you are working out of your home. Make your home-based office a *business-only* room, and with hard work and a little luck, your business will outgrow it. But while you have it, it's all business.

Small Office Startup

When you are starting a business that requires an office outside the home (not a store), the beginning expenses can be somewhat overwhelming. You'll need all the office equipment, computers, and furniture. If you'd rather use your resources for marketing than for equipment, consider starting your small office in an executive-suites environment. This type of office space is usually small—one to four rooms—and is sometimes furnished. You'll probably need your own computer, but most other equipment will be available (for a fee, of course).

Such office suites usually provide a receptionist and a reception area that is used by all tenants. There should also be a conference room available for use on a reservation basis. This is where you'll want to talk to customers and prospective clients. Reserve it far enough in advance that there's no conflict with other tenants.

Make sure that the main door to the building is open and available when *you* need to work. Normally, you should have access to your office 24/7, but the reception area may only be open during normal business hours. Ask questions like these before you sign a lease.

Many such suites will also provide free coffee, a refrigerator, a microwave, and a break room with vending machines. There will also be a mailbox in the general area for your suite and a place for outgoing mail. Cleaning services and energy costs should also be part of the lease. Normally, you can get a lease as short as six months or one year, but anything is negotiable. Rent will be somewhat higher than for regular office space because of the services provided.

It's a good idea to talk to a few other tenants in the building before you sign a lease to see whether they're experiencing any problems, such as noise from neighboring suites. Generally, the only drawback to this type of setup is that you have little or no control over the receptionist or building personnel; they are *not* your employees, and they take orders from the building management only. So you'll have to learn to live with the rules until you're ready to move to a larger office.

When it's time to move to a bigger office, consider an older but well-kept building, because rent will be more reasonable than rent for an office in a brand-new building. Many such buildings will offer a common conference room, which can save you from paying for more space. You'll want to negotiate cleaning services to be included in your lease, which will normally run from two to five years. The longer the lease you sign, the more perks and better rates that can be negotiated into your lease.

Whatever you agree on will be in force for the term of the lease, even if the current owner sells the building. You likely will be asked for a one-month security deposit in addition to the first month's rent. If the building owner asks for more than a one-month deposit, I advise you to look elsewhere; you just can't afford

If you're starting a small office, consider leasing an executive suite. The ready-made space and services offered will take your mind off routine tasks and let you concentrate on building your business.

When you decide that you can't operate your business office from home, it is better to pay a reasonable rent than to risk losing business. You'll also likely find that your stress level will be lower and you'll be able to concentrate more on building your business.

to tie up that much money. Also, if you're not moving in right away, you can suggest that you'll pay the security deposit when you sign the lease and the first month's rent 10 days before you take occupancy.

You can also ask how long it will take to get your security deposit back at the end of the lease. And always ask for a right-to-sublease clause in your lease, in case you sell your business or want to move out early. If this is your first business lease, you may want to have a local lawyer review it and point out any technical information or fine print you need to consider. The normal fee for reviewing a lease for a small office should not exceed about $150, and if you're not familiar with reading a business lease, a lawyer may save you thousands in the future.

Your New Retail Store Location

A critical part of opening a new retail store is deciding where to put it. Most likely you will be renting, but a select few new owners will be able to buy. Either way, if you pick the wrong location, you'll regret it for as long as you're in this business. You could always move, but that means you'd have to pay for the build-out again and hope that your customers follow you. Also, consider the cost of moving and installing all your equipment. Obviously, if you do your homework first, you'll have less remorse later.

Take your time selecting the location for your new retail store location—a little forethought now can save you from picking the wrong place for your new venture.

Allow yourself enough time so that you're not rushed into taking a location that isn't exactly what you want. You'll want to be where your target customers can find you easily—not in an obscure location where they'll get lost and head for a competitor.

We've all heard the phrase "location, location, location," but can you really afford the very best location available? You need to decide what type of location you *need* and can *afford* to find a happy medium. Overextending your budget on rent is just as bad as choosing the wrong location. Your business may have its sales ups and downs due to seasons, economic factors, or other unexpected situations, and you must be able to pay your rent *every* month. So evaluate your best and worst sales periods when making your site selection, and make sure your budget can handle the rent.

Does your type of business need to be in a high-traffic area, or will customers look for you in the phonebook or on the Internet and drive to wherever you are? If you're planning a good-size store, you may be able to be the anchor in a strip mall a little off the high-traffic area. If you're the biggest store in a strip mall, you may be able to negotiate a few extra perks from the landlord and get the biggest spot on the monument sign. Or, is there a large national store near a location you're considering that will bring your type of customers into the area?

A good commercial realtor should be able to show you all the currently available spaces plus any that may be coming on the market in the next three months. Don't look at just one or two spaces and make a decision; look at *all* that are available. This will be your business home for several years, and you'll be spending a lot of time there. Take the time to investigate seriously.

Just because a space isn't empty today, there's no reason why you shouldn't consider it when it does become available. If it's a great location and a reasonable price, wait for it—you'll be happy you did. You'll only get one chance to make your decision on your new location, and once you sign the lease, the decision is made. After signing, though, forget about it. Don't second-guess yourself; just start building your business.

If you're opening a franchise, the franchisor should have someone assist you in finding a store location. If they don't, you may want to consider this when deciding which franchise to sign up with. The franchisor should physically visit any space you're consider-ing *before* you sign the lease. They can draw on their experience with other units in their organization. The franchisor should have as much interest in your success as you do and will be your best advisor on site selection.

You'll also want to check the demographics within a five-mile radius of your proposed location. This will tell you not only how many people are in the area, but also the type of people. It will show income level, education, age, and several other factors. You can then decide whether these are the customers you're look-ing for. A good commercial realtor should be able to provide these demographics at no charge and explain them in layman's terms. If your target customer isn't nearby, why would you want to locate your business there?

> Check the demo-graphics near your potential store and make sure your target customers frequent the area. Also see whether the area has been growing over the past five years, which will give you an insight into the future.

And then there's the mall: the one-stop shopping center where you can visit 150 or more stores in a single location. A place where you can shop and eat and shop and eat and go to the bathroom all in one trip. They even have benches where you can sit down and count how much money you have left. Most people who visit a mall stop at more than one store; it's too much of a hassle to go for just one thing.

I believe that many shopping malls will disappear in the future because of high expense and online purchasing. One concept that might work is turning them into retail condos that businesses can own and pay a management fee for common-area services. For most startups, the cost of rent and expenses is more than their budget can bear, so they look elsewhere.

However, space rental in a mall comes at a price. When considering a mall for your new store, realize that the rent will be 20 to 50 percent higher than that of your typical street location. See whether there any available spaces close to a large anchor store that will generate a lot of traffic past your store entrance. Other good positions are in the center where wings of the mall converge, on a corner, or near the food court.

Find out how many stores have recently left the mall, and if it's more than 10 percent in a year, this should raise a red flag. Find out why they left. If you can, find out who the stores are and call the person who was in charge of that location. There may be a general problem or a lack of interest by the mall owners that could hurt all tenants. You don't want to sign a lease and find unpleasant surprises later, so check out things in advance.

How does the mall look on the outside and the inside? Is it well kept? Do they decorate for the holidays? Do they have special events inside and outside that draw people? Visit some of the stores that are the size yours will be and talk to the owners. Are they making money? Do the mall owners or the landlords promote the mall on radio or TV? If it's located near an interstate or a major highway, is there an exit within a mile of a mall entrance? Is it easy to get into and out of the mall, and is there enough parking?

Location for a retail business is important, but some stores will have the same sales even if they're located around the corner. There is no prestige in having a fantastic location and a negative cash flow.

An all-important question is whether your type of store will benefit from mall-style shoppers. Sit on one of the benches and watch the people go by during the day and in the evening. Are these the kind of people who will shop at your store? Will they purchase your products? And most important of all, can you make a profit after paying all the expenses?

Most locations will also charge a triple net (taxes, repair, maintenance) or CAM (common area maintenance) fees in addition to rent that must be paid monthly or quarterly. These can be from 2 to 15 percent of the rent, and you need to compare them to those of other nearby locations to make sure they're in the ballpark. These charges generally cover common area maintenance, landscaping, snow removal, and costs for other services.

The things that the triple net covers should be itemized in your lease, so learn what they are. You should also get a quarterly report that itemizes all the CAM expenses. Most people consider this as part of the rent when planning expenses. Your rent will likely increase a little every year, so check the escalation amounts in your lease before you sign it. If the landlord's estimate for the expenses and taxes is lower than they really are, all tenants will get a final invoice after the end of the year.

Take your time choosing your location, because you're going to have to live with your decision and pay rent for a long time. A little advance investigation will give you much peace of mind later. If you are doing an expensive build-out, you may want to have a clause in your lease giving you first rights to renewal. This prevents the landlord from replacing you if business is very good in your current location and the landlord decides he wants a different (perhaps higher-paying) client in that space. You will have the first option to renew at the current rates so that you can protect your business location.

Once your location is selected, stop thinking about it—the decision has been made. It's time to get on to the purpose of your new business. Why are you in business, and what makes you different from all the other companies in the same industry? It's time to write your mission statement, which is your overall business objective.

Mission Statement

Why are you in business? Why should you make any money in your business? Why should any customers buy from you? What do you want to provide to your customers in the way of products and services? Why did you open or purchase your business in the first place? Does your staff know the purpose or mission of your business? A good mission statement will distinguish your company from all your competitors and give you and your employees the focus to attain your goals and objectives. If your only mission is to make money, you won't have much of a mission statement— and maybe small business is not for you.

You can use your computer to print signs with your mission statement and have them laminated at most mailing or office-supply stores. Hang several copies in your business or store, where your employees will see them every day. You can also display a general

Use simple, clear language when writing your mission statement.

mission statement for your customers. Keep the wording easy to comprehend so people with all levels of education will be able to understand it. You want everyone on your team to be working toward the same goals.

In our past ice cream and sandwich shop, we liked to think our mission was "to provide premium-quality specialty dessert and deli products in a *fun-to-visit* family atmosphere." When everyone in your business knows and understands your mission statement and goals, it's easier to work together as a team.

You can modify or adjust your mission statement as the business changes or grows in new directions; just inform everyone and explain the new statement. Your employees need to believe in your overall mission for the business and work to accomplish it every day. Make sure everyone is informed and headed in the same direction to achieve your business objectives. And by the way, money is not an objective. Financial rewards will come naturally to successful businesses.

When you have a clear mission statement, it's time to think about a marketing plan.

What's Your Marketing Plan?

Your marketing plan defines where you're going and how you'll get there. Many businesses will change their marketing plan often because of new ideas, market changes, and unexpected results.

Without a plan, how will you get there? Get where? You won't know without a plan, nor will you know when you've achieved it. Many small-business owners don't write down a marketing plan—they just want to have more sales than last year. But does more sales mean more profits? Not if payroll, rent, distribution, postage, and other business costs and expenses increase as well. Even a rough marketing plan is better than none—it's something you can refer back to often to see whether you're on the right track. Did you ever hear of a general going into battle without a plan? Or a football coach without a game plan? A homebuilder without plans? You need to define to yourself and to your employees where you're going and how you're going to get there. Without it, there's no telling where you'll end up.

Here are five steps to help you set up your marketing plan and then work with it:

1. **Define your objectives.** Make your objectives challenging but still within reach. It's useless to plan to double sales when in the past your best annual increase was 20 percent. Perhaps you want to add new products or services, or move to a larger distribution center or a bigger store?

2. **Establish a time limit.** When do you want to reach these objectives? Setting a time limit that is too short or too long will not give you accurate results. Try selecting six months, one year, or a selling season. Make your time limit reasonable and possible to achieve.

3. **Identify your target market.** Define your customers and where they are. For a retail store or restaurant, they might be shoppers or diners within a five-mile radius. For a mail-order company, it could be the entire U.S., North America, or the world. And who are these customers? Teachers, consumers, engineers, homeowners, manufacturing firms, insurance companies, bookstores—whoever is most likely to purchase your products or services. Do you want to expand your customer type and add new groups? If so, decide which ones you will pursue.

4. **Plan a marketing mix.** How do you want to achieve your objectives—by advertising, direct mail, telemarketing, signs, in-store classes, coupons, or press releases? Decide on the best strategy that is in line with your budget and then follow through. Test different approaches and expand on the ones that show the best results.

5. **Analyze and review.** After you start working with your marketing plan, you need to watch the results as you go. Is your business progressing toward your objectives the way you planned? Do you need to make adjustments or change your marketing mix? Do your employees believe in your mission statement, or do you need to make some changes?

You can't just go into business and say that you'll sell anything customers want to buy. Who are these customers, anyway? Have a startup plan for what you are planning to sell and to whom.

You may want to consider also writing a long-term marketing plan for three to five years out. This will include several of the aforementioned short-term plans. You can alter the longer-term plan as conditions change and new opportunities arise. You can keep changing your plan as often as necessary to keep up with the times, but you'll have nothing to change or review if you don't write the initial plan. Make everyone in your business aware of any changes as soon as you make them. Include everyone in your marketing plan—you won't reach your goals if you don't involve everyone.

Naming a New Business

Selecting a new business name that's short, descriptive, and easy to remember can be a real challenge. Or, you may want to start a new branch of an existing business, but that new branch needs a separate name. Where do these names come from? Who thinks of them? Large corporations hire agencies to name new ventures—for this, they spend more money than you want to know. But a small-business owner can easily save that money and name the business himself or herself.

Start by writing down words or phrases that define your products or services. Check a thesaurus to find more words related the ones you come up with. From this list, start combining the words until you see a word or phrase you like. But don't stop there; you need several choices before you can make a final selection. If you can combine words, then try to use the acronym to make another word, and you've got a real winner. For example, what about Real Insurance Specialized Knowledge, or RISK. Have friends and associates look at your final list and give their opinions.

A name that's short and descriptive is the key to being remembered.

After you select one or more names you're happy with, conduct a search on your computer to see whether the name is being used by anyone else. You should also check the online yellow pages. If the name is too similar to that of another company, you'll need to change part or all of it.

Your final step before you start using your new name is to have your lawyer do a complete name search—this can be done on a state or national level. This will keep you from having to change your business name later if a business with a similar name threatens you with a lawsuit.

Above all, make sure you're really happy with your new business name, because you don't want to have to change it later. As the business grows, you may want to consider getting a trademark or service mark to protect it. Most of the time a small TM or SM after the name will deter others from using it, and after several years it may hold up in court because of continual use. But you could also have your lawyer file the papers to make it official if your business is growing rapidly.

Merchant Services for Credit Cards

One task that is required when you open a new business or an additional location is setting up your system to accept credit cards. All types of businesses accept credit cards now, and you likely will lose some customers if you don't. Most bank debit cards will also work through this merchant system. In fact, these days most merchant services will even let you use gift cards on the same machine.

In today's marketplace, accepting credit cards is a must. The percentage you pay to accept them is minimal for the additional business you receive.

There are three components to complete this process and get your merchant system up and working:

- The application
- The physical machine
- The software

The application consists of your basic company and owner information, which must be approved by the merchant service provider's main office. The best place to look for a service provider is the bank where you have your checking account. You can also check rates and fees at other providers, but be very cautious of many of the unsolicited calls you will get. Always compare the transaction fees, the startup charges, and the early cancellation fees. These can vary widely and may be spelled out in the small print on the contract. If in doubt, just ask the representative to show you exactly where they are in the contract.

I always like to work with a company that has a local representative I can meet in person. Remember that you are obligating your company and yourself for the term of the contract, and due diligence is necessary. You should also use a provider that can troubleshoot your service for any problems 24/7/365 via an 800 number. Ask for references and check them if possible.

Accepting credit and debit cards is an essential part of doing business with consumers and other businesses. Always know about the merchant service you will use and what *all* of their charges will be. The safe and smart way is to consult your bank before you sign a contract with anyone.

The next step is to acquire a credit card machine to do all the processing. The service you are signing up with will have a couple of different ones available, and most new applicants just buy or lease them there. But wait—there is a better *and* cheaper way! You don't have to buy the machine(s) from the service provider. For our last business, we found out the models we could use that would accept the software and went looking and comparing prices. We found

MerchantWarehouse.com had what we needed at 40 percent less than the service provider was offering. This can be a big savings, especially if you need more than one machine. Merchant Warehouse is just one such company—you can find others as well. This is not an official endorsement of them, but they did a good job for us. You can order online or by phone and pay with a credit card, and they ship within 24 hours if the item is in stock.

You will need a separate, dedicated line for the machine that is not connected to your regular phone lines. We use the fax and credit card machine on the same dedicated line because seldom do we need both at the same time.

Getting your processing software should be the least of your worries, because the service provider you have selected will download it over the phone lines. Because your representative from the service provider either makes a commission or has a quota, let them do the software download for you. It usually takes 15 to 20 minutes, plus the several steps to get the software started. Before you sign the contract, tell the rep that you want him to come to your business and do this for you. Also request that he instruct you and your staff on how the system works.

You should also get a verbal commitment that the rep will be available for at least the first 30 days to personally assist you with any problems or questions. You don't want the rep to tell you to call the customer service number and wait on hold forever.

Accepting credit and debit cards is a necessary part of most consumer and business sales. You can decide whether you want to accept only MasterCard and Visa or also add American Express, Discover, and others. Your lowest processing rates and fastest deposits will be from MasterCard/Visa. However, if you are marketing higher-priced or luxury items, you may need to consider accepting the other cards as well. Just find out in advance how much each transaction will cost you and how quickly the money will be in your account. Most banks will deposit the money from MasterCard/Visa charges at 12:01 a.m. the following day. American Express usually takes three days and charges a higher fee. But you should confirm all of this in advance of signing the application or contract. Credit card payments can be fast and easy for both sides of the transaction, but as with anything else in business, you must do your homework first. Search until you find the best rates *and* the best service.

Startup Blues: Nothing Will Happen without Marketing

You're opening a new business. You've rented the office or store and ordered the furniture and equipment. You've received your business cards, letterhead, and other forms. You've hired and trained your staff. You've turned on your "Open" sign, but no one comes in or calls. What happened—where's the line outside your door? Did you forget something? What about the marketing? Did you do enough or any?

No marketing equals no customers. If potential customers don't know who you are, where you are, and what you have to offer, why should they consider buying from you?

Everything else is useless without customers, and you'll have no customers if you don't do any marketing. You need to devote at least 20 to 25 percent of your startup budget to marketing. You must tell your target customer group who you are, what you do, and why they should buy from you. And you must tell them over and over again. You need to plan well in advance of your opening so you can have some potential customers excited and waiting for your grand opening.

Here are some marketing ideas to help you get started:

- Take out a yellow pages listing or ad (but don't overspend on this, because many people now find what they're looking for online).
- Have your website up and ready.
- Send direct mailings to potential customers.
- Distribute coupons or special offers.
- Send press releases to newspapers and magazines, as well as radio and TV stations.
- Create and hang Opening Soon banners.
- Pass out flyers (or menus, if your business is a restaurant).
- Hand out business cards.
- Join a leads exchange group.
- Find cross-promotion partners.
- Place ads in papers or trade journals.
- Join the Chamber of Commerce.
- Host an open house.

- Use the Welcome Wagon service. (The Welcome Wagon visits new homeowners and businesses and offers information and coupons for local businesses.)
- Use billboards and posters to advertise.
- Make sure you're listed in web search engines.
- Tell everyone you meet about your venture—in other words, network.
- Place ads in church bulletins.

Set a projected opening date so your new customers will be ready when you are! Post or advertise your open-for-business date for the most exposure.

You're almost ready! Now you need some street-smart ideas to jump-start your opening.

Jump-Starting Your New Business before It Opens

You have started marketing your own business, and you hope to be a big success. You've made the commitment, spent all your savings, spent your investors' money, taken out bank loans—now what? Do you have all the customers you'll need to be successful, just waiting for you to unlock the front door and turn on your phone? You'll need customers right away—a lot of them!

You need to have customers waiting before you even open for business. Start marketing to them before *you open your doors.*

Getting customers is the most difficult part of opening a new business. You have no past customers, no prospects, and no referrals—and you will need all of them. As your business grows, these will all fall into place and form a foundation on which you can build.

Marketing and sales promotion should start *before* you are ready to officially begin your business. Once you've made your decisions on store layout, office construction, and/or home business equipment, it's time to start getting those first customers, who are so important to all new businesses. Without them, you'll have bills to pay and no money coming in to pay them. Your startup capital will be depleted very quickly without a decent cash flow in the beginning. Don't let this happen to you! Go after customers early and use several different methods to see which work the best.

Here are some ideas to consider and have in place *before* you actually open for business:

- **Have a toll-free number.** It can feed into voicemail or your home phone number so customers/prospects can ask questions and request information. Later, you can have calls go to your office or store phone, where you can answer them during business hours. A toll-free number can make your business seem larger than it really is.

- **Get your email started.** Send email to—and receive it from—prospective customers to create interest for your opening day.

- **Start direct mail.** Send letters, flyers, menus, and so on to your biggest pool of prospects in advance. You can do this yourself on a smaller scale or turn the task over to a mailing house that can select the correct lists of prospects and do the entire mailing for you. This first mailing will make future customers aware of you, create some sales, and make it easier to contact customers later.

- **Offer free literature.** Use response cards, email, and a toll-free number from which prospects can request free information. Your literature should explain what your company is all about and why people should buy from you. Describe products and services that will be available and explain how they are different from and better than competitors' products or services.

- **Set sales appointments.** Set sales appointments in advance, so you're busy visiting prospects from day one. You can use your home phone to set meetings with the most receptive prospects. If you have friends with businesses, offer to pay them for a desk and phone until your office is ready. If the sales appointment is more than a week in advance, you can mail a postcard a few days after your call to remind the customer of your appointment.

- **Start telemarketing.** You, your staff, or an outside firm should start calling your most likely prospects as soon as possible. Tell them about your new business, when it will open, and why they should be your customers. You can also accept advance orders if you know what your prices will be. However, don't promise delivery or store pickup unless you are absolutely sure you can do it. You don't want to break your first promise to a customer.

■ **Announce introductory offers.** Entice people to try your new business with special offers, but don't give away the farm—it will cheapen your image. Make offers that you can afford and that prospective customers will value. Always set a time limit or an offer-end date, or else your introductory offer will become your regular offer. You want people to try your product or service and then return to buy at regular prices.

■ **Offer gifts.** Include something extra for the first 100 or 500 buyers to get the cash register ringing. Everyone likes to get a gift as long as it's usable and has some value. Try to find things that relate to your business either directly or indirectly. After you open, you can have a special prize for the 1,000th or 10,000th customer and make a big deal about it.

■ **Have a contest.** Offer a contest with no purchase necessary to get people to try your product or listen to your sales pitch. Be sure to follow all state and federal rules. It's wise to offer one big prize to attract attention and several smaller prizes so there will be more winners. If you're having a drawing, announce the time and day far enough in advance that you can have as many people in attendance as possible—they may make a purchase while they're there. Make the contest duration short—four to six weeks is desirable—and enter any names on a mailing list when it's over.

■ **Offer a free trial.** Get prospective customers using your products by giving away free samples. Nothing sells better than the actual product or service, especially when the user doesn't have to pay for it. If it's as good as you say it is, it should sell itself. Don't provide such a large sample that it supplies all the customer's needs for a long time—you want the customer to purchase more as soon as possible.

■ **Place advertising early.** You'll want your print ads to be out when you're ready for business, and many publications and magazines have a one- to two-month lead time. This is the time for any introductory offers or grand-opening sales to be in buyers' minds. Always check with the publication to find out when the ad will actually hit the public. Often the November issue will be released the second week of October, for example, so be sure to ask when the issue will be out.

- **Send press releases.** Find something newsworthy about your opening and send it to newspapers, magazines, trade journals, radio, and TV at least a month in advance of your opening. They may be interested in a revolutionary new product or even a contest if the prize is unusual. Read the inside pages of related publications to get ideas from what they are printing.

- **Offer a free consultation.** This consultation should include quotes, estimates, samples, and advice. Get that face-to-face contact and close the sale. You can do consultations in your store, at your office, or at a neutral meeting place for breakfast or lunch. Promote your expertise in your field to create confidence in these first customers.

- **Hold a seminar.** Make the seminar free and convenient and include demonstrations and an informative agenda. About 60 to 90 minutes is enough to create interest in your new business, and much longer than that may have the opposite effect. You can also learn what new products or services your attendees are interested in and find a way to offer them.

- **Stress your guarantee.** Make a big deal about your guarantee so first-time buyers can feel comfortable—no one likes to be a guinea pig. Some customers may be apprehensive when it comes to a new business because of past experiences. You need to assure them of your commitment to the highest standards and back it up.

- **Offer cash discounts.** Gifts or discounts for immediate payment in cash can increase your short-term cash flow and make your purchasers feel as if they received a good deal. If you can't ask for the total amount in advance, try requesting a 50 percent deposit on the first order and the balance on delivery or within 10 days. Any money you receive early will help with expenses and paying suppliers and any employees you have.

- **Start networking.** Go to all the meetings you can—find them listed in your Sunday or Monday newspaper. Bring plenty of business cards and give them to as many people as possible. Explain how your new business is different from your competitors and ask for referrals or permission to call for an appointment. Always keep at least 10 business cards with you.

- **Offer advance-order specials.** Offering extra quantity, discounts, freebies, and/or free delivery can result in a pile of orders waiting for your first day. You may make less profit on these orders, but you'll have a cash flow, which is extremely important in any new business. Offer whatever you can to get those orders without taking a loss. A small profit is better than no customers at all and will build loyalty plus word of mouth.

- **Teach a class.** Local colleges and business schools have short-term classes and clinics in various subjects. Offer your services in your field of expertise for little or no pay. People in your sessions will want to know your current business, and it may produce some new customers.

A new business that waits until the day it opens to start promoting will have more expenses than sales. Why not have cash flow from early sales by using all the ideas available? The sooner you start promoting, the sooner you'll see results.

You want to create a sense of urgency for prospective customers to act now—they may lose the offer if they don't act quickly! The early new business and customers will give you much-needed cash flow and will increase your chances of success. Be aware that special offers, contests, and discounts will reduce your profits on the beginning orders, but this loss can be made up with repeat business. It also starts the *free* word-of-mouth advertising working. Don't overlook or set aside the task of getting those first customers—they are very important.

Making a Wish List

When starting a new business, you may not be able to purchase everything you would like to have; you may only be able to afford the things that you *must* have. You can make a wish list of items and services to consider buying as your business starts growing.

Better yet, make two wish lists—one for you, the owner and manager, and one for your employees. You probably won't be able to buy everything you want when starting or growing a newer business. With the resources you have, buy the things that are essential to effectively run your business. Undoubtedly, there will be several other items or services that you know will help you be more efficient or will reduce your workload, but you just won't be able to afford them right away. So make a prioritized list of what you really want or need and keep it handy.

A business owner/manager's wish list might include items such as an extra computer, a new company car, new office carpeting, a new copier, or a monthly accounting service instead of a quarterly one. If the item is something you can't do without or you must have now, you'll have to borrow or set up a lease to get it. Otherwise, wait until you have extra profits or a great quarter and buy it with cash.

Prioritize your wish list so that must-have items are among the first you acquire.

An employee's wish list might include such things as a microwave, a comfortable chair, a refrigerator, a new sound system, or a holiday dinner at a local restaurant. Let employees know that their customer service and care will help them earn those things on their wish list. Allow them to add new things to the list if at least two employees agree to it. Post the list in your break room or in employee restrooms, where your staff can see it regularly, and it will inspire them to do their best job.

Don't forget to add some sort of new marketing to your wish list so you can pursue even more profits. Take a little off the top and use it to test ideas for getting new customers and increasing the loyalty from your current customers. You could even have a third wish list of marketing, direct mail, or advertising ideas that you want to try. If some of your new ideas work, you'll have even more sales and profits in the near future. Creating wish lists can provide short-term rewards for all the hard work that you and your employees put into your business.

Making a Bigger Impression

Many consumers and businesses may be reluctant to be the first customers of a new, untried business. But there is no reason why you have to let them know you are a small business with little or no track record. There are ways of making your new business look larger than it really is, and this is a reasonable strategy as long as you are providing the great products and services that your customers are interested in buying.

Here's an idea to make your new business look bigger and more established than you really are: Instead of starting your invoice numbers with 0001 or 1001, try using five digits and a starting number like 22001. It will look as if you've been in business for a while and have had a lot of customers. You can do the same thing with purchase-order numbers so suppliers won't realize that you're too new. Suppliers and manufacturers consider a new business a higher risk and may require prepayment or a deposit. I would never suggest lying, but creating an impression of a more established business will make a new business run more smoothly.

If you have delivery trucks and vans, number them Van #6 or #12, even if you only have one. That way, you'll look as if you have a fleet of vans and a lot of business. No customer likes to be the test case when there's no track record for the business. Try to give the impression, even if you're new, that you have many satisfied customers. You'll create a more comfortable feeling for those first buyers and suppliers. And when you serve your new customers well, word-of-mouth advertising will start on its own. You can also consider pricing a little lower for the first few customers so your team will gain some quick experience in processing orders.

Working with Suppliers

You'll need to open accounts with manufacturers and distributors to acquire the products you want to resell. Or, if you're manufacturing yourself, you need raw materials and other items. Even if you're going to open a service business, you'll need some supplies and office equipment.

Honesty is always the best policy when dealing with payments to suppliers.

Most businesses purchase these items and products on credit and pay in 30 days to conserve cash and use their resources effectively. But starting a new business raises a red flag because many suppliers have lost money on new businesses that closed quickly and never paid their invoices. So when you're opening new accounts, be prepared to pay something in advance for your first few orders or to make a preorder cash deposit. This will ease as time goes on and you establish a favorable track record. You will get a small credit limit, and it will gradually increase the longer you are in business and pay on time.

One way to use credit and still satisfy the supplier is to apply for company credit cards. This will give you 25 to 30 days of free credit if you pay your balance in full. Some company cards will even give you a small cash reward or allow you to earn miles for free travel. Keep in touch with your suppliers and don't be afraid to inform them of slow times or if you will be a little late on any payment. And if you can't pay in full, a partial payment will buy a little more time. Straightforward honesty will keep your account in good graces. Remember, you need them as much as they need you, and long-term relationships will always help your business grow.

Finding New Suppliers

When starting a business to sell products, you may have an idea of who you want to buy from wholesale. But are they the best source with the best price and delivery? Can they supply all the products you want to market, and do they continually come out with new, improved, or related items? (The more related products and add-ons you can sell to your regular customers, the more profit you'll make.) Will they deliver on time or offer rush service if necessary? When you need new products or more competitive costs on large orders, where do you find them? This is always a challenge, but if it were easy, everyone would be in your business. Finding the best suppliers can be the key to a successful, growing business.

Make a list of what products or services you're looking for and always be on the lookout for new suppliers. Don't stop looking when you find one; keep looking to see whether there is a better supplier with better costs and products. Here are some ways you can start your search:

- Scan industry trade publications.
- Ask at your Chamber of Commerce.
- Visit tradeshows in your industry.
- Ask current suppliers about non-competitive products.
- Search company directories in your local library's reference section.
- Search online directories by industry.
- Search the Internet by keywords and phrases.
- Look in your local and large city phonebooks.
- Check out associations for your industry.
- If you know someone with a similar product, ask where he or she got it.

Always be on the lookout for new and better suppliers to enhance your product offerings for your customers. As your volume increases with current suppliers, ask for better discounts, prices, and delivery options. Remember that they need you as a customer who will buy continually from them.

Always be on the lookout for new suppliers.

Finding new suppliers for products you want to sell can give your new business a big boost and may save your business if your products are becoming obsolete. What you're looking for is likely out there; you just need to find it. If it's hard for you to find, it will also be difficult for your competitors to find. And many of your competitors won't have the perseverance to keep looking.

You can also ask any suppler if you can have an exclusive right to sell their products in a certain area. They may not agree right away, but you may be able to work out an agreement when you reach a specific sales level. Many new businesses will find a better way to market an existing product (or a private label) and become successful quickly. But you must be aggressive with your marketing to achieve these goals. New suppliers often have new products that will allow you to expand your market and pursue new customers.

Pursuing New Customers

Finding new customers is a pressing need for any business, but it is especially so for a new business. Think of all the sources to find new customers and use all the methods and tools you have available to go after them. Some customers will only be casual shoppers, and others will become loyal regulars; you need both to survive and keep your cash flowing in the early stages. Even the best and largest businesses lose customers who move, change jobs, change interests, and so on. You will need to replace customers regularly and add more so your business will grow and survive.

Your expenses will continue to increase, so you must keep increasing sales to stay ahead and prosper. Getting new customers is absolutely essential for any startup business to survive. Make it your top priority every day by finding and testing new marketing ideas. Never feel confident that because business is good today, you don't need to attract more customers. This mistake could cost you dearly when there are quick economic changes that you didn't foresee.

Without a constant flow of business from new customers, a company can quickly come to a standstill or, worse, show negative growth. There are always new people you can sell to, but you need to pursue them. Have an ongoing marketing program to attract new buyers and be on a constant search for new target markets.

Keep testing until you find areas to which you are not currently selling. The following chapters in this book will provide many ideas you can use for marketing and sales.

Action Plan

✓ Decide whether you will be an in-home or an outside-the-home business.

✓ Find a business leasing agent and explain your startup goals.

✓ Check the demographics of your target market.

✓ Write your mission statement.

✓ Decide on your marketing plan.

✓ Choose a business name that's easy to remember.

✓ Find your primary suppliers and backup suppliers.

"Starting a small business is like going into a lion's cage with a small whip. It's your positive attitude that will keep you alive."

—BT

Chapter 3

Franchises

- What Franchise Should You Choose?
- Where Do You Find a Franchise?
- Questions about Buying a Franchise
- The Franchise Agreement
- The Franchise Manual
- The Training Period
- Big Brother Is Watching
- Is There Any Risk?

If you want to be a business owner, but you don't want to go it alone, a franchise can be an excellent alternative. Established franchisors feel as if they have perfected an almost surefire success plan in a given industry. They may or may not own stores or businesses themselves in the franchise organization.

When franchisors sell you their plan and their idea, they expect an ongoing return for their information. This return is called *royalty*, and it is usually paid monthly or quarterly, normally based on sales volume. Regardless of whether you make a profit, the royalty is due. That's why it's based on sales instead of net profit—these people aren't stupid! Generally, they won't guarantee that you will even make a profit, but they will show you other franchisees' past performance.

A franchise is great for most people, but headstrong entrepreneurs can have problems with them. They can't handle the corporate direction and the need for permission to try new ideas. Such entrepreneurs would be better advised to take the risk of opening a business on their own.

There are many laws governing what a franchisor can tell you, so if one guarantees you'll make a big profit or income, you should quickly slam the door and go on to the next one. Profits are usually made by following the plan exactly and adding your own hard work.

The growth of the franchise industry in the last few decades has been explosive. Just look up and down any busy street in your town and count the franchises. I'm not just talking about fast food—it's everything! But remember, just like a marriage, it's a lot easier to get into a franchise than to get out of it. When you pay your franchise fee and sign the agreement, you're part of their family. Make sure you're comfortable with the people at the top and bottom of the organization. Give yourself *all* the choices before making the final decision. And don't let anyone talk you into a specific company—*you* make the final decision. Just be sure you don't think you can change your mind later and easily switch to another franchise. It just doesn't work that way.

Do all your homework to make sure you select the right franchise the first time around.

There are books and magazines that list hundreds of different types of franchises, their sizes, necessary phone numbers, and the investment needed. Check your library or your local bookstore's magazine rack and do some comparisons. Numerous websites also offer information. Just search for the term *franchise*, and you'll find a lot to check out. The more information and knowledge you acquire in the beginning, the more likely you are to succeed.

One consideration when choosing a franchise as your business is that there are rules and guidelines that you must follow. You're not an employee, but you have to go along with the gameplan. There are specific ways of doing things, mandated décor, reports to file, and guidelines that you will be expected to adhere to. You may also be restricted as to what you can sell, what to charge, and how you can accept payment. These are all parts of the proven success pattern and will be in the contract you sign. Some franchisors are more lenient than others, so you need to discuss what's expected and whether you can live with it. The following section lists some questions you should ask to be sure you're entering the type of business environment you really want and can live with.

What Franchise Should You Choose?

First, you need to decide the industry or type of franchise you will select to make all your dreams come true. You need to ask yourself some serious questions before you choose the franchise or the industry in which to invest.

- What are my realistic goals in owning a business?
- Do I want to use skills I already have or learn new ones?
- Do I want to sell to consumers or just to other businesses?
- Do I want to work outside of my home in a store or office?
- Do I want a lot of employees, just a few, or none?
- Do I enjoy training employees and supervising them?
- Do I want to dress in a suit, a uniform, or just casual attire?
- Will family members be working with me?
- Do I want a lot of supervision and guidance from the franchise home office?
- Would I like a large national chain or smaller local or regional one?
- Do I like working early in the morning or sleeping late and working into the evening?
- Am I content and relaxed selling, or do I want customers to come to me only from advertising and promotions?
- Will I work weekends or only Monday through Friday?

Just because you think you're an expert in one industry, that doesn't mean you should choose that type of franchise. Look at related areas where you can use some of these skills and also be involved in something new and interesting.

- Am I going to work in the business myself or be an absentee owner?
- Do I want more than one location—now or later?
- How big do I really want to get?
- Will I consider co-branding two or more franchises?
- How much do I have available for the initial investment?
- Am I planning to keep the franchise for the long term or build it up and sell it?

Chances are you're never going to get everything you want from any one franchise. But if you can find most of these things plus the most *important* ones (in your mind), then you're ready to take the next step. Select three or four franchises, request their literature, and start to investigate. They may seem similar on the outside, but they may be very different when you examine them closely.

Where Do You Find a Franchise?

There are numerous franchise companies around; investigate several before you make a decision.

If you want to invest in a franchise business or at least investigate the idea further, where do you find franchise opportunities? We all know the common ones we see when we drive down the street, but what about the others? There are thousands of franchise companies out there, and you should look at *many* in your area of interest before making any final decision.

So, where do you look? Check your local bookstore for directories that are printed once or twice a year with a hundred or more of the most common franchises. Magazines are issued several times a year that list some of the newer franchises. Small-business magazines have many ads to entice you to open a small business, but you need to do your homework first.

Your other source is your computer, which will allow you to search numerous websites. You can find general information and links to franchise company sites at:

- www.franchise.com
- www.franchiseinfomall.com
- www.franchise.org
- www.franchiseopportunities.com
- www.worldfranchising.com
- www.franchisedirect.com

You can search by type of product, industry, or startup capital needed and get information on many franchises to investigate. You can also get connected to sites that offer home-based franchises. Email for free information from all the ones that interest you.

Check out the large and smaller companies in the field you're interested in and compare startup costs and royalty amounts. Some newer franchises will offer more incentives and perks, but they also come with higher risk. Most franchisors will tell you up front the amount of initial investment needed, so you'll know whether it's in your price range. If they don't tell you outright or they are unsure or hesitant about answering, be very wary of them. They should be straightforward and direct with all the answers to your questions.

Find the time to research and investigate as many franchises as you can *before* you make a final commitment. And be careful of an untried or unproven franchise that's *too* new. Collect information and compare many companies to narrow down your search to a few and then do your due diligence.

Questions about Buying a Franchise

A franchise is great for people who want to own their own business, but have little or no idea how to start it. Like anything else, there are good and bad franchise companies competing for your investment. So when putting your hard-earned and long-saved money into a franchise, you want to be sure that it's what you really want to do and that you'll be successful. As I said earlier, no franchisor will guarantee results (if they do, start running) but you can be reasonably confident if you do your homework first. Here are some questions you'll need to have the answers to:

- **Are the products or services something you enjoy personally or have an interest in?** This is the beginning of your new business life, and you'll have to learn the industry and work long and hard at it regularly.
- **Is your franchise company a leader in its industry or at least well known?** It's hard to get new business customers if no one has ever heard of the company or the brand.

- **Are the product selling prices competitive in the marketplace?** A high-priced product or service at a new business will take more selling and longer to catch on. But prices that are too low will mean lower profits per sale and perhaps lower quality to the buyer.

- **Is the startup cost within your budget?** You can usually add 15 to 20 percent extra for unexpected expenses. You will also need additional capital for advertising, marketing, and promotion of your new business. Don't select a franchise that will drain all your available resources right in the beginning.

- **Does the franchisor offer a protected territory or area?** You need something in your contract that stops the franchisor from opening another location within a certain number of miles from yours. It's also nice to have an area where you alone can open additional locations for a two- or three-year period. Ask before signing and have it put in your contract.

- **Does the franchisor have company-owned stores or services?** Are any near your location or selling area? It will be hard to compete with the home office for business when they have much bigger resources.

Most franchise companies are reputable, but a few are not. Ask questions and talk to current owners. Don't let the franchisor suggest which owners you should contact; ask for a list and select them yourself. Ask the owners how long it took them to become profitable in the beginning.

- **Are other franchisees making money?** The franchisor should readily give you a list of other owners with contact information. Request a list of 50 or more and select at least five to talk to. If the franchisor is reluctant to give you much information, it's time to look elsewhere for a different franchise.

- **Can you visit other franchise locations and observe their operations?** You should be able to see whether this is really what you want to do and how it's done. Any hesitation here by the franchisor, and it's time to hit the road. You might even work at another franchise location for a few hours to get a hands-on feeling.

- **Can you live with the hours it takes to run a new business?** Are you willing to put your personal time and vacations aside until the business is on its feet and you can hire and train competent personnel? A new business is more time consuming than you may think.

- **Are there reduced startup costs if you open more locations?** If the franchisor doesn't have a regular policy on this, you can request something in your contract that reduces the fees for additional operations.

- **Are there any restrictions if you decide to resell?** Can you resell at any time to anyone who is financially qualified and of good moral character? Is there a transfer fee, and how much is it? Will the new owner get the same first-class training that you did?

- **Is the royalty reasonable for the industry?** You can compare by visiting competitors' websites to see what their percent of sales is or send them an email requesting the information. One or two percent either way is not a big deal, but five percent is a lot.

- **What type of initial training does the franchisor offer?** How long is it, and where is it done? How many people can attend the training, and who pays for it? Do you receive reference manuals as part of your franchise fee? Is there a toll-free help line available 12 to 24 hours a day?

- **Does the franchisor provide onsite training and supervision when you first open?** Will people from the home office be there to assist you in your first few days or weeks of operation? You can't run to the training manual with every situation that arises. Plus, you want those first customers to be treated well so they'll return.

- **Is the franchisor constantly looking for new products and services to offer?** Markets change and so do consumers. Has the franchise kept up with changing times in the past? Will the franchisor consider your ideas if you submit them?

- **Does the franchisor offer assistance in selecting a site?** When you have narrowed your location to a few possibilities, will the franchisor review demographics, rent, and area to advise you on which area will be the best for your success? Will they send a representative in person to see the final choice?

- **Is the corporate office financially stable?** Can you call company suppliers to verify good relations? Are there any lawsuits pending that would cause concern? Is the franchisor having disputes with any franchisees?

- **Does the franchisor have store layout or construction plans available?** This will save you money because you won't have to start from scratch with an architect. You can use any money saved for marketing and grand-opening promotions.

- **Are there restrictions on what you can sell?** Local markets can vary, and additional products may sell well in your area. How hard is it to get permission to add more or new products? Does the franchisor have discounts set up with national suppliers?

- **Does the franchisor offer help in financing, if necessary?** Do they have agreements or programs with any national banks or finance companies that are familiar with the franchise? Can they offer a basic business plan you can use or modify?

- **Does the franchisor do national or regional advertising?** You may have to pay a small monthly percentage for marketing and advertising. How are they using this money? Do they provide in-store signs and promotions? How often?

- **Are all franchisees treated equally?** Or are the larger ones with several locations getting preferential treatment? You don't want to be the last in line just because you're new. Ask another *newer* franchise owner how he or she feels about this and his or her experience.

These are just a few things you'll want to know before writing that *non-refundable* deposit check. It sounds like a lot to find out, but remember that you're investing much of your life savings and your time. Most franchises are very reputable businesses and should open all the doors to their operations and answer all your questions. To get more information and literature, you can contact the American Association of Franchisees & Dealers or the American Franchisee Association.

A franchise can give you a ready-made plan or a turnkey operation, which eliminates a lot of the headaches of starting on your own. You just need to be sure it's what you really want, because once you sign the agreement, you'll be partners for a long time. Check it out, ask all the questions, and be sure you understand the answers. Double-talk and vague answers are not signs of a reputable franchise company. Demand clear answers to your questions quickly or walk away and look elsewhere.

The Franchise Agreement

When you've selected the franchise company with which you'll spend the next several years of your life, you must sign on the dotted line. Franchise agreements of today have many pages and need to be reviewed by a lawyer with some previous exposure to franchise documents. Franchise laws are different and unique, so don't use your family lawyer—get an expert. It's worth the money (usually from $150 to $300) to know exactly what you're getting into and to be able to ask for changes to the franchise agreement. Most smaller and medium-size franchisors are somewhat flexible on some items and may agree to a few reasonable changes that your lawyer suggests. The big national chains will probably say that everything's written in stone—sign it as is, or you're out!

In some cases you may be able to change a few items in the franchise agreement, so take a chance and ask. Your lawyer can make a list of desired changes, and if you get 20 percent of them, you're ahead of the game.

A few things you'll probably see in the franchise agreement are:

- **Royalty.** This is a percentage of your gross sales (not profit) usually paid monthly or quarterly. There is often a minimum amount due, even if you're having a slow sales period. However, you can ask to have a no-fee-due clause if your business is temporarily closed due to weather or disaster. Compare the royalty to others in your industry to be sure it's inline with them. There should be a five- to ten-day grace period without a late penalty for royalty payments. Some franchisors offer automatic debits from your bank account so you don't forget to pay.

- **Minimum purchase.** If you're selling a corporate product or only approved products from the corporate supplier, you may be required to purchase most or all of these items from agreed-upon sources. There may also be a minimum you need to buy in a given selling period, so make sure you feel comfortable with this.

- **Initial franchise fee.** This fee is the first payment you'll make. It opens all the doors, but it's usually non-refundable, so be very sure of your intentions before you hand over this check. Get rid of any hesitation before you make this payment so you can go full-steam ahead into your franchise. This money will allow you to receive all the secret systems and procedures that the franchisor holds dear, and it covers legal and accounting costs involved in setting up your franchise.

- **Renewal fee.** Normally, your purchase of a franchise has a time limit built in—10 to 20 years in most cases, but it can be longer. You may want to be sure that if business is going great, the franchisor can't refuse renewal and take it away from you. The renewal fee will be less than half of the initial franchise fee, you may be able to negotiate it even lower based on performance.

- **Protected territory.** You will be given an area or a number of households upon which another of the same company franchise will not infringe. In a retail environment, there should be a certain radius within which another company franchise can't be placed. Of course, you can't predict where customers will shop, but most will frequent a store close to their home or workplace.

- **Product restrictions.** The franchisor will have an established line of products and services that you will be expected to promote and sell. But usually (except with large national companies) the franchisor will permit you to add related items that would sell well in your territory as long as you include the sales in the gross receipts. It's good to get written approval first so there are no disagreements or problems later.

- **Access rights.** The franchisor will want to inspect your premises and review your procedures from time to time. A representative will arrive (previously announced or not) to check things out. The rep will look at things such as daily reports, employee records, and store cleanliness and will observe employees in action. The rep may make recommendations on the spot and/or send you a report of the findings within two weeks.

- **Non-compete.** You'll need to guarantee the franchisor that you won't open a similar or competing business once you're a franchisee. This protects the company from revealing all of its systems and procedures to you, only to have you use them without paying royalties. This non-compete agreement will extend even after you sell the franchise—for anywhere from one to three years—and it can have a distance restriction as well. Make sure that you're very clear about this to avoid future problems.

These are just a few sections of the agreement you need to be aware of and consider when making your decision to open any franchise. Your lawyer will point out other items for you to consider and review. You should be able to get a draft of the agreement before you make your initial fee payment, so don't forget to request it. Don't neglect to read all of it even though it may be long.

The Franchise Manual

Upon execution of your agreement/contract, you should receive a complete manual or handbook of all the company's systems, procedures, and guidelines. You may have to wait until you go through training to receive the manual, only because the franchisor will need to explain it thoroughly. You invested a lot of money and time for this franchise, so be sure to read the manual often and refer to it when in doubt about any of the company's procedures.

Refer to the franchise manual often. Chances are, it will answer many of your questions about running the business.

The home office should send you new or replacement pages as things change, and they *do* change. I've seen a few franchise owners put the manual on a shelf and ignore it once the business is open. This isn't a good idea. You need to refer to the manual often so no question in your mind goes unanswered and you're operating the franchise as it was intended.

The manual will also include problem-solving ideas that you'll need as the business grows. Others have already asked many of your questions, and the answers should be in the manual. Besides, the manual is available 24/7, and you don't have to wait on hold or get voicemail as you would when calling the home office.

The Training Period

Included in your initial franchise fee should be the training you need to operate the business according to the proven franchise system. This training usually will take from two days to a month, depending on the franchise company. Some training likely will be at franchise headquarters or another approved location, and some will be in other stores or offices already in the franchise system. Recordkeeping and management techniques are normally taught first, along with information about the reports you'll be expected to submit periodically. Then there's usually hands-on training at an established business or a model site.

The training for your franchise will be by the book because it has always worked before. But if you don't understand something, stop the trainer and ask him or her to go over it again until it's clear to you. After all, you are paying for this, and you need to understand it thoroughly before you open your franchise.

The training will be required before you're allowed to open your doors for business to make sure that you're following the system right from the start. The franchisor should offer instruction or assistance in hiring your beginning employees at your site and should help with training them. This is the time to ask *all* your questions pertaining to running the business, because you won't have the individual attention of the complete franchise staff all together again.

A good and growing franchise should have ongoing training sessions for new products and procedures. You paid for this training, so learn as much as you can. The more you know in advance, the more confident you'll be when your new business opens.

You paid for the franchise and the training that goes along with it, so take advantage of that and get the most you can out of the available training.

Another form of ongoing training is field support. Usually quarterly or even more often, a home-office or regional representative will visit your business to observe and offer suggestions. This person will likely carry a checklist of predetermined criteria to look for. He or she can also offer assistance and training in any new products or services the franchise is offering to its customers. This is a great time to get hands-on answers to any questions or procedures you're not sure about. Because you won't be paying for this visit, take advantage of the free help. Plan in advance or make a list of questions, and don't waste any time while the rep is there.

Big Brother Is Watching

Recognize that the franchisor's level of control in the operation may vary—so be sure you're comfortable with the fact that the franchisor may hold a strong hand in your venture.

Some franchise owners feel more like employees than businesspeople. Why? Because they didn't do their homework when they purchased the franchise. They became involved with a franchisor that has tight control over franchisees, and they don't like it. Every franchise has a proven method for their business, and franchisees need to follow it in process and spirit. That's the purpose of buying a franchise in the first place. But some franchise companies enforce less control than others, and they let the franchisee make some decisions on his or her own.

There's nothing wrong with either approach, and you must decide which works best for you. Some people just want to follow the program without making any decisions at all. But if you don't want someone controlling all your activities, then maybe you should forget the franchise and open your own independent business. With a franchise you're not really a subordinate, but the franchisor *does* hold a higher hand.

Is There Any Risk?

In a word: absolutely. Each geographic location has its challenges and problems, based on demographics, unemployment, and economic changes, among other factors. There are few, if any, surefire businesses where you can pay your franchise fee and be a multimillionaire in six months. Even the largest and best-known franchise companies close stores or offices from time to time. But with a franchise, you have a partner—someone who wants you to succeed and who will show you how to run a successful business and help you along the way. Your obligation is to follow the plan with a realistic approach and confidence. Don't be apprehensive about calling the main office when you have questions or problems. Starting a franchise usually has a much higher success rate than starting a business on your own. So if you're not quite ready to start from scratch, consider a franchise. Thousands of people have—just look up and down your Main Street.

Action Plan

✓ Decide whether a franchise is for you.

✓ Find several franchise companies in your area of interest.

✓ Ask all the necessary questions before committing to anything.

✓ Have a lawyer read the franchise agreement.

"Don't think that operating a franchise is trouble-free; it's hard work, just like any other new business."

—BT

Chapter 4

Advertising

- Setting an Advertising Budget
- Advertising to Four Levels
- Print Ad Copy Questions
- Headlines
- Hot Words
- Where's My Ad?
- Competitors' Advertising
- An Advertising Agency
- Where's Your Business Card?
- Sign of the Times
- Do It Outdoors
- Your Moving Billboard
- TV Direct Response
- Let's Try an Infomercial
- Message on Hold
- Piggyback—Cheap!
- Co-Op Advertising
- A Final Thought on Advertising

Y ou see them everywhere: ads, ads, ads. Most people, on an average day, are exposed to 500 to 1,000 advertising messages. Look inside your shoe—is the brand name in there? That's advertising, plain and simple.

Advertising is everywhere, and you can't escape it! Companies and people are spending gazillions of dollars to make you remember them and buy their products, but is it really working? The quality and creativeness of advertising are what will reap rewards for the company investing in it. Probably more than 90 percent of the advertising that you see every day is immediately forgotten. Can you remember more than 10 of the 200 display ads that were in today's newspaper? Can you remember any?

So how, as a small business, can you use this medium? How can you create a lasting image of your business in your prospective customers' minds? You likely don't have a huge advertising budget to compete with the big boys and stay constantly in the faces of consumers with your products and services. But you can compete effectively if you set a budget for advertising, develop a plan, and use your available resources wisely. Smart advertising means using your advertising dollars where they will result in the best chance for increased profits. That's the purpose of this chapter—to point you in the right direction and give you workable ideas that you can afford and that will pay off.

Setting an Advertising Budget

Set a spending limit and allocate it across the most productive areas of your target markets.

Most small-business owners use seat-of-their-pants spending for their media presence. They see or hear of a new place to advertise, so they try it once and mentally write off the cost. The best approach is to set a spending limit and spread it across the most productive areas of your target markets. But how do you determine how much to spend?

A lot of it depends on your goals for the business and what you want to accomplish. What gross sales levels and amount of profit do you want to accomplish? Will more advertising result in these numbers?

You can also consider what your competition is spending in your target market. (By target market, I mean where and who you want to sell to.) If you have a hot-dog stand in North Cleveland, you don't want to spend money advertising in Cincinnati or even in South Cleveland. You want to advertise only where it will do the most good and reach the people most likely to buy from you.

If your direct competition is advertising like crazy, you may have to do the same, but be as selective on the media as you can and use every dollar effectively. A general rule of thumb for an advertising budget for small businesses is from 2 to 8 percent of gross sales, but you need to fine-tune those numbers to fit your own situation.

Promoting a new product will require more advertising dollars initially to get the product off the ground. Be prepared to make this investment when considering a new product or service. You may have the greatest thing since sliced bread, but it won't sell if no one knows about it. Monitor your results, and you may be able to get more exposure for your dollars than your competitors are by selecting the best media and the best timing.

And don't let your media salesperson talk you into a long-term contract *before* you see the results of a few ads. The salesperson's job is to tie you in for as long as possible with no guarantee of the outcome. Test before you commit, even if the cost is lower for a longer contract. You can still get that deal after you try a few ads. Don't get talked into a long contract at the beginning, or you'll risk being stuck with poor results and a contract you can't get out of.

Advertising to Four Levels

When dividing up your available budget to spend on advertising for the quarter or year, you should consider looking at four levels. Here's an approach for using your money wisely and effectively:

- **Existing customers.** You're already making money from them, and it's likely that they will spend more or purchase new products. Keep them informed of all changes and innovations in your products and your company. Repeat business is the name of the game. Regularly spend 40 to 50 percent of your advertising budget on existing customers.

A lot of business owners never have a budget for advertising. If they hear about a new idea that they like, they jump in and test it without a plan. Then, when the advertising doesn't show quick results, they abandon the whole idea. This is not the way to use advertising; it is often just a waste of money.

Small-business advertising is a large topic—far too vast for me to cover in great depth in this one chapter. For more information about advertising for your small business, an excellent source is Mark Hoxie's *90 Days to Success Marketing and Advertising Your Small Business* (Course Technology PTR, 2010).

- **Serious prospects.** These people have not yet purchased, but have come close. They've made several inquiries, browsed your store or website, or received a quote and need a little nudge to be a buyer. Spend 25 percent of your budget on serious prospects.

- **Casual prospects.** These people have made one inquiry, sent back a postcard, or perhaps requested literature, but you never heard from them again. They need more prodding. Spend 15 to 20 percent of your budget on casual prospects.

- **The rest of the market.** These are people in your selling world you have never heard from, and you're not sure whether they would ever be customers. Spend the remaining 5 to 20 percent of your budget on them.

Advertise to four levels of people: existing customers, serious prospects, casual prospects, and the rest of the market, known as suspects.

The part of your budget you're spending on each of the last three levels is trying to move people to the next highest level until they become customers. The part of your budget you're spending on the first level—your customers—is to keep them as customers and attempt to sell them more. Keep separate lists on your computer for each level and move prospects from one list up the ladder, hopefully to the customer list. Be sure to delete prospects from the lower-level list as you move them up, or you'll be duplicating prospects and wasting valuable advertising dollars.

Print Ad Copy Questions

Before you start to write the copy for an ad or a direct-mail piece, you need to answer a few questions. These answers will set the basis of your offer and present all the advantages of your product or service to the prospect. You should have answers to all of these questions before you commit your precious advertising budget.

- What are all the benefits of the product?
- Who will buy this product?
- How will my target audience respond to this ad?
- What type of payments will I accept?
- How long should the ad copy be?
- Should I offer a guarantee?
- How can I create an urgency to buy now?
- Can I use any testimonials?

- How is the product different from competitors' products?
- What price or offer is my competitor using?
- Can prospects easily afford to buy?
- Is there any discount for multiple purchases?
- Can we handle an unexpected number of orders?
- How quickly can we ship or restock the store?
- Can I sell upgrades at the time of sale?
- Is the product for personal or business use or for both?
- Can I tie in a holiday or special event?
- How easily can a customer order or buy?
- Are there any accessories or add-ons to sell?
- Will the product sell locally, regionally, or nationally?
- What payment options can I offer?
- What headline will best draw attention?

These are some general questions, and the answers to them will you help to write productive and responsive copy. You should add even more questions that apply to your industry or products. Being prepared in advance can eliminate much revision later—or, worse, something that you left out. Consult associates to help answer the questions or have a roundtable discussion.

Advertising is not cheap, so you want to use the most effective copy from the very first ad forward. If you need help preparing your ad, there are many professional copywriters available. Ask your printer or check the phonebook or Internet for creative writers.

Headlines

No, it's not Jay Leno's bit—it's what you need to draw attention to your advertising and direct mail. Without a great headline, the rest of your copy isn't worth nearly as much. And what good is great body copy if no one reads it?

The headline may be the only thing a prospect sees when flipping through a magazine, perusing a newspaper, surfing the web, sorting the mail, or watching TV. The purpose of the headline is to catch the viewer's attention and direct him or her to the rest of the copy with a hint or idea of the benefits of the product or service. In the headline, you'll want to state your strongest benefit or advantage. Words and phrases such as "How to," "You can,"

Your headline should catch readers' attention and hint at the benefits of your product or service. You may only have one second of their time to do this.

59

"You will," "Fantastic," "Easy," "Fast," and "Sale" are good attention-getters, but you must follow them with some informative words to hold the prospect's attention.

You want your prospects to remember what's in the body copy and the headline. The headline's purpose is to get them to read the body copy where the real information is.

Appealing to a specific group can make an effective headline, such as "Attention Restaurant Owners," "Homeowners Beware," or "Parents Read This!" They will see something that hits home with them and feel the need to at least read more.

Being too clever or wordy or using rhymes can actually hurt more than help. Being clever is great for slogans and jingles, but slogans are not great headlines. Jokes and cartoons are not for headlines either, and they can actually do more harm than help. Some of the most entertaining, award-winning commercials failed to increase sales and were dropped after a short run. A small business doesn't need awards; it needs sales and profits. Remember, the purpose of the headline is to get people to read on and find out what you really have to offer. It's not intended to entertain people. For that reason, slogans, jingles, jokes, and cartoons, if used at all, should be deeper in the body copy for readers to see *after* you have their attention.

> Put a "wow" or shock phrase in your advertising headline to attract attention. People will pay attention long enough to want to know more. But remember that if you make a promise in a headline, you must keep it or lose credibility. Another tip is to always be positive and never use the word "if." You want the reader to be sure about what you're saying.

Always write down several headlines before you use them and select the best one for your copy. Ask associates, friends, and customers what they think. Your headline should reach out and grab your prospects and make them want to know more. Don't let prospects turn the page or leave the TV until you've told your entire story. Remember that the headline is the most important part of your advertising—without it, there is no advertising.

Hot Words

Following are some words and phrases to use in your advertising copy to draw attention to the rest of your message. Use them often!

It's Here	Revolutionary	Wanted
Free	Guaranteed	Easy
New	Worry-free	Fresh
Beautiful	Extra	Super
Improved	State-of-the art	How to
Best	Announcing	Updated
Warning	At last	Final offer
Special	Time-saving	Fast
Clearance	Low-cost	Wow
Magic	Breakthrough	The truth
Sale	Reduced	Discount
Grand opening	Simple	Unique
Unusual	Secret	Exclusive
Bulletin	Homemade	Just out
Incredible	Warranty	Savings
Amazing	Outrageous	Fail safe
Handmade	Just released	While supplies last
Fantastic	Pure	Outstanding

The secret to successful advertising is to attract your prospects' attention and hold it until you can convey your entire message. Browse through magazine and newspaper ads and see what attracts you and makes you want to read the whole ad.

Keep in mind that each industry is different, and some words are not tasteful or appropriate for certain businesses. Would you want to see your dentist advertise a sale on root canals or your doctor advertise rectal exams? Use words that your potential customers will likely understand and respond to.

Where's My Ad?

When placing a print ad in a magazine, newspaper, or trade journal, placement can be a major factor in determining the response rate. The best ad, with the best product, at the best price, can't draw as well if it can't be found or seen easily. Publishers will rarely guarantee a specific placement unless you're buying the front or back cover or are a regular big-bucks customer. However, you may be able to get an appropriate placement if your ad is big enough or runs long enough. Some things you might request are:

- **Placement in the first 10 to 15 pages.** This area generally draws better response than later in a publication, but you'll need a larger ad to even be considered for this location.

- **Placement as the only ad on a page with an article.** If it's a great article, you'll get a lot of exposure. Better yet, if the article pertains to your business, you'll hit the jackpot!

- **Placement of your ad on a right-hand page.** More people tend to look at this side. Your ad even has a better chance of being seen when people are flipping through if it's on a right-hand page.

- **Placement that is not on the same two-page spread as a competitor or a similar product.** You will want to be several pages away from a competitor's ad, especially if the competitor's ad is larger than yours. Make this a serious issue when discussing your ad with the publisher's ad department.

Half-page ads can draw as much attention as full-page ads if the placement is in a spot where the ad will be seen easily.

Full-page ads can be way over a small business's budget, so consider half-page or quarter-page ads if you can get desirable placement. Many half-page ads will draw attention almost as well as full-page ads at a far reduced cost.

Always request a sample of the publication ASAP so you can check the location of your ad and check for any errors in printing. If the publisher makes the error, they will usually run the ad again at no charge. If there's a mistake in your contact information, for example, the ad is really useless.

Is It an Ad?

An unusual but effective type of ad is when you make it look like an article in a newspaper or magazine. The ad can look like a news story on a subject of interest to most readers. Many people will start reading the ad because they think it's part of the publication—it will take them a moment to realize it's an ad. You can get your message out if you put the benefits right in the beginning, so people will read on. The publication's editor may put "advertisement" at the top of the page, so readers won't be confused, but some people won't see that. Just make sure your body copy is truthful and non-deceptive, or you may turn off readers and destroy your response rate.

Competitors' Advertising

The amount of advertising you need can depend on what your competitors are doing. If you had no competitors, you would only need to show directions to your business once in a while. But unfortunately, business life is not usually that easy, so you need to keep your eyes and ears open all the time. Here's what you should be doing regularly.

- Listen to and watch closely all your competitors' radio and TV commercials. How often are they running, and do you think the sales they generate are enough to justify the cost of the spots? Can you compete in this medium, or is it way over your budget?

- Clip out all of your competitors' print ads and make files by company name. Take each company's ads and spread them out on a table, a desk, or the floor. Study them. What are the headlines? Do they use short or long copy? How are the ads different from yours? Can you get ideas that you can use to improve your ads?

- What benefits do your competitors stress, and are you targeting the same market with the same or different benefits? Can you afford to spend as much on ads or to use more targeted ads and publications?

- What other or unusual media are your competitors using? Can you be creative and find advertising sources where competitors have no presence? Do you think your competitors are growing faster because of their advertising?

Monitor your closest competitors' advertising. Make a file for each one and save clips of recent ads. Look at them when planning your own ads, so that your ads are competitive and not the same as theirs.

An Advertising Agency

You don't need a high advertising budget to hire an agency. Some specialize in small businesses. They may be able to group-buy space or time for several companies in the same medium. If you're advertising on a regular basis, it's probably taking a lot of your time or one of your staff member's time to talk to salespeople from all the media and publications. A good agency can take some of that burden, as well as offer suggestions on ad copy and new media sources. They may also be able to get you last-minute deals when extra ad space is available close to a publication's deadline.

A small business should look for a small agency that has some knowledge of or past experience in your target market. Many of them make money as a percentage of what you spend with the medium, paid by the medium.

Don't rule out using an ad agency. Some specialize in small businesses, so you don't need a high budget to hire them. But be sure to find out what you will get for the money you spend before you sign any contract.

An agency can develop an advertising plan or a complete campaign, depending on your budget. But once you hire an agency, don't be a backseat driver and question everything they do. Don't nitpick every detail along the way—just let them show you what they can do. They will bring you in for your comments and review when the time is right. You hired them for creative ideas and results, so let them apply their expertise while you assess the outcome.

There are several ways an agency can get paid. The most common is the 15 to 20 percent commission they receive from the media for placing your advertising. If your budget is small, they may ask for creative and artwork charges to pay for the formulation of your ads. Another method is a front-end fee or a contract with monthly billing to allow their staff to devote time to keeping your ads current and changing what's not working.

If you're only selling retail to a local market, find a one- or two-person firm that knows the market well and has a lower fee schedule. Just realize that your agency needs to make money and pay their staff too, so be fair when dealing with them.

Where's Your Business Card?

Always carry extra business cards with you, no matter where you are.

Business cards are now inexpensive, and many people save them in files for future reference. There is very little cost difference between two-color and full-color business cards, so why not go all the way? Also, you can use both sides for additional information and photos.

I can't believe all the professional people I meet who don't have extra business cards with them *at all times*. I assumed it was a no-brainer to always have some with you, but I guess I was wrong. It's really free advertising, because most people will accept your card. When going on a sales call or entertaining clients in your office, business cards are part of the procedure. But what about non-working hours? Do you refuse to discuss business and not meet a new prospect or client? Can you only find a new customer during working hours? Of course not—we meet all types of people during our everyday lives, all the time.

Your first line of offense is usually your business card. And if you don't have one with you, it may make the person you meet wonder how prepared and organized you are. If you can't even produce a business card, how can you be expected to do the job you represent? It doesn't matter whether you're in sales; you are your company when you are discussing business.

One evening when I was working at our ice cream store, a couple came in and sat in one of the booths. It being a cold weeknight in January, business was slow, so we started discussing small business.

The man told me that he was a CPA and specialized in small business. Because I had a couple of other businesses and felt neutral about my accountant, I thought it would be a good idea to save his business card, should the need ever arise. After all, it's sometimes difficult to find someone who specializes in small-business clients by looking in the phone book.

So I asked for his card, and he fumbled around looking for one. When he couldn't produce one, he asked for something on which to write his information. I handed him one of my cards, and he wrote his name and phone number on the back. His printing was a little sloppy, so one of the numbers was difficult to make out. And of course there was a small ice cream stain from the hot fudge sundae he was eating.

I took the card, put it in my pocket, and didn't really expect to call him or save it. If he didn't value his own service enough to have business cards with him, why should I value his service? And by the way, he didn't even ask for one of my cards so he could follow up himself.

This gentleman may be a good accountant, but not too many people will find out. His business will likely grow slowly because he's not taking advantage of all the opportunities that are available. Why pass up a chance to acquire a new client or customer when the effort is so easy? You should always have extra business cards in your pocket, purse, wallet, and car for those unexpected meetings. Be ready when the opportunity presents itself so you can grow your business.

Sign of the Times

One of the oldest methods of marketing and advertising is the use of signs. Probably the first use of logos was hundreds of years ago, when a craftsman would put a picture of his work on a sign to advertise to uneducated people or those who spoke a different language. If you saw a picture of a man shoeing a horse, you knew it was a blacksmith. If you saw a picture of a man making bread, it was a bakery.

Not a lot has changed over the years in that respect—signs are used everywhere and by every type of business. They are a cost-effective way to advertise and help people find your business. You pay for a sign once, and it lasts five years or more—what a deal!

Signs are a cost-effective way to advertise and build brand awareness.

Just be sure you put up enough signs or banners that they can be seen from all directions. You can change banners and posters for different promotions. Local regulations will dictate where and how many you can use, but there may be ways to get around the rules if you want more signage.

One idea is to piggyback on a sign of a non-competitor, which draws more attention to both signs. Most towns ban flashing signs (unless you're in Las Vegas), but a bright neon sign with different colors will attract more attention. However, if you're a home-based business, your neighbors might object to a big neon sign on the roof, so where can you use signs? On the sides of your delivery vehicles, perhaps. Or you can put magnetic signs on your car— you can easily take these off during non-business hours. Also, if you're doing tradeshows, expos, or seminars, an attractive sign can get more attention than the one the promoter supplies with the booth. Established sign companies can provide assistance in design and get any permits you need.

A well-designed and well-placed sign will attract new customers and remind current customers that it's time to buy again. Compared to other forms of advertising, a sign can be an inexpensive way to promote your business.

When purchasing major signs for your building, always get at least three estimates and find out what guarantee the company offers. Six months down the road, you don't want a burned-out light or hail damage to create new expenses. After the initial guarantee period, you may be able to negotiate a long-term maintenance contract with the sign company to take care of everything. If it's affordable, it's one less thing you have to worry about while you're trying to run your business. And when you have a problem with your main sign, you want a quick response to get it repaired and working properly again.

Do It Outdoors

Billboards provide 24/7/365 advertising for your business.

If your business can use outdoor advertising, it can be a very effective way to convey your message. Unlike on radio or TV, your ad is available and on display 24/7/365 for as long as you run it. You can rent billboards on main highways to reach a general audience or in specific neighborhoods to reach a particular ethnic group, for example. A great place to reach prospects and consumers is on an expressway or a busy street where traffic backs up during rush hour. Depending on local regulations, you may be able to add neon lights or raised and extended copy over the edges. There are even changing signs now that you can share with a couple of other businesses. These should cost less than if you paid for the entire space yourself.

Billboards work for impulse buying or building a brand. They must contain short, targeted messages and easy-to-remember contact information. Always put your phone, email, or web information in a big, bold font. With a billboard, you only have from roughly 2 to 30 seconds to capture your prospect, depending on how quickly traffic is moving past your sign. If it's near a stoplight, you will even get longer exposure.

Anything that attracts attention over and over will give better results and draw more business. Keep your billboard copy short, large, and to the point. Let pictures do some of the talking when you can show people using your product or service. Entice prospects to take action with phrases such as, "Call 1-800-555-5555," or "Turn right at the next corner." How about this idea: "Order a pizza on your hands-free cell phone now and pick it up 10 miles ahead at Joe's Pizzeria"?

Don't use long website addresses on your billboard, because passersby will never remember it and will not be able to write it down.

Finally, keep information current. As seasons and holidays change, change your message. Don't keep running a Christmas ad in January.

Outdoor advertising can be much less expensive than the newspaper, radio, or TV and can give much more exposure. Billboards are great when you're opening a new business, so that customers will know that you're open and how to find you. Further, billboards are also still affordable for small businesses if you're selling to a local or regional audience. Some of the biggest users of billboards are fast-food franchises: They attempt to attract motorists to stop along the way. Talk to billboard owners to come up with ideas to make billboards work for you and your budget.

Other methods of outdoor advertising include bus and train benches and shelters, sports stadiums, city buses, taxis, your vans and trucks, the outside walls of your business, and walls in airports. People are spending more time in their cars and sitting at traffic lights these days; they might as well look at your message instead of at the car in front of them.

Remember that placement of your ad can be just as important as the ad itself. Find the best location that your budget can afford.

Your Moving Billboard

Your company vehicles are free billboards, so make use of them!

Where can you get free advertising that moves around your selling area spreading your message? On the sides of your company vehicles, of course. You can also use magnetic signs with your company logo and phone number on your car. This works great for home-based businesses. If you can use this type of advertising, you're getting great exposure at a low cost if it's done correctly.

Here are a few ideas to help you get the greatest benefit from this type of advertising:

- **Keep it clean.** What impression do you get when it's a sunny day and you see a truck or van with a company name and phone number, and vehicle is filthy dirty? Not a very good one. Wash your company vehicles often.

- **Don't say too much.** Make letters large and easy to read. A quick glance by another motorist or a pedestrian should leave the person with something he or she can see and easily remember.

- **Drive carefully.** Put a "How's my driving?" sticker and a phone number on the back of your company vehicles. Use only drivers who are safe and courteous and who won't likely irritate potential customers.

- **Don't block other cars.** When you're unloading deliveries, don't block other cars so people can't get out of driveway entrances to businesses. This creates ill will, and some people may remember not to buy from you because of this. Remember, your company name is there for all to see.

- **Park to be seen.** When they're not in use or after hours, leave your company vehicles where they can be seen by passing motorists—don't hide them in a back parking lot! Your vehicles are free billboards, so use them.

When used correctly, company trucks and vans can be great vehicles (sorry!) for promoting your business at little or no cost. The next time you're driving, look at other trucks or vans to get more ideas. Don't forget to use your logo and slogans when deciding what to paint on the sides of your vehicles. Some businesses will use a large decal for lettering instead of painting. If you're not sure how to design the copy, ask a local graphic designer to help you with the layout. Get your ad rolling—at the speed limit, of course!

TV Direct Response

When purchasing by-spot television ads of one to three minutes, you need to maximize your message in the time available for the resources you have to spend. We've all seen TV ads for things such as garden widgets, CD sets, and household cleaners. You don't have to be a giant company to use these direct-response ads. Placing your commercials during non-prime time and on non-network or cable stations can produce great results if you do your homework first. Here are some factors you must consider when planning your direct-response TV ads:

- **What products to offer.** The ads must appeal to a mass general audience or to the people watching a specific cable station.

- **Special offers.** Make prices attractive and offer something extra if people call within a certain number of minutes. Tell viewers when the special offer will end.

- **Fast-moving copy.** Get your message out quickly and repeat it often so you don't lose viewers or bore them. Keep repeating your contact information.

- **A known personality.** Can you afford someone well known to endorse your product? If you are on a local station, then a local celebrity will work fine.

- **A spokesperson.** Who will speak most of your script, and how does that person look on TV? Do a screen and voice test first.

- **Specific stations and times.** Where can you get the most for your resources and still hit a target audience? Test locally first to estimate response.

- **Inbound call service.** Who will handle the incoming calls, and what do you want them to say? There are companies who specialize in this service; review several before you select one.

- **Whether you can upsell.** Upgrade to better models or offers for people who call in to order. Perhaps they can buy two for a discount price or add an accessory.

- **Payment strategy.** Can you offer "easy payments" or free delivery and handling if an order is paid in full on the spot? Can the person's credit card automatically be billed monthly?

- **Fulfillment.** Who will process the orders and ship in a timely manner? Review several fulfillment companies for both cost and service and then monitor them to make sure they're meeting your needs.

- **Aftermarket sales.** Can you re-mail or call your past customers with other offers later? Or can you sell your lists to other firms?

There is no surefire method that guarantees outstanding results. In fact, you'll probably fail to break even more times than you succeed. But when you hit it big, you'll forget the failures and reap the rewards you've earned. One big winner can cover all your previous losses and then some! Sounds a little like the stock market or the lottery, doesn't it?

Let's Try an Infomercial

When considering advertising on television by doing an infomercial, you need to make sure what you're selling is the right type of product for your audience. Many local stations have reasonable rates for half-hour slots during late nights and weekend mornings. Try to make a balance between what you can spend and when your best target audience will be watching. Select the correct channel to do your infomercial—for example, you probably don't want to be promoting oil-change equipment on the Food Network.

There are other factors you will need to know before you spend the big money it takes to put an infomercial all together. In a small business every dollar counts, so here are some guidelines:

- Your markup will need to be 400 to 500 percent (or more) to come out ahead.

- Your product should appeal to a mass market. Don't waste money on viewers who would never think of buying or using your product.

- You should be able to demonstrate the product and show its uses. Make it look easy to use.

- You need to be able to handle a flood of orders if you're lucky enough to get them.

- You must have the money in your budget plus about 25 percent extra to pay up front for most of the costs.

- You should offer a satisfaction-guaranteed refund policy and mean it. Keep an escrow account for this purpose, and process refunds quickly.

- You need to show people who have purchased or are currently using your product and are really delighted with it and excited about it.

- You need to be sure you're adhering to all FTC and FCC rules and regulations. Your TV station representative can help you with this.

- You should select a time and station to give your product the best chance to succeed. This should take into account when some of your target audience will be watching.

- Can you afford a local or national personality to attract attention?

We'd all like to advertise during the Super Bowl, but that's not realistic for a small business. You must start small and see what the results are before you invest more money. If this sounds like a lot of hard work and expense, it is. However, a good media consultant can help you get started on your first infomercial.

If you're willing to spend the money, take the risk, do the work, and try the tube, good luck! If an infomercial is done correctly and if you have the right product at the right time, it can result in high profits achieved quickly and great exposure. You can also attract the attention of large stores and distributors that you couldn't even get in to see before. Television opens a lot of doors if you use it wisely.

Infomercial guru Ron Popiel had several businesses using infomercials and is still going strong today. He follows the rules that you must have a knowledgeable host who is likable and easy to understand and who builds trust in the product. The late Billy Mays did the same thing, and millions of people bought the products he talked about. Hundreds of infomercials air weekly on all types of channels, and most of them produce a profit.

Message on Hold

One powerful way to advertise at a low cost is to use your already installed phone system. When people call your business and need to be transferred, they are usually put on hold. If the person or department they're waiting for is busy, they just sit there listening to a void. This is not only boring for the caller, but it also wastes a valuable selling opportunity for your business. A pleasant advertising message with a little music mixed in while people are waiting will solve both problems.

Using an on-hold phone message is another inexpensive, effective method of advertising. People are a captive audience while they are waiting.

These hold-message systems are attached to your existing phone equipment and can be very reasonably priced. For $500 to $800, you can purchase the necessary attachments, have them installed, and produce a professional recorded message.

You can change your recorded message as often as you like for a reasonable fee. While your callers are waiting on hold, you can point out products and services that they didn't know about. Many times you'll hear, "I didn't know you did that!" when you answer the transferred call that was on hold.

On-hold messages are a great business booster that you already have access to in your office or store. Even if you're not busy, you can put the caller on hold for 30 to 45 seconds, just to let them hear your message. (Naturally, don't *tell* the customer you're just putting him on hold so he can hear your message!)

You'll find companies that offer on-hold message services in your phonebook under the Telephone On-Hold Services heading or through your local phone company. Get competitive prices and compare any special services.

Piggyback—Cheap!

Look for inexpensive ways to piggyback on a non-competitor's advertising. It can be both a benefit and a cost-saving method for both businesses.

Here's an idea you can use for almost any retail store in a strip mall. We had an ice cream/deli store and wanted advertising ideas that weren't expensive. (I think *cheap* is the word.) Our ice cream store was next to a larger auto/phone/stereo store that did a lot of advertising. On occasion, they had a radio remote on the weekends—this is where the radio station comes to a store, broadcasts for a couple of hours, and entices people to visit the store. Because we were non-competitive with the other store, we were able to give the DJ three $5 gift certificates to our store to give away on the air. We also offered the radio personalities samples of ice cream or yogurt so they could taste our high-quality product and comment on the air.

There are many ways that you can share the cost of advertising with others in your target market. The only limit is your ability to create a new idea. Just remember that when sharing ad expenses, all parties involved must have a chance to profit.

We made the gift certificates good for only that day, and the winners were able to pick them up from the radio person doing the remote broadcast, so everybody won. How else could we get our business mentioned a couple of times on the radio for all of $15? The people who won the gift certificates usually spent more than the $5, too, so we had a chance to break even. What a deal! We also picked up some regular customers who may not have been in our store before.

Co-Op Advertising

I'm guessing that about 50 percent of you don't know what co-op advertising is, and that's a shame. Free money and benefits are slipping through your fingers, and you didn't even know it! Now is the time to jump on the bandwagon and get all you can.

When you're selling products that you didn't manufacture yourself, co-op advertising can be an effective and cost-saving tool. Many large and well-known product manufacturers are willing to provide cost-sharing or reimbursement programs for promoting their brands. Such programs are used in most media, such as print ads, radio, TV, and even phonebooks. In some cases, the supplier will even help with the production costs of the ads if they know you'll use them more than once. Each supplier has its own set of rules and restrictions you must follow to collect the funds or credits.

The co-op funds or refunds can be returned to you in several ways, such as a check rebate, a credit to your account, or additional products added to your orders. If you're selling different brands of the same item, let the manufacturers know that you will feature only the one that offers the best co-op plan. The manufacturer or supplier becomes your partner because they have a vested interest in seeing you do well. They are investing their money, products, or efforts to help you achieve more sales of their products or services.

> Always get any agreement you make on paper so there are no surprises later, especially if there are personnel changes at your supplier.

It's best to get any agreement you make on paper so there are no arguments later about what was promised. In most cases, you'll need to ask your suppliers whether they have a co-op plan and how it works. Even if your suppliers haven't done it before, there might be some interest from their marketing department to start by working with you. It never hurts to ask, and it could stretch your advertising dollars, which will result in more sales for both your company and the manufacturer or supplier.

If you're working with an advertising agency, they can do most of the routine paperwork for you and make sure you get the most out of co-op advertising that you can.

A Final Thought on Advertising

The most important thing to remember when advertising is to test, test, test. Don't put all your quarters into one slot machine if it's not paying off. Selecting the correct medium and then testing and monitoring the response will make your ad dollars go the furthest in producing results.

Don't be afraid to cancel an ad or change directions early if the expected returns aren't happening. And don't let media salespeople talk you into something that isn't working. Their job is to get you to spend your money with no guarantee of results. It's your business and your advertising money, so spend it wisely—you make the decisions.

Advertising can and will work if you put in the necessary time to investigate all the media relevant to your business. Stay with the media that work and drop the losers as quickly as you can. Once you advertise, sales reps will be calling constantly for reruns and renewals. Don't be talked into continuing with a medium that's not working and that will not help your business grow.

Action Plan

✓ Decide what you can spend on advertising.

✓ Take the time to write great headlines and copy.

✓ Always check your competitors' advertising.

✓ Be on the lookout for new ways to advertise.

"Don't let excessive advertising eat up your marketing budget; test before you overspend."

—BT

Chapter 5

Publicity

- Publicity versus Advertising
- Press the Press
- Tips for Getting Publicity
- If a Reporter Calls
- On-the-Air Publicity
- Publicity by Speaking
- Publicity by Writing
- Do Something Outrageous!
- One Final Note

Wow, something for nothing—the idea is great! Why should you pay for advertising when you can get it for free? Just send in the copy and wait for the results. Why didn't you think of this before? Well, Mr. or Ms. Businessperson, think again—it's much more difficult than you might think to get free publicity, but it's not impossible.

Don't let me discourage you—when it happens it's great, so be persistent and go for it! Many times it can happen when you least expect it. A good entrepreneur uses all the tools available, and publicity is certainly one of them.

Publicity, sometimes referred to as *PR (public relations)*, is the media coverage of your business, products, services, or yourself. In some cases, publicity can be in the form of news, and in other cases it can be in the form of an entertaining or learning segment. Whenever your business is referred to, mentioned, or named in print or air media, that's publicity.

But how do you get the media to mention your business in a positive way? After all, their source of revenue is from advertising, so why should they give it away? If you could find the elusive answer to that question, you wouldn't need more publicity; you'd be very rich already. Timing, your pitch, and who you know can be big factors in getting your business name in front of the public without paying for it. For example, you could be called upon for commentary as an expert in your field. If done with a positive angle, this can also mean an endorsement of your business by the media presenting it.

Media for publicity can come in several forms, such as newspapers, magazines, trade journals, television, and radio. You can contact them by phone, fax, email, or regular mail with your press releases, but if they've never heard of you, mail is your best first choice. It gives people a chance to read any literature you have sent and become familiar with your company. You can follow up shortly after by phone, and they might even remember your mailing. Timing your release for a slow media day can also help if you're a new and unknown business.

Publicity versus Advertising

Publicity and advertising both bring your name and/or business in front of the public or target audience, but there are big differences between them. When you're paying for advertising, you have control of the message and when it's aired or printed. The message is conveyed the way you submitted it or requested it. With publicity, the control is in the hands of the media. Your message may be changed and could even be seen as negative. Because you're not paying for publicity, you may have little influence over how your message is interpreted after you submit it. You won't have much control over when it's run or aired, either. The best thing you can do is make sure your press releases and events are clearly defined and accurate and that your releases have contact information so anyone can confirm the facts.

You have more say in the content and placement of your advertising than you do for your publicity. But the advantage of publicity is that it's a third-party endorsement of you or your business.

Always leave the door open for further explanation and encourage the media to call, email, or visit you. Make sure that an informed person (preferably you) is available to answer questions at all times, or the media will just go without your explanation. Having one of your staff members answer questions incorrectly and give the media the wrong information is *not* a good thing. Designate only certain people as the ones who can talk to the media. Anyone else on your staff should not answer questions; they should just refer the media to the correct person(s).

You need both advertising and publicity for an effective marketing mix. So have plans for both and execute them regularly. But in most cases, positive publicity will reap even more rewards than advertising will.

Press the Press

Press releases are a good idea to send anytime and all the time. Most newspapers and magazines are always looking for good and interesting copy to fill vacant space or to catch their readers' attention. But in larger markets, they get tons of press releases every week and may not be able to sort through them right away. You should always use a 9×12 envelope, preferably white, so your internal sheets are not folded. If the person at the newspaper or magazine opens your envelope and lays your press release on his or her desk, you don't want the release to curl up where it was folded, covering your headline.

Mail your press releases in a flat 9×12 envelope so you don't have to fold the internal sheets. This will make a more professional first impression.

You can also use email to transmit your press release, but it's very easy for the recipient to delete an email without giving it his or her full attention.

If the media outlet publishes your item, it needs to be newsworthy, informative, new, innovative, or of public interest. If you write it to sound like an advertisement or a commercial, you've just wasted your time. The media outlet is fully aware of why you sent the press release to them, and they will use it only if it's informative or different. They can't stay in business giving away free advertising or publicity, but if it's newsworthy, there might be a place for it.

Physical press releases need to be double-spaced and on white paper. (Double-spacing leaves room for editing.) They should include a contact person's name at the end with a phone number and/or email address. Don't send generic press releases or photocopies to Attn: Editor; personalize each release letter with a person's name. You can look up the correct person's name in *Bacon's Media Directory* or simply call the publication and ask.

You can enclose another sheet or two with information on your product or service, but don't include too much. You need to pique their interest with one main news idea and not confuse or frustrate them with needless literature.

An editor or reporter may call you with questions. You need to be available, as he or she may not call back. And get to know reporters and their deadlines—they may contact you when they need advice in your field. You could go on file as an expert when big news in your area of expertise is happening.

Send press releases only to publications that have an interest in your field.

So where do you send press releases? To the publications that would have an interest in what you do. You're wasting your time and money if you send a press release on a new cat-litter product to an industrial news magazine; you want the pet magazines. Every industry should have several publications you can approach. Look for specific publications and address your packet to the appropriate editor or reporter by name.

Be patient; you may not get a response for one to two months, or sometimes even longer. And just because you didn't get a response the first time, that doesn't mean you can't try the publication again. But don't overdo it and send something every week, or the editor may just toss the envelope without opening it as soon as he or she sees your return address. Sometimes timing can be a factor if they need fillers and you're lucky enough to be there at the right time.

Following are some sources where you can find publications on all types of industries and subjects. Most of these should be available at your local library in the reference department:

- *Bacon's Newspaper and Magazine Directory*
- *News Media Yellow Book*
- SRDS Newspaper Advertising Source
- SRDS Business Media Advertising Source
- *Working Press of the Nation*, Vol. 2

You aren't able to check out most of these directories and others, so bring paper and pen with you or some change to use the library copier. Plan to spend some time; there's a lot of information to search through. Revised editions of many of these directories come out every year. If you find that press or news releases are working well for you, consider buying one of these directories or subscribing on the Internet for easier use in your office or store.

Tips for Getting Publicity

Use these tips to increase your chances of getting the publicity you seek. Even if it doesn't work the first time, that doesn't mean you shouldn't try again.

- Check the editorial policies and needs of each medium in the media directories and adjust your press release accordingly.
- Direct your material to a specific editor or reporter by name.
- Keep in mind that timing for certain holidays or slow days will increase your chances of being used.
- Know who reads, watches, or listens to each medium to be sure you're hitting your target market directly.
- Follow up with a phone call or an email if your release pertains to an event on a specific date.
- Take print-media plant tours or studio tours to meet and get to know editors, reporters, and on-the-air personnel.
- When calling the media, assume that you may be taped, so be aware that everything you say is on the record.
- If you work with a certain medium on a regular basis, know when its deadlines are.
- Always have a contact name and a toll-free phone number or an email address in bold print at the beginning and end of your document.
- Follow up to see who's using your release, when they're using it, and whether it's accurate.

- Request a copy of the publication or airtime so you can be sure the information was used correctly.

- If your information and material concerns a national audience, send the release to wire services and news services.

- Remember that timing for a publication's editorial calendar can greatly increase your chances of being used at that time.

- Include some backup information to support your ability to be an expert in the field of the release.

- Use 1-1/2 or double-spaced copy so editors have room to make notes easily.

- Make sure you have interesting news copy and that it doesn't sound like an advertisement or a sales pitch.

- If you're announcing a product, show how it's different from others on the market and offer to send samples for media review.

- Offer your free appearance on radio or TV to be interviewed or to take audience questions.

- If your release relates to breaking news, send all materials via FedEx or UPS overnight.

- Before going on a live show, try to spend a few minutes with your host to get a feel for his or her personality.

- If your host is acting hostile or asking antagonistic questions, respond in a cool, professional manner.

- Always demand quickly a correction notice or a retraction for any print publicity that's inaccurate or was taken out of context.

- Just because the media hasn't used past releases, that doesn't mean you shouldn't keep sending them. Persistence may pay off.

If a Reporter Calls

Try to tie in your press release with a reporter's story angle or a national concern or issue, if possible. They're always looking for expert commentary to include.

Reporters won't even bother to contact you unless they see an angle for a story in your material. They're always looking for news that's accurate, informative, and happening now. They know their audience and what will likely interest them better than you do. If you can tie your message in with the reporter's perceived angle, you have a good chance of being used and getting publicity. Or, can you tie in material with a national concern or a major issue? A good reporter always likes a new angle for popular subjects in the news. You need to be a little creative on how you present your press releases and be prepared to discuss them further.

What do you do if a reporter asks negative questions about your business or finds fault with one or more of your products? Well, you don't run and hide, because the story will be done with or without you, and it's better to include your input. Confront the accusations and problems head on and explain your position. If the accusation is false, you must show proof or explain completely your side of the story. The negative article may run anyway, but it should be accompanied by your rebuttal.

A prosperous and growing business can be stopped in its tracks by negative publicity, so don't ignore it; explain as soon as possible. Don't admit guilt until you know all the facts and they are verified. If the accusations are correct, offer some type of apology and be willing to do any restitution necessary—and do it *now*. Don't wait, because the consumer—the public—will only remember the problem, unless a solution accompanies it.

If you have trouble talking to the media under pressure, use a spokesperson, but be sure he or she knows all the facts and is available on the spot. The only things I know that benefit from negative publicity are some movies and the wrestling industry. Trust me, you don't want it.

Whether the story is positive or negative, you want to read it. If it's in a local publication, you should be able to acquire it easily—don't wait until it's sold out. If it's a national magazine or newspaper, be sure to ask the reporter when it's coming out and request a copy of the publication or at least a tear sheet. Mark your calendar to be sure you received your copy or delegate the responsibility to an assistant to follow up. If a few days go by and you haven't received your copy, get on the phone or email and remind the publication.

Don't say anything "off the record" to a reporter, because it won't be. Be honest and straightforward, and don't say anything that you don't want used in their report. Discuss the facts as you see them and don't volunteer any unusual information.

You need to see the story or article ASAP to respond to any phone calls or email concerning it. You also want to be sure all the facts are correct and immediately contact the reporter about any errors. If the publication needs to acknowledge any errors in print, make sure you also get a copy of that. Save these printed articles and stories and put together a portfolio when you accumulate several of them.

On-the-Air Publicity

Some of the biggest audiences you'll ever get will be on radio or television. We'd all like to be on a national talk show to discuss and promote our company. But what are your chances? You may have a better chance of winning your state lottery than of landing a spot on such a show. Only the best, the hottest, and the most spectacular will get that chance of a lifetime.

Start local! You may be able to get a spot on a local radio or TV show. They often have empty time on slow news days.

But don't walk away with your tail between your legs. There's still a chance to get on the air at the local level, so that's where to start. Send a letter similar to a press release to the radio station manager or the on-air personality stating that you're an expert in your field and would be available to be a guest should the need arise. Offer to take calls from callers on your specialty and to give free advice. Question-and-answer segments are very popular with most audiences.

Send your letter to all the radio stations within an area you can get to easily on short notice. Many stations will keep your letter on file and will call you unexpectedly when a news story or public-interest questions in your field come up. Radio is a great place to start because if you're nervous, no one can see it except your host, and the host isn't going to tell. After a few of these spots, and if you know your subject well, you'll be relaxed and ready to try television.

Before you go on television, preview your material with friends, family, and staff.

Television is the big time, where people not only hear your voice, but they also see you, your actions, and your body language. So start small and build confidence in yourself and your presentation. The key to getting on any of these shows is what you have to offer to the audience to keep them engaged and interested. You should preview any material that you plan to use with your staff, friends, and relatives. You don't want to sound boring, or your time will be cut short, and you won't be asked back.

Find the best local stations to approach for your target audience. You can look in one of the directories mentioned earlier or check your local phonebook. Many local stations have talk shows on Saturday and Sunday, early in the morning. Contact the show producer—not the station manager—to offer your appearance and availability. Larger regional or national talk shows may monitor local shows to find new and interesting guests they haven't seen before. For example, Jay Leno has people on his staff go to local comedy clubs to find new talent. If you don't take the chance and you're not there, they'll never find you.

When you've done one or more of these shows, you'll find it's infectious—you'll want to do more. Every three months or so, contact the producers for the shows you most want to guest on, offering a new angle each time. They may use you as a backup for a famous person who cancelled at the last minute, so be ready.

When you're starting out, don't expect to be paid or to receive anything other than public recognition. After you become famous and receive many appearance offers, you can negotiate reasonable fees. But publicity itself is usually a big payoff.

Publicity by Speaking

Being in front of your target audience gives you the status of being an expert in your industry. Take the opportunity whenever you get a chance, regardless of whether it's for a paid engagement. Make your presentation entertaining as well as informative. People remember speakers who tell stories and make them laugh.

Donate your time or charge low fees for speaking engagements at colleges, Chambers of Commerce, business associations, and libraries. Have a clinic on your specialty at a library; do it twice— once in the morning and once in the evening—to accommodate everyone's schedule. Question-and-answer sessions in your area of expertise are generally popular.

Donate an hour at a retirement home, but instead of speaking on your business subject, read a short story and bring popcorn for everyone. Or pick a nonprofit organization you believe in and offer to be their spokesperson. You never know when you'll have a chance to be publicized when the organization is in the news.

Whatever you choose, don't forget to let the media know. Send emails or press releases and/or have one of your staff call the news stations in your area. If it's a slow news day, you might get coverage. Local newspapers, magazines, and radio usually have some space and time to fill, so the opportunity is there.

Press releases or interviews will let people know that you are well informed or an expert in your field. This can lead to speaking engagements at local or regional meetings. One speaking engagement will probably lead to others, so be prepared for future requests. The more you accept, the more attention you'll bring to yourself and your company. If you are new at speaking, you can join your local Toastmasters club and gain some quick experience.

Speakers automatically make themselves experts in the field they are talking about. Offer to speak at local clubs, leads groups, and service organizations to get publicity and credibility.

Publicity by Writing

Writing informative articles for magazines, business journals, or newspapers can also give you and your company needed exposure. My experience has shown that offering several different articles in a subject area works best. Most editors use articles that are 800 to 1,500 words long and submitted on paper, CD, or email.

Do any advertising in your byline, *not* in the actual article.

If you're using paper, make sure it's plain white and the copy is double-spaced (or at least 1-1/2 line spacing). The article should be interesting, informative, and, when possible, entertaining. Don't make anything in the article sound like an advertisement; save that for your byline.

You can send letters to an editor with your *free* articles listed and numbered for their easy selection. Some background data or a short bio can show your experience and expertise in the field. You can also offer to accept assignments from them in the future, which normally includes payment for your work. But normally, they will want to see your free articles first.

When you're submitting requested articles, make it clear that they are free as long as the article includes your byline. You should write your own byline and try to keep it to about three lines so it won't be edited to make it shorter. Include your name, title, company name, toll-free number, email address, and website URL if you have one.

Don't offer an exclusive to any one publication unless you're being paid fairly for it. And always request a copy of the publication in which it's used so you can check for any errors.

Do Something Outrageous!

One way to get *free* coverage from newspapers, TV, radio, and other media is to stand out in the crowd. Plan an event or stunt that's not seen every day, and depending on the amount or seriousness of the news that day, you may get free publicity. It takes research, planning, and a little luck, but it's worth a try. The least you can expect is to be noticed by passersby, but hopefully you'll attract some media attention, too.

The media is interested in subjects that are out of the ordinary and newsworthy. However, what's newsworthy can be interpreted differently by each source. So if you don't appeal to one medium, it doesn't mean you won't be of interest to others.

The key is to be different and innovative for your area and target market. You may have to get out of your comfort zone. Don't copy a competitor and do something similar—you'll look silly and will just remind everyone of your competitor's event. You want to be first or don't bother, so try to come up with a new idea. If you've seen or heard of an event in another city, consider it for your local area. As long as your market hasn't seen it, it's new.

Don't borrow an idea from a competitor; come up with something fresh and exciting. If necessary, brainstorm with your employees and customers to get those new ideas.

Alert the media well in advance and again when you're only a few days away. Here are some ideas you can consider or change to fit your business:

- Compete in a local event to win an award.
- Give an unusual donation to a local charity.
- Try to break a Guinness world record or sponsor someone who is trying to do so.
- Use a hot air balloon (if they're not often seen in your area).
- Host a theme day where employees dress up as unusual characters.
- Rent wild animals (in cages) and have a special weekend zoo in the parking lot.
- Hire parachute stunt people to jump holding banners with your message or logo.
- Give away your products during certain hours or for a whole day.
- Hire a celebrity to entertain or sign autographs.
- Announce a new model of a big, expensive product and give the first one away free. (Try to split the cost with your manufacturer.)
- Have Christmas in July and give away gifts.
- Give away tickets to a circus or other family-friendly event to children of low-income families.
- Have the World's Largest…something in your parking lot or store.

- Have a bingo party at a nursing home and give away prizes.
- Hire a well-known sports figure to give a clinic at your location.
- Sponsor an unusual show or event at a local hospital.
- Offer free meals to police officers, firefighters, or soldiers for a day.
- Hire a known entertainer for the children's wing of a local hospital.

Many small-business owners don't bother trying to get publicity because they think that it won't happen. But submitting good stories, ideas, and case studies will pay off eventually. Don't overlook the opportunity to promote yourself and your business when the price is free.

Find any ideas you want to use? If not, read them again and think about how you can change them for your business or industry. Remember to be different, be first, and be outrageous to get the media to notice you. And be sure to send press releases announcing the event.

Action Plan

✓ Mail and email press releases often.

✓ Find the best sources for your publicity.

✓ Let the media know you are an expert.

✓ Write and speak to groups for publicity.

"Luck comes to those who leave many doors open."

—BT

Chapter 6

Direct Mail

- Mail Your Customers
- Effective Direct Mail
- Mailing Lists
- Consumer Targets
- Consumer Direct Mail
- Business Direct Mail
- Layout and Design
- Evaluate Your Response
- Direct Mail Timing
- Co-Op Direct Mail

W e all know what direct mail is because most of us find it in our mailbox every day. Receiving advertisements and flyers in the mail has been going on for decades and will probably continue for a long time. I've been sending direct mail for more than 30 years and have not seen that many big changes. Most of the basics are still the same. The only improvements I've seen are better printing quality and better refined, corrected, and targeted lists.

Whether you're a retail, service, professional, manufacturing, or medical business, there should be some direct mail in your marketing mix. No business can afford to get complacent and let lack of attention reduce its customer base. Customers will leave for a number of different reasons, so you must add new customers regularly. One way to do that is with direct mail.

As much as we complain, postage in the United States is much less expensive than almost anywhere else in the world. And if you presort your outgoing mail, you can reduce the cost even more. (Besides, the postal service would have a hard time existing without all the business mailers.)

Many people argue that email doesn't need a stamp and thus should be used over direct mail, but do people really respond and buy as a result of email offers? Many people won't open or read unfamiliar email because they're afraid a virus may get into their computer. Unsolicited email, or *spam*, may have a place in some businesses, but it's not for the mass market yet.

Almost any business can benefit from using direct mail.

Almost any business can use some form of direct mail, even if it's a postcard thanking customers for their orders. And, of course, on the same postcard you can put another offer or product information. Dentist and doctors use direct mail as well, to remind you that your next visit is due.

If you're not using direct mail now, spend a weekend thinking about how you can incorporate it into your business. Regular contact with your customers and prospects is an essential part of staying in business and growing. Find a way to use some form of direct mail for your business, and the results should pay for themselves. Even the smallest business can afford some literature, stationery, and a few stamps.

Mail Your Customers

You need to keep in contact with your customers at least once every 90 days, and the easiest and most economical way to do so is through direct mail. It doesn't matter what type of business you are, you must do this or risk the chance of losing some of your customers. Your competitors are likely mailing or calling your customers as their prospects.

In the retail business, you might not keep a record of your customers' addresses. And, if you're a restaurant, the same may be true. So how do you get your customers' names and addresses? Have a drawing that requires an address to enter, give a preferred customer card that requires customers to fill out an info card, or ask customers to fill out a coupon and mailing list form. Tell them that periodically they will receive discount coupons or special offers in the mail.

If you accept checks, you have the customer's information right there. Record the address in your computer before you deposit the check. If you have so many different customers that it's impossible for you to keep track of them, then let someone else do it. There likely are many small mailing companies in or near your location—just look in the yellow pages or on the Internet to find them. Mail to customers and your best prospects in your general selling area at least quarterly to keep your business familiar and in their mind.

Direct mail your customers roughly every 90 days to keep your business fresh in their minds. Always have something new to say each time you mail them.

To get a prospect list, contact two or three mailing-list brokers and get quotes. You'll want to specify selection parameters for consumers, such as income level, ZIP code, age group, home value, and so on to get the target audience you want. For business-to-business (B2B) mailings, you can select by ZIP code, area code, type of business, SIC code, number of employees, yearly sales, and so on.

One of the best sources for general consumer and business lists is ReferenceUSA. They have most of the phonebook listings from the entire country available and are reasonably current. They have most new listings in their database long before the next phonebook comes out. Most list brokers can also get information on consumer and trade magazine subscriber lists that go to your target customers. The minimum order for most lists is 5,000 names, so plan your printing accordingly.

Whatever you send to your lists, don't send the same thing two mailings in a row. Restaurants can send out a small version of their menu with a coupon for new items. B2B mailers can offer businesses free shipping if they order by a certain date.

Effective Direct Mail

Direct mail will be the most effective if you follow a few guidelines. Just using it blindly will not produce the results you want from all your efforts. Here are some ideas to get the most from your direct-mail campaign.

- **Target the right audience.** Your current customers are your best audience. But prospects who have an interest in or a need for what you're selling, can afford to buy it, and can be motivated to buy now are your next best audience. Without a great mailing list, you've wasted some of your direct-mail dollars. It's better to spend a little more on a great targeted list than to waste printing and postage costs on a mediocre one. You need to test different lists to find your best response and your correct audience. You can spend a fortune on the greatest mailing piece, but what good is it if it's not in front of the right potential buyers? Effective lists will both save you money and make you money.

- **Use high-quality material.** What you send can be almost as important as who you send it to. I've received mortgage offers on a faded photocopy sheet with my name written in. There's no way I would risk my home by dealing with the person who sent something like that. Be professional, colorful, and informative. Have a graphic designer set up at least the main sheet for high impact. An attractive and eye-catching piece will entice potential customers to read it and act.

- **Make an irresistible offer.** Consider offering a big discount, something free, a gift with order, free installation, a two-for-one sale, a high-value coupon, a free sample, extended terms, or special personal service. Make your offer early in your material and several times more as customers read on. You need your offer to entice the prospect to take action, and they won't do so if your material is tossed out. Make your best offer in your headline and make it stand out so your prospect will want to continue reading. Your offer can also be a new, innovative product or service that your target audience has been looking for. Above all, you must keep potential customers' attention if you have any chance at getting them to take action, so give them something to think about.

- **Be persistent.** Mailing your prospect or customer list once and forgetting about it is not the correct approach. You need to mail every quarter or three times a year to the same audience for the best results. People may not need or want what you're selling the first two times they receive your mail, but by the third time they may be in the market. I've mailed to the same companies for several years, and I always get someone who calls and says, "I've been looking for products like yours. Where have you been?" I just throw up my hands and get on with the sale. Afterward, I check my lists to see who we haven't mailed in a while and get busy mailing them again.

- **Create urgency.** You want your recipient or prospect to take action now and not put down your material and forget about it. To create urgency, use phrases such as "limited-time offer," "while supplies last," "price increase coming," "sale ends," "not all sizes available," "sneak preview," "before open to public," "call now for," and so on. Customers' attention spans will be short, so you need them to act now, or they never will.

- **Make it easy to respond.** Not everyone wants to order the same way, so be flexible. Some want to come to a store and browse, some want to browse your website, some want to mail you their order, and some want to call, fax their order, or email. Make as many of these options available as you can. If you're selling outside your local area, you must have a toll-free number. Customers expect it, and some might not call if you don't have one. Toll-free numbers are much less expensive than they were years ago. Your local phone company or long-distance provider should be able to provide a competitive rate. Make it easy and comfortable for your new and old customers to contact you.

- **Make it easy to pay.** Accept as many different credit cards as you can and advertise this. Some people will want to pay by gift card or debit card, which can be set up on your current credit-card machine. Others may want to send a check or use the electronic check service that allows businesses to accept a check over the phone. Decide whether you can afford to offer a small discount if the customer pays promptly or in advance or with cash.

A mailing is of little use if your staff members aren't trained to assist customers appropriately when they respond to the piece.

- **Foster employee awareness.** Does everyone in your business who would have contact with your customers know what's being sent in your direct mail? If there are several different offers being used at the same time, do your people know about all of them? Have they actually seen the mailing piece so they know color(s) of ink used, so that when the customer calls about the blue flyer he or she got in the mail, your employee knows what the customer is talking about? It doesn't matter whether you're a two-person business or you staff 100 people, your employees should know more than the customers—or at least as much.

Mailing Lists

Mailing lists for your direct-mail program come in many shapes and sizes, but the best lists you can use are ones you build yourself. Your number-one list consists of your customers. These people already purchase from you and are usually open to new promotions and products.

Your number-two list contains the prospects who have responded in some way but have not become customers yet. They should still be responsive to your future mailings and promotions.

Always test 2,000 to 5,000 names before investing in an entire list.

Your number-three list consists of new prospects you have never heard from or have never contacted before. Look at your type of current customers and find a list that has other people or companies like them on it. You should always test at least 2,000 to 5,000 names first to evaluate the response before investing in the entire list. Some list companies have a minimum order, but you may be able to convince them to let you test a smaller number. Sometimes, the list or your offering will pull more at certain times of the year, so plan in advance and have enough staff available to handle the response.

Good sources for lists include list brokers and yellow-pages lists. If you can use yellow-pages lists, the best source is ReferenceUSA. You can buy these lists on disc or labels, with or without contact names and phone numbers. List brokers can supply lists of magazine subscribers and other private lists. Your cost per 1,000 will vary with the amount of detail or refinement you request and the quantity you order.

Another source for lists is a company that serves the same market as you do but is not a competitor. You may be able to swap lists and incur very little cost, but always get an agreement that the company to which you give your list will not resell it or merge into their other lists. You don't want your customer list to indirectly get to your competition.

If you want to mail a large list, it's best to test a few thousand names before you invest in the entire list. Purchase a test sample using the *nth* name, which is a random selection and gives the best overall test. The right list used at the right time can increase your business quickly. You wouldn't see all the direct-mail offers in your mailbox if the system wasn't working for the senders.

If a list works for you, and you get the response you expect, don't hesitate to mail it again in three to six months. A good list doesn't wear out; it keeps producing good results. Each time you use the list or purchase it, there should be some new listings and some bad addresses taken off. Even with higher postage rates these days, direct mail is still the most economical way to reach prospects and customers if you use the correct list with the right offer at the right time.

Consumer Targets

When selling to consumers, spend your direct-mail dollars when you have the best chance for profitable returns. Consumers buy for many different reasons, and you have to zero in on what's best for your product or service. Ask yourself these questions when planning your mailing:

- Are your competitors mailing to the same lists that you are?
- Do the people on your list buy regularly by mail?
- Have they ever bought by mail?
- Can they buy at your store, on the phone, or at your website?
- Are they the correct age group to respond?
- Is your offer gender related? Or ethnicity related?
- Can your recipient afford to buy your products?
- How will the consumer want to pay for the purchase?
- Does the consumer need your products?
- Does the recipient's location make a difference for service?

- Has the consumer purchased similar or related products?
- Are your prices higher or lower than your competitors' prices?
- Have you mailed this list before, and what response did you get?
- Can you buy a more refined list for better results?
- How will recipients receive their purchase—by pickup or shipping?
- Will you offer coupons or a discount?
- Is this list reliable?

You can send consumer direct mail more often than you can to businesses. People expect to find it in their mailbox and give it a quick glance before reading more or tossing it. Always change a few colors and the headline if you mail consumers often.

A good list broker can help you find the answers and the lists you need at prices you can afford. By a good list broker, I mean someone who wants to build a business relationship with you—not just take your first order and forget about you. As a small business, you won't be buying a million names—maybe only thousands—so explain that you will continue to use the same broker if they give you the service you need. Insist on knowing about all the lists available in your target market before making your final decision. Great lists can produce great results, so look at all that are available.

Consumer Direct Mail

The amount of advertising mail a consumer gets depends on many factors, such the number of magazines he subscribes to, how many credit cards he has, and what he has responded to in the past. Or he may be on a list that was sold from one mailer to another.

Your consumer direct-mail piece should be eye-catching so the recipient doesn't just toss it out with the junk mail.

So why do people open some mail and toss out other pieces unopened? Something catches their eye or creates a desire to know more about what's inside certain pieces. You must decide how much you want to spend on copy and printing, but even low-budget mailings can be creative and can pull good response.

Most items in consumer mail are lower priced if the mailer is looking for an immediate sale. Chances are slim that any person will immediately pick up the phone or go to a website and order a $1,500 sofa or an expensive diamond necklace as the result of a direct-mail piece. However, lower-priced goods, where there is less risk, are more likely to inspire a quick sale.

Big-ticket direct mail to consumers usually tries to create the desire to visit the store in person to get a hands-on demonstration. Whichever approach you use, you want the consumer to take some action as an outcome of your mail piece. As with print, radio, and TV ads, there must be a need or a desire for your products and the financial ability to buy before the consumer will act.

Here are a few ideas for consumer direct mail:

- If you're sending a business-size envelope, use First Class mail; you'll get double the response. And if you're *not* sending via First Class, you won't get undelivered mail returned, so you won't be able to update your list.

- Self-contained or fold-open mailers that are colorful can be sent by bulk or standard mail for postage savings.

- Use a current list. People move often, and consumer lists become outdated quickly. Buy a current list within 30 days of each mailing for best results.

- If you're buying a new list, wait until right before your mailing to buy so that it's the most current list available.

- Don't use only black and white unless you're selling Dalmatians. Even a third color will make your piece stand out.

- Show a picture of your product in your copy on each page.

- If you're a service business, show someone providing the service with a smile on his or her face.

- Use "hot" words in your copy, such as "free," "new," "easy," "fresh," "improved," and so on.

- Make a special offer—be creative and different.

- Give several ways to buy—over the phone, in person, by fax, or on your website.

- Get several quotes from printers on the production of your mailing piece. A broker can sometimes find the best factory for your type of project.

- If you're using a mailing house, the total cost after sorting should be no more than if you sent it yourself. Compare prices and find out how long it will take the mailing house to get it out the door.

- If you're using different lists, code your responses so you know where they came from. Some lists will pull better than others, and you'll want to use those lists again.

- Do test mailings to your best target customers before you spend your money on the others. You may want to make some changes or adjustments before the big mailing.

- Talk to several list brokers to get the best lists. Each may have different recommendations and ideas. Ask them to fax or email a couple of listings before you buy.

- Lists should be submitted to your mailing house on disc or electronically so they can be easily sorted for the lowest postage. Ask the mailing house for their preferred method.

- Do mailings of fewer than 500 pieces yourself, in house. There will be little or no savings if you outsource these small mailings.

- Have a follow-up mailing to send to all who become customers. If they are satisfied with their purchase, they are likely to buy again soon. Mail them with a different offer approximately 30 days later and another in 60 or 90 days.

- When people buy something, they like to receive it quickly. You'll get better response if you offer a shorter delivery time—four to six weeks is too long. Free delivery is a big selling point; offer it if you can.

- Make your products and offers *now* items. Don't try to sell winter coats in August or beach balls in January, like the stores do. Direct mail is a right-now, today, pick-up-the-phone-and-order proposition.

A small business needs to use its direct-mail dollars wisely to get the most orders for the dollars spent. Make your copy more consumer-friendly and leave out the heavy technical jargon. Be creative, unique, and urgent for the best results. When it works for you, consumer direct mail can be a great and inexpensive way to build your business. Because consumers are always buying, why shouldn't they buy *your* products instead of your competitors'?

Business Direct Mail

The first goal of direct mail is to be delivered, so use the best list you can find and afford, because it won't get opened if it doesn't get there. Businesses move less often than consumers, but you must be sure your list is not more than a year old; six months or fewer is better.

Address your business direct mail to the correct person in the organization. That person should be a decision-maker in the company.

As with any type of business marketing, you want to target the correct decision-maker—by name, if possible—for your product or service. Does a customer service rep really care if the company saves money on long-distance service? Not really; you need to reach the boss, who watches the expenses.

Some lists are available with the name of a person and his or her title. If names are not available, you can send your piece to the attention of the title of the person you're looking for, such as CEO, Chief Engineer, Office Manager, Marketing Manager, President, and so on. When the piece is delivered to the correct person, you've increased your chances for a sale.

Business direct mail should be more professional than consumer direct mail—save the wild colors.

Here are some more ideas for effective business direct mail:

- Never use an address label on a business-size envelope—it's unprofessional. Do use your return address.

- If possible, use commemorative stamps on your envelopes instead of using a postage meter. Not all marketers agree with this, but I believe that it still looks businesslike but has a more personal touch.

- Always send #10 envelopes First Class if you can afford to.

- Laser-print or type addresses on envelopes; handwritten envelopes are not professional.

- Have a response card or an order form with a toll-free phone number, fax number, and email address. People like to respond in different ways, so make it easy for them by offering several choices.

- If you have a website, encourage prospects to go there for more information.

- If you're sending several sheets in an envelope, at least one sheet should be full color and should be the one seen first.

- Bright-colored envelopes don't work for business; white or off-white is much better.

- Offer something free or on sale to get quick attention. If your headline and first sentence don't capture potential customers, they probably won't read on.

- Start with a personalized letter if you have a target name or title.

- Get right to the point of the mailing near the beginning of your letter, or customers may lose interest. Don't use deceptive or unbelievable copy. Be direct, honest, and informative.

- Ask for a response early and often in your copy and give the recipient several ways to respond.

- State some type of deadline, such as "Please reply by…" or "Offer expires on…."

- Be unique and different but still businesslike and professional.

- Test different letters to see which one gets the best response.
- Offer extended terms or billing rather than cash up front. Ninety days same as cash is a good incentive and often is successful.
- For higher-priced items, offer to set an appointment for a demonstration or a test model.
- Don't make letters too long; businesspeople often have less time to read them than consumers do.
- Stress your guarantee. No buyer wants to be stuck with a bad decision and reprimanded by his or her boss if something goes wrong after the purchase.
- Use testimonials (if you have them) from other satisfied business customers in your copy.
- If you're using direct mail to generate leads, stress free samples, a free consultation, more information, no obligation, a free seminar, and so on.
- Update your mailing list from any returned envelopes before you use it again. You'll save not only on postage, but also on literature and labor.

Layout and Design

When designing your direct-mail piece, you want to be as user- or recipient-friendly as possible. You also want the post office to find the address easily and expedite your mail. Following are a few things to consider when planning your mail package.

- Will the address show clearly? Black or dark type on a white or light background is the best option.
- Is there space for the nine-digit (carrier route) ZIP code?
- Keep the envelope size within the post office limits so you don't need to put on extra postage.
- If you're using a letter, does the paper match the envelope?
- Are you folding the letter copy-in or copy-out?
- Make sure any response or order form fits easily in the reply envelope.
- Are any perforations easy to tear and positioned correctly?
- Does any personalization line up perfectly with the envelope window?

- How does the piece look when it's folded?
- If you're using a window envelope, make sure there's enough room for the postal barcode.
- If you're doing a larger mailing, does your design conform to most inserting machines?
- Is there a return envelope for any remittance? Who pays the postage?
- Is your envelope easy for the recipient to open?
- Did you check and recheck all copy for spelling and grammar mistakes?
- Did you check and recheck any prices?
- Are your headline and hook phrase easily seen?

If you're sending only a few hundred to a couple thousand pieces, you can design your own copy on your computer. For larger mailings, you may want to hire a graphic designer with experience in direct mail. You should talk to more than one and review some of their work. Fees can vary quite a bit, but the cheapest is not always the best. See how many other projects the designer is working on and whether he or she can meet your mailing deadline.

For larger mailings, consider using a graphic designer who has experience in direct mail. The designer may have ideas you didn't think of that will improve the possibility of your mail being opened and read.

If you like two different designs, consider using both and dividing your target list in half. Answering all these questions and checking everything in advance will save you headaches and mailer's remorse in the future. So, do your preparation before you spend any valuable marketing money.

Evaluate Your Response

Getting response is the name of the game. Whether it's an order or lead generation, you need response to make your direct mail worthwhile. How can you afford to continue mailing the same offer if the response doesn't make it pay off? The answer, of course, is that you can't. At least one of two things has to change—or both.

The first possibility is that the offer may not be appealing enough or may not be professionally prepared. Review it and alter it as necessary. The second possibility is that your list is not the right target audience for your offer.

It sounds simple, doesn't it? But in reality, it takes much fine-tuning to make a list a winner.

To analyze your response cost, add up all the expenses involved in doing your mailing—postage, printing, stuffing, addressing, and any mailing-service fees. Divide this total by all the responses you received from this mailing within 60 days. After 60 days, the mailing becomes stale, and few (if any) customers will respond to it.

Determine your CPR to evaluate the response you get from your direct mailing.

The number you get after you divide the cost by the response is your *cost per response (CPR)*. Can you make a profit with this CPR? Maybe you can break even and make a profit from quick reorders. Can you sell other products to the responding people? You will need to evaluate these numbers to see whether more changes are necessary for your mailing.

Direct mail is not an exact science; the numbers can be different each time you mail. After several mailings, you'll see a percentage range into which your response rate will fall. The question to ask yourself is whether you can be profitable and grow your business at this rate. And then, you can adjust as necessary.

Direct Mail Timing

Good timing is critical for direct mail; constant testing will let you know the best mailing times. Always monitor when you mail versus the total response.

Let's all mail on January 1 and July 1 and go on vacation 90 days later. Sounds easy, doesn't it? Well, you can forget that idea now. Good timing is important, and only constant testing will show you the best mailing times. You need to mail prior to when your customers will need to buy your products or services. Don't set up your lemonade stand outside when it's 10 degrees; there won't be any customer traffic. And anyway, your lemonade will freeze, and so will you.

Research from 2010 showed that Americans between the ages of 18 and 34 prefer to receive offline marketing information instead of online.

Get on your competitors' mailing lists and find out when they send their direct mail. Then you can decide whether you want to start before or after them. If you're just not sure when the timing is best, do half of your mailing on one date and the other half 30 days later. Your response will give you the answer for the future.

Are your products seasonal, and have you tested previous mailings to determine how early to mail? Can you do off-season promotional or clearance-sale mailings? Maybe your products can easily be sold year round by direct mail with good response. If that's the case, and you're on a limited budget, then split your mailings into six or eight parts and spread the cost while profiting from previous mailings.

If your products sell better in warm or cold weather, then divide your list by ZIP code to separate the northern and southern parts of the country. Mail to one part of the country prior to potential customer needs and wait on the other half until the weather is close to changing.

Timing helps you use your resources to their best advantage and get sales when customers are most apt to buy. Watch what your competitors are doing and keep testing, monitoring, and adjusting your timing.

Co-Op Direct Mail

When you start figuring all the costs for doing a mailing, they do add up:

- Designing and copywriting
- Printing and folding
- Purchasing lists
- Stuffing and addressing
- Sorting by ZIP code
- And let's not forget the postage…

So why should you pay all these costs yourself when often you're promoting a manufacturer's products? Similar to co-op advertising, which was discussed in Chapter 4, direct mailers can use the same concept. Your suppliers and manufacturers may offer to assist you or pay for some of your mailings. Many larger companies have in-house art departments that may be able to design your complete mailing piece or brochure for you at no cost. They have all the art and photos available for their products. After all, you're trying to sell more of their products, so why shouldn't they help you? They may also have a mailing service they use regularly that you can use at a discount. And see whether your suppliers have a regular printer that you can use at a better cost than you could get on your own.

However, your suppliers aren't going to do anything to help you unless you do one thing—ask! Remember, you are their customer, and they should want to keep you happy and increase the amount they sell to you. If your mailings provide a big chunk of your sales, then they also contribute to your suppliers' sales. Explain this to them if they don't get it right away. You'll need to talk to someone in their marketing department or a sales manager, rather than your sales rep or customer service. If you're a valued customer, they should do something for you, but don't forget to ask.

Action Plan

✓ Start a program to mail to your customers regularly.

✓ Find new mailing lists and test them first.

✓ Design your mailing piece so it has a good chance of being opened.

✓ Monitor your response from every mailing.

"If you can't get your foot in the door, at least get your mail in there."

—BT

Chapter 7

Business Promotions

- Coupons versus Rebates
- Show Off Your Logo
- Collaborate with Your Strip Mall Neighbors
- Special Discount Days and Nights
- Fast-Food Delivery Convenience
- Stick with Magnets
- Sponsor a Nonprofit
- Nonprofit Your Way to Profits
- Cross-Promotions
- Have a Contest
- Don't Be Unoccupied
- Celebrate Your Anniversary
- Feature Kid Art
- A Weekend at the Mall
- Some Other Fun, Profitable, and Outrageous Promotions

Something you don't see every day, something out of the ordinary, something outrageous, something fun, something educational, something informative—all these are promotional activities you can use to build your business. Promotions are activities or events outside of your normal business routine that entice people to participate for their enjoyment and your gain. Tie in special offers with unusual holidays, or make up a cute holiday and then make a big deal out of it. You can stand out from your competitors and see a short-term increase in your market share and profits. Bring in new buyers with fun and money-saving ideas that your competitors aren't doing.

Promotions also can be an ongoing process where you reward your customers for repeat business. Make a promotional offer on your website and have customers refer to a phrase or code to receive a discount when they order. Change the offer often to encourage repeat visits and offer printable coupons.

Let's find some other things a small business can do to bring itself into the limelight and be remembered by customers and prospects. Remember, you can use ideas you've seen elsewhere and change them to fit your business. Promotions can be fun and profitable while they encourage new and repeat business and referrals.

Coupons versus Rebates

Why use a coupon over a rebate, or vice versa? What's the difference between the offers, and what's the advantage?

Coupons can be a form of advertising or direct mail and also available to print out at your website.

A coupon is printed and freely distributed in advance of a purchase, with the hope that it will motivate a potential buyer to purchase a specific product or service. The coupon can offer a discount at the time of purchase, a free gift, an upgrade, or some other type of bonus. It can also be given after a purchase to be used on a subsequent purchase within a given timeframe. Coupons also remind people of your business and can be used as a form of advertising or direct mail or as a print-out from your website.

Some industries, such as fast-food establishments and restaurants, are great candidates for coupons and use them often. Not many people will buy a pizza without a coupon—they're available everywhere. But coupons need to have a reasonable perceived value for the buyer to use them. If the coupon value is not enough to make it worthwhile to purchase a certain item within a time limit, customers won't use it. And if the customer doesn't like the product or has no use for it, he or she probably will discard the coupons immediately. You should direct-mail coupons to people who need or want your products and can afford to buy them.

A rebate is an after-the-sale refund of money that has already been paid. It's generally given by the product manufacturer or the home office of the seller's business. Rebates are usually offered on larger purchases or products where continuing service fees are charged, such as a cell phone or smartphone purchases.

Coupons offer discounts *before* a customer pays; rebates offer a refund *after* the customer pays. Both of these assume that a purchase will be made.

To qualify for the rebate, customers usually have to fill out a card asking for personal information about themselves, their buying habits, and their household or business. The manufacturer or home office doesn't really *need* this information to send the rebate—they want it so they can decide what else to try to sell you. Based on the customer's answers, his or her name and address will be assigned to one of the business's mailing lists for future use. The customer will start receiving mail or calls about extended warranties, add-ons, or other products that should relate to their income level and lifestyle. They also may end up on mailing lists that are sold to other companies.

Many people will buy a product because of the rebate but never send the rebate in, which is essentially more money in your pocket. A rebate doesn't work for every type of product or service, but if it can work for you, consider it. Ask the manufacturers of your popular products whether they offer rebates or plan to in the future. You can win in two ways—you get the sale and the mailing list for future purchases.

Show Off Your Logo

If you have a logo (and you should) or a special type style for your company name, you must put it on everything and put it everywhere. If you need a new logo, contact a local college's art department to find students who will help you design one at a reasonable cost. Professional firms can create logos for you, but you'll have to search for one that's not too big or expensive and get a couple of quotes first.

A local college's art department can help you design a logo at a reasonable cost.

A point to consider: The more colors you put in your logo, the more it will cost to print. When you first get a new logo, ask for many copies of it—black on white paper. The black on white can be used to print in any color. If you're using more than one color, you'll need separated artwork so that each color can be printed independently. You'll also want to have different sizes of your logo.

You always want people to remember your logo or special type style for your business name. Look for ways to use it everywhere. Buy a stamp or labels so that you can apply your logo to all literature and correspondence. Your logo will build your brand just by being there and being visible.

Be sure to save it on your computer and back it up on a CD or other storage medium. Keep copies of your logo in several places and take a disc home—don't take a chance on losing the only copy and having to start over again.

Make sure you're satisfied with your logo before you accept it; you don't want to change it often. Your logo should become familiar to customers and prospects, and changing it could hurt your identity awareness. When you have the logo just the way you want it, start using it *everywhere*. Here's a list of places where you can use your logo:

- All envelopes and mailers
- Business cards, letterhead, and business forms
- Fax cover and memo sheets
- Advertising brochures/literature
- Product packaging and cartons
- Product instructions
- Invoices, purchase orders, and checks
- Uniforms and hats
- Company shirts and wearables
- Promotional items and giveaways
- Promotional backdrops, displays, and materials at tradeshows
- Signs, posters, and billboards
- Your door or nameplate
- Website pages
- Display windows
- Vehicle lettering
- Magnets and labels
- All correspondence and communication
- Direct-mail pieces
- All print advertising
- All TV advertising

The more times your customers and prospects see your logo, the more confidence they will have in buying your product or service. They will remember your brand more easily and think of your business when they need that type of product or service. You want to create a buying *comfort* level that comes with seeing your logo over and over.

Using your logo everywhere should be automatic, so that it will stand out in your group of competitors. Even the smallest business can and should have a logo or a special type style that looks unique. It's an inexpensive way of placing you and your company in the minds of everyone who sees it. Looking unique to your target market also can create a feeling of your company being larger than it actually is.

Collaborate with Your Strip Mall Neighbors

If you're in a strip mall, get together with as many neighbor stores as you can and have a parking-lot or end-of-the-season sale or an entertainment event. Just be sure to check with the building owner to see whether there are any local restrictions or objections before you spend a lot of time planning. Also, check with your city to see whether you need any permits and with your insurance agent to see whether you need any special insurance for the event.

Collaborating with neighboring businesses for a promotion is a good way to draw more people to your event and share the expense.

Start planning and promoting at least four to six weeks in advance so the event doesn't disrupt your regular business. There will be several other merchants involved, so you can share the expenses, making costs lower for everyone.

Giant balloons or searchlights can easily attract more attention; use them if you can. There's no way to predict the weather, so if you can afford to get a big tent, it's a good idea. People will see the tent going up and may be curious enough to come back. The more things that make your area look out of the ordinary or unique, the better. Check with an event planner/rental agent for other ideas.

Make a checklist and keep adding to it as new ideas come up. You can have short after-hours brainstorming meetings with the other business owners to get everyone's input and find out what each can afford to spend. Consider two days for your event and longer hours so your investment will have plenty of time to pay off. Get BIG banners for all entrances to the strip mall and put them up seven to ten days in advance. Better yet, start promoting the event when you first have a definite agreement with the other stores.

By the way, that agreement should be on paper and signed by the other store owners or managers.

Here's an idea to start creating early interest; people are intrigued by the mysterious, so try this. Get five banners and put one each week on the busiest nearby street. Start with the fifth week prior to the event and change the banner every week.

- Fifth week prior: *It's coming soon!*
- Fourth week prior: *It's coming in four weeks!*
- Third week prior: *Music and fun in three weeks!*
- Second week prior: *Two more weeks—mark your calendar!*
- Final week prior: *Bring the family next Saturday and Sunday!*

By not using dates on your banners, you can use them again next year if the event is a success.

Line up some type of entertainment or a radio remote. Have contests and games for the kids and include a nonprofit raffle to make it more than just a shopping experience. Try to get the local chapter of the American Heart Association, the Red Cross, or the Juvenile Diabetes Research Foundation to set up a free testing area. Depending on the size of your city, you may even get the Chamber of Commerce to join in or set up a booth.

If the strip mall has a fast-food outlet or restaurant, they can serve outside with portable tables and chairs. If there isn't a fast-food store, invite one from a nearby strip mall to participate. They'll probably jump at the opportunity. (Remember, you want to involve a small business, *not* a national chain.)

Send press releases to all the local newspapers, TV stations, radio stations, and churches (which may put a notice in the weekly bulletin for their congregation). Do this at least three weeks in advance, so these media outlets will have plenty of time to use the release.

Start putting up decorations, pennants, searchlights, flags, and more signs about two to three days in advance to attract pre-event attention. Make sure you have enough extra products on hand for increased sales. You'll also need to schedule more sales staff and a clean-up crew. If you get everyone to do their part and you promote enough, the event should be a great success. You'll get the attention of many new customers who never knew you existed and who may return with repeat business.

Special Discount Days and Nights

For a retail store or restaurant, attracting attention is the name of the game. You can have special discounts for normally slow days and nights that will make people aware of your business and will help you cultivate new customers. Serve refreshments and have music or even door-prize drawings. You might even get newspapers or radio stations to cover a big enough event. A few ideas for special events or discount nights are:

- Uniformed military night
- Senior discount day
- Little League/soccer night
- Police and firefighter night
- Family night
- Couples night
- Double-coupon day
- Honor student night
- Two-for-one day
- College student day
- Twins or triplets day
- Singles nights
- It's your birthday!
- 50% off night
- Meet the mayor night
- Amateur talent night
- 1960s dress-up night
- Newlywed night
- Big family discount day
- It's your anniversary!
- Boy/Girl Scout night
- Chamber of Commerce night
- Veterans night
- City workers night

There are as many more possibilities as you can come up with. You don't want to have the same discounts too often, though, or those customers will never come back when they have to pay full price. Be sure to promote the event well in advance with in-store signs, window signs, and newspaper ads if they are in your budget. And don't forget to send press releases to the media—you might get lucky and get some coverage.

When you have special discounts or gift nights, you make people feel important if they qualify. Post a list of dates when discount days are coming and mention them to customers so they spread the word. Any time people are talking about your business, they're also promoting it.

Not only do events like this get people talking about your establishment and bring in new customers, they also create goodwill with the group getting the discount. Everyone likes to get a discount, but the long-term objective is to increase sales and acquire new and repeat customers.

Fast-Food Delivery Convenience

For many food establishments, delivery orders can add 10 to 20 percent to overall sales totals. For pizza places, it's typically more than half. So why not make it easy and pleasant for your customers? Ease of ordering and timely delivery can keep your current customers coming back and can entice new ones. Find ways to provide the outstanding service that your competitors are not offering.

If you're a restaurant, adding delivery service can yield increased sales and bring in new customers who might never come in person.

You can set certain hours for delivery so you won't need to have a delivery person available all the time. But those hours should be liberal, such as 11 a.m. to 2 p.m. for lunch and 5 p.m. to 8 p.m. for dinner. Put these hours on all your menus and literature and post them in the restaurant. And if people call a few minutes before the cutoff time, don't refuse their order if there's any way you can get it to them. You can also offer free delivery with a minimum order total or delivery for just a nominal fee of a dollar or two. Remember, deliveries can result in extra business, so treat them like an ongoing promotion.

Encourage early ordering for lunch so you can plan ahead and get orders delivered on time. There will be some last-minute orders, so be prepared by getting the early ones ready to go and waiting. Make it easy for your customers to place their orders by phone, fax, or email. You can also start a list of fax or email addresses for frequent customers and send out daily specials in the early morning. Many of your business customers will wait for the message so they can decide what and where to get lunch. You'll get orders you might otherwise not get, because you'll remind customers about your establishment. If they want to stop receiving the faxes or email, just give them an easy way to get off the list.

Hire reliable and competent delivery people, because they are visiting *your* customers. Require their appearance to be clean and neat. Most businesses that get lunch deliveries give good tips, so your delivery people should make a fair amount if they get there on time and are courteous.

Any time a delivery is more than 10 minutes late or something is forgotten, offer some restitution right away—either a free meal or sandwich or perhaps free dessert on their next order. Fax or email the customer something he or she can use to remind you of this in case you forget. And keep those deliveries moving so you can make those extra dollars.

Stick with Magnets

Do magnets still work as promotional items? It depends on your business, but overall, they're an inexpensive way to keep your company name and phone number immediately available to your customers. Magnets are useful not only for consumer sales, but also for any business that wants a quick response when it's time to order. And they're convenient for emergency numbers when seconds matter.

Order magnets that are attractive and colorful, so they will be saved and used by your customers.

The business-card size and shape of magnet is the most popular and the least expensive, but many shapes are available. For example, a local florist uses large heart magnets on the sides of their delivery vehicles. Ask your salesperson for a catalog.

Magnets are also available affixed to postcards for fast mailings via First Class or standard mail. The latest idea in magnets is the magnet-coupon combination card. These cards are usually 8-1/2×3-1/2 or larger and can easily be used in direct mail. The top portion has magnetic material on the back, and several perforated coupons are below. After the coupons are torn off and used, the top magnetic portion remains with the customer for future reference. These combo cards work great for fast-food restaurants, pizza parlors, maid services, computer stores, or any other business that offers coupons. They can also be used as a self-mailer postcard; check with your promotional supplier for ideas.

Here are a few other ideas of businesses for which magnets might be useful:

- **Pizza parlors.** When you're ready to order, don't you look on your refrigerator door rather than drag out the phonebook? Is there a magnet there?

- **Drug stores.** People put these on medicine cabinets for pre-scription reorders and questions.

- **Animal hospitals.** Magnets can provide emergency phone numbers and hours for office visits.

- **Schools.** These might include snow-day phone numbers. Or, they may be given as recognition to students for academic excellence and/or strong attendance.

- **Realtors.** You never know when someone will be ready to buy or sell. A magnet comes in handy for them to send referrals to you or to check current prices.

- **Towing companies.** Towing companies might give magnets to restaurants and building owners for the removal of unwanted cars.

- **Office supplies.** Customers can put magnets on filing cabinets for quick and easy ordering of supplies. You might also have a large magnet with a to-do list or a list of things to order.

- **Professional offices.** You might buy magnets in October with next year's calendar on them, or just use them as business cards.

- **Oil change and repair.** Magnets could serve as a reminder of when a person needs to change his or her oil and when it was done last. (Static-cling stickers are also available.)

- **Florists.** Magnets might include where and when to order flowers and may promote non-plant items and gifts.

Magnets have been around for quite a while, but they're still an inexpensive way of making your business visible and easy to contact when needed. Give magnets out freely and offer to put a stack of them in your cross-promotion partner's store or office.

- **Restaurants.** You might advertise your specialty and the number to call for reservations or carry-out orders. You could also sell magnets for a dollar or two and use them as a 10 percent discount on any guest check over, say, $10. Make these good for multiple use, but they should have an expiration date.

- **Banks.** Magnets might include info on how to check balances by phone, pay bills, transfer funds, and so on. They can also include hours of operation and web addresses.

- **Parts supplier.** You might put magnets on your customers' filing cabinets for quick phone ordering.

- **Sports teams.** Magnets might feature schedules of games and phone numbers to call for tickets.

This list provides only a handful of ideas for how magnets can promote business. Look at your customers and prospects to see whether magnets will help you promote new business and get reorders. Make it easy for customers and prospects to find and use your phone number, website, and email address.

Sponsor a Nonprofit

By sponsoring an organization in your selling area, you can get not only personal satisfaction, but also a boost in business. Select something you believe in, such as a boys' or girls' club, a homeless shelter, an elderly activity group, or a "keep my town beautiful" organization. Something local will bring more attention to your company and will generate free publicity. Avoid the large national organizations where you're just one of thousands supporting it. And remember that sponsoring can mean making donations, giving your time, or running a fundraising event.

> Sponsor a local organization, rather than a large national one. It will generate more publicity for your company, and you'll be doing something good in your community.

Whatever you decide to do, be as visible as possible and send news and press releases to the media. You can bring attention to your business plus motivate other companies and individuals to jump on the bandwagon with donations and help.

To find the right nonprofit group for you, look in the yellow pages for associations and organizations or just search the web. Then call a few and ask questions. You want to make sure that your time and money are going to something worthwhile. You don't want some executive getting a large salary taken from the donations.

A long-term relationship with a nonprofit will make your name and company synonymous with the organization. You'll always be in the foreground or background when something newsworthy occurs concerning that nonprofit organization.

Depending on your time and abilities, you may even get on TV to promote your cause and be introduced using your company name. Always make any donations in your company name, not in your name. And if your employees are ever phone volunteers for a telethon, make sure they're wearing company T-shirts or polos. If you don't have shirts, get them quickly; there are many sources available.

At nonprofit meetings, you may also meet other prominent businesspeople in your area. Networking with them surely can't hurt.

Nonprofit Your Way to Profits

An independent supermarket in suburban Chicago is using a promotion that benefits a local school and their store. Every month, the school buys $20,000 worth of $10 cash cards (2,000 cards) that are as good as money in the store. They get a 5 percent discount, or $1,000 off, which the school keeps for special projects and general expenses. The school has parents who have committed to purchasing all the cash cards every month, so that the school quickly gets its investment back, including their $1,000. Because the families need to buy groceries every month anyway, they now shop at that supermarket and use the cash cards to pay for part of their purchases. The store then resells the numbered cash cards back to the school the following month, and the cycle goes on.

The supermarket is getting a lot of customers that probably would have gone to the bigger national stores, and the additional business easily pays for the 5 percent discount. The store also makes some of the discount back because people never redeem all the cards, and people buy more than $10 worth of groceries per trip. The store is helping the school and promoting their business at the same time.

You could do something similar with several schools at one time or with any other nonprofit organizations. Have signs in your store inviting anyone interested to inquire about participation in a program that can benefit both of you.

Cross-Promotions

Find a non-competing business that has the same target market as you and work out some cross-promotion strategies.

It there a business that wants to reach and sell to the same customers as you do—but is *not* a competitor? There are always other businesses that serve the same target market you do but that have no interest in your type of business or what you sell. Why not work together and expand your horizons even more?

You can put flyers with coupons in your cross-promotion partner's store and even print "Compliments of…" on them for a nice personal touch. In return, you can give out information or have a small display where your customers can be referred to your cross-promotion partner. Some businesses naturally go together very nicely, such as:

- Hair salon and tanning parlor
- Printer and graphic designer
- Wedding photographer and tuxedo rental
- Health-food store and exercise club
- Clothing store and shoe store
- Travel agency and car rental agency
- Employment agency and daycare center

- Fast-food franchise and candy store
- Liquor store and deli
- Casino and jewelry store
- Furniture store and interior design firm
- Auto-parts store and tire store
- Bookstore and coffeehouse
- Video store and pizza delivery service
- Hotel and restaurant
- Pet store and veterinarian
- Golf course and sporting goods dealer
- Florist and funeral home
- Chiropractor and massage therapy
- Auto-repair service and towing service
- Realtor and mortgage company
- Computer store and software company

See the relationship between each one? They both sell to the same customers, but they supply a different product or service. Find your best cross-promotional partner and talk to the owner.

This scenario works best for two small businesses because store managers for large companies usually don't have the authority to make these types of decisions, and they may think it's too much trouble to take it higher up. And besides, we want to help and promote our fellow small businesses, and we hope they feel the same way, right?

It's important get to know your partner(s) and be sure they provide quality products and services. You're giving an endorsement by referring customers to other businesses, and you don't want it to backfire on you.

Have a Contest

Contests are fun, attention-getting promotions if you advertise them correctly. You can set up the contest yourself or use a consultant who specializes in them.

Keep in mind that your prize(s) must be of value to your participants for the contest to work. The prizes should be something they probably wouldn't buy for themselves or something that is out of their price range.

If you want to run a contest, remember that the prizes must be something of value to your customers, or they will just ignore the contest.

One thing you can try is scratch-off game cards that offer discounts and free products. Scratch-offs are becoming a fad, and businesses of all sizes can use them. They give the customer a feeling of participating and a chance to win something.

You may be able to get other stores or businesses to donate prizes in exchange for the free publicity. It never hurts to ask, and you may be pleasantly surprised by what you receive. Just keep in mind that when running a contest, you must adhere to the Federal Trade Commission rules and guidelines, which include:

- **Ensuring randomness.** You need to show that no person or thing can affect the contest outcome.

- **Providing full disclosure.** You must provide complete contest rules to all participants, as well as the odds of winning (if they can be determined or will be determined by the number of entries). You need to specify how people can participate without buying anything.

- **Awarding all prizes.** If you award all the prizes you advertise, it's safer and less of a hassle than trying to explain why you didn't award all prizes.

- **Not discouraging non-buyers.** Make it very clear that all who enter have an equal chance to win and that everyone should enter.

If you're doing a national direct-mail contest, be sure you're not running a lottery!

If you are planning a national direct-mail contest, you need to be sure you're not running a lottery. Many states still prohibit lotteries, and you'll also be in violation of postal regulations. A lottery has three elements:

- Chance
- Prizes
- Consideration

To be sure you're not running a lottery, you need to eliminate one of those elements, and consideration is the easiest. Legally, consideration means buying something in order to enter the contest. Also, a requirement that a person must be present to win can be interpreted as a consideration.

Why go through all this trouble just to give away prizes? Increases in responses of up to 35 percent are not uncommon to the offers that accompany a contest. That doesn't necessarily mean buyers, but with that much increase in response, you're sure to make more sales. Contests also bring attention to your company and may get more people talking about your business. So follow the rules of running a contest, and you could be the big winner in sales and customers.

Whenever you have a contest or a giveaway at your store or restaurant, make a big deal out of the winners. Have the drawing at a time when most people who want to can attend and be sure to take lots of pictures. Send a press release or call the newspapers, radio stations, and TV—if it's a slow news days, you might get coverage. After all, you can't get a "no" or a "not interested" if you don't at least try—and you certainly can't get a "yes." Any time you can get your business mentioned in the news, it's exposure you didn't have to pay for.

Don't Be Unoccupied

What do you do if your promotion isn't working? Perhaps you thought you had a great idea to bring a lot of people into your business, but all you can hear is an echo instead. Maybe you sent out press releases saying what a big event this is would be, and it's a slow news day so the media shows up—but no one else is there.

When you invite the media to an event you're having at your store or office, be sure that there are enough people there when the media arrives. Invite friends, relatives, neighbors, sports teams, and anyone who will attend. Serve refreshments to make people more comfortable so they'll stay for a while. Tell people about the food and/or drinks in advance; everyone likes a free meal.

If you arrange an event that will attract the media, make sure people show up to the event! The promise of free food or stuff for kids can lure a crowd.

If your business is nearly empty, the media will assume you're not successful and will report that or not even cover the event at all. But by all means, don't cancel the event after you advertised and alerted the media. Go on as planned for the people who *do* show up, and learn from the experience for the next time. Experience is a great teacher, and you're sure to learn what will work and what won't. So have your promotional event, but plan for any outcome in advance—especially if it's the first time you're having such an event.

Celebrate Your Anniversary

No, I don't mean with your spouse—I mean with your business. Your anniversary comes around every year, and you might as well get some recognition from it. And, unless you opened your business on a national holiday (which isn't likely), no one else, including your competitors, will be using that day. It's your one special day to get some attention for your own business, so don't pass it up.

Celebrating your business's anniversary demonstrates that you're successful enough to survive in your field. This will give customers confidence in your company.

Besides, anniversaries can make customers more comfortable, because they're a sign of your longevity in business. Remember that many companies don't make it past two years, and some don't even survive the first year. By having some type of event, you're rewarding your loyal customers and picking up some new ones, as well as celebrating your success. You may even get some free publicity if you've been in business for a long time, so alert the media.

Retail, mail-order, and B2B companies can all celebrate anniversaries. The kind of celebration or event you have will depend on your type of target customer. What will your customers be attracted to? Perhaps a sale, a parking-lot party, free gifts, or fun entertainment. You can use a free offer for mail-order customers, such as 20 percent more product if they order during your anniversary week. If you have local business customers, you can have your salespeople deliver a box of candy, donuts, or a specific usable item made just for your anniversary. Be sure to use a label so your company logo or brand is on the delivery.

You could also use the occasion to announce a new product or service that your target market has been waiting for. Make pre-announcement statements in the paper or through direct mail to build anticipation. If your customers are all around the country, consider making a video or CD of your presentation and sending it to them. Many companies make these announcements during tradeshows, and you will draw even more attention if you tie it in with an anniversary.

If you have a retail store, you can roll back prices on some popular products to what the prices were when the store was founded. Set up only certain hours for this promotion and be ready to handle a crowd. This can all tie in with a mini-party and free soda, food, and games for kids. A free raffle for an expensive item can be a temptation to pull in new customers. Have banners made for the occasion—and remember that if you don't put a date on them, you can use them again in the future.

Start planning a few months in advance to give yourself time to come up with ideas and a way to use them. Ask others on your staff for their input and let them follow through on the ones you like. You're going to have your anniversary anyway, so you might as well use it to your advantage. And consumers enjoy any type of celebration, even if it's not their own.

A Weekend at the Mall

If you're starting a new business or you have a home-based business, here's an idea for some additional public exposure. Most shopping malls are looking for extra income wherever they can find it and will allow you to do temporary selling at a reasonable rate. You can usually get a draped table and two chairs for a two- or three-day weekend for a nominal fee, and you can use that to present and sell your products. If you feel this amount (usually around $250 to $300) is still more than your budget will allow, consider sharing it with another person who is trying to reach the same market. Also, sometimes you can negotiate a lower rental price from the mall if you contract for three to six weekends.

Almost everyone shops the mall, so your type of customer or client is likely to walk by. Get a sign with a headline that will attract your target customers and get them to stop at your table.

This is also a good way to test new products and see whether there is any customer interest. You can give a small sample of your product or show a video of your service, which may also attract passersby. Watch people to see how long their interest lasts and ask them to join your mailing list.

You might be surprised by how reasonably priced it is to set up a table and chairs to display your products or services at your local mall. Always select the busiest mall days to increase your exposure.

If you're selling big-ticket products or services, you can use this get-acquainted process to set up appointments at people's home or office. When setting an appointment, write the date and time on the back of your business card so your potential customer won't forget it. Give people at least one piece of literature they can take with them and read at their leisure. And be sure to follow up exactly when you told them and be on time for all appointments.

If this strategy works at one shopping mall, try it at others in your area.

Some Other Fun, Profitable, and Outrageous Promotions

Promotions can come in any size, shape, or form and are only limited by your imagination and resources. Here are some ideas you can use or mold to your business objectives. But don't stop with these; try anything you think will work for your business.

- **Organize a parade.** Find a theme that everyone likes, get a city permit, and start and end the parade at your business parking lot. Offer refreshments and entertainment afterward.

- **Have a band play outside.** Find a band or combo that fits in with a holiday theme, such as St. Patrick's Day or patriotic songs for Flag Day (June 14). Many local bands want exposure, so the cost can be low.

- **Hold an art exhibit.** Have local artists display their art and sell it at reasonable prices while you promote your regular business. Put an ad in the paper or contact local art stores, and you should get an abundance of artists interested in participating.

- **Have an ice cream social.** Invite people to a local ice cream store, encourage, say, 1960s clothing, and hand out information on your business. Play music from the era, too.

- **Hire a balloon sculptor.** This is great for retail stores that sell children's products. Arrange for the sculptor to be at your store for three to four hours on a Saturday and Sunday, and make sure you publicize the event in advance.

- **Sponsor a record breaker.** Many people want to get into the Guinness book, so have the record broken at your place of business and get a crowd or even media coverage.

- **Reward yellow-pages clippers.** Give a 10 to 20 percent discount if customers clip and bring in your biggest competitor's yellow pages ad—the original only. The next time customers look in the phonebook, your competitor's ad won't be there—and your smaller ad will remind them of your business.

- **Do CD/book exchanges.** People who leave one get to pick one that others left. Any leftovers can be donated to a retirement home or a civic organization.

- **Have a drawing.** Maybe it's a free lunch at 12:45 p.m. every Tuesday for people already in your restaurant. Give away one big prize and use entry forms to build a mailing list.

- **Have a trivia quiz.** Use the almanac or search the Internet for questions and answers; give discounts on products for correct answers. Have a final quiz where others come and watch.

- **Feature costumed characters.** Hire one or two dressed-up characters to play with the kids and tease the adults. They can also hand out coupons for future purchases.

- **Celebrate unusual holidays.** There are websites for "Fundays" and "Crazy Holidays." Find out when Hat Day and National Garden Month are, for example. Then use them in your promotions to attract people.

- **Run a dance contest/marathon.** You'll get some unusual-looking dancers that will entertain your customers. Just be sure you're willing to stay until it's over or set a predetermined ending.

- **Host a cutest baby contest.** Take pictures and let other customers be the judges. Put the pictures on a bulletin board for everyone to see. The proud parents and relatives will come back to see them.

- **Have a bagel-/donut-eating contest.** These are usually inexpensive—or maybe free if you make a deal with the baker to advertise for them. Supply free coffee/milk to the participants.

- **Have a guess-the-number contest.** Have a big bowl of gumballs, sticks of gum, screws, paper clips, or any other small item. Have people guess how many of the items are in the bowl. Remember, you have to count them to determine the winners. Use names on the entry slips to build your mailing list.

- **Give the lottery.** For big-ticket sales, you can give $25, $50, or $100 in scratch-off lottery tickets. The recipient might even win his or her entire purchase price back! If the person wins a big prize, you'll get some great publicity.

- **Have kids' games.** Children love to play games of any type and are happy with even small prizes. They will keep asking their parents to bring them back to have fun again.

- **Reward the 10,000th customer.** Figure out a way to keep track of the number of customers in a given time period. Host a big event to celebrate the winner, take pictures, and alert the media.

- **Give game cards.** Mail out scratch-off or lift-off game cards for prizes, free items, or discounts. There should be no purchase necessary to play, but the cards should be redeemed at your business.

- **Have a storyteller.** Do this on Saturday morning for kids and their parents. Usually a bookstore will send someone at no cost. This is a great idea when you're promoting youth-oriented products.

Action Plan

✓ Find different types of promotions to draw in business.

✓ Design a logo that people will remember.

✓ Plan an event with your retail neighbors.

✓ Keep looking for new promotional ideas to use.

"When every day seems like a rainy day, start selling umbrellas."

—BT

Chapter 8

The Website

- Purpose of Your Website
- Some Design Ideas
- Website Don'ts
- Promoting Your Site
- Luring Visitors Back with Interesting Bait
- Order Follow-Up
- Getting Attention
- Don't Let Your Site Get Stale
- Being Charitable
- Social Media And Blogs
- Don't Quit Your Day Job
- Asking Permission First

If you're in business, you can't ignore the web; it's not going away, and it will only get bigger. How big? Does anyone really know or care? The only things people care about are how easy your site is to use, how informative it is, and how quickly it loads when they visit it.

The web is ever-changing; in fact, what I'm writing about in this chapter today could be out of date by the time you read it—such is the nature of materials written about technology. So, to avoid this as much as possible, I'll keep to the general aspects of your website, what your customers want to see when they visit, and how to get them to return.

Customers' wants and needs won't necessarily change much—but how you offer to fulfill them might. You want a visit to your site to be a pleasant experience and encourage people to explore what's new since their last visit. Whether you're taking orders or providing information, it should be done easily and quickly. People use computers in large part because they're convenient and fast, so don't let your site slow them down.

The price of designing and setting up a website has come way down in the last few years, and it is now affordable in most small-business budgets. Many creative and technologically savvy people design sites as a second job, and their services are usually very reasonably priced. Talk to a couple of them before you make a decision on hiring one. Or, you may already have a website design program on your computer. If not, you can purchase one at a reasonable cost. If you enjoy and understand the software, you can design your own website and change it often.

When selecting a web host, get several quotes and references. Ask friends or other businesses which one they use. You want to be sure that the host provides enough space for all the things you want to include on your site. Also, find out the monthly or quarterly cost from your web host and how you are supposed to pay it. Will they email you an invoice, or do you have to remember to make a payment on your own? Some may ask to keep your credit card on file and automatically charge your fees every month. You might also consider automatic checking-account withdrawal so you don't forget to pay them. You don't want your website shut down because of an oversight about payment.

You can have your site open while you're designing it; just put "Under Construction" on the homepage. Allow visitors to send you an email to get additional information before it's up on the site.

Purpose of Your Website

After you've made the decision to construct and operate a company website, you must design it for the purpose intended. Many startup home-based businesses want to run their entire business as a website, which is fine. The basic idea is that the cost to start such a site-based business is relatively low compared to starting a business with a physical location. If you're using your home for your business, your rent and utilities are already taken care of— plus, you may be eligible for a tax deduction.

There's more involved in setting up a website-based home business than you might think.

Sounds great, right? But there may be more involved than you think, because doing everything on your site means:

- Advertising your site (with search engines and offline)
- Presenting and marketing your products or services
- Taking the order and answering inquiries
- Changing prices and specs as necessary
- Accepting payment and providing secure-site assurance
- Processing the order correctly
- Providing customer service for questions and inquiries
- Performing follow-up maintenance on orders
- Providing information and facts

If you want to start and finish the sales transaction on your site, can you provide all of the above? How long will it take you to set up a site that can do all of these things? Is there software available that will fit your needs—or that you can adapt to? If one part of the process goes down, can you still serve your customers? What about customers who won't order without actually talking to someone—are you equipped to handle them? Will you have a toll-free number and be available to answer calls?

Another approach is to provide all the information, sample requests, literature requests, and basic order information on your website. Then complete the order by phone, fax, or in person. If your product or service would sell better with a personal touch, give the customer the option of a human contact. You will be more successful if you conduct the transaction the way your customer wants it done, rather than simply doing what's most convenient for you.

Keep the process simple for even non-tech-savvy customers. Remember, they have the money you want, so keep them happy while they're spending it.

Some Design Ideas

Whether you're going to hire a web designer or create the site yourself, certain factors will help you make a site that customers and prospects will want to visit over and over again. And if your site is going to be a big part of your business, then satisfied visitors will be very important. Consider these ideas and add more of your own to be sure your site is appealing to everyone who visits.

- Choose a domain name that's easy to remember but not so long that it's difficult to type in. Don't use difficult or foreign words; keep it simple.

- Don't overload your homepage. Encourage visitors to click on links to pages they're interested in. Create a good first impression with your visitor.

- Stack your links on the side vertically, the same way the page is viewed.

- If you're using a background scene or color, use the same one on every page.

- Use just enough graphics on your homepage to catch your visitors' attention without requiring a long load time. Simple yet attractive is best for capturing people's interest.

- Use drop-down menus so people can easily navigate your site.

- Have a contact or email link on every page.

- Encourage everyone to bookmark your site for future visiting.

- Keep text short and to the point; visitors aren't there to read a book.

- If you're selling a product, have pictures of it in use.

- Describe your products and services in easy-to-understand terms.

- Give visitors options for how you can ship their order: standard mailing, expedited shipping, or overnight.

- Specify whether you sell locally, nationally, or internationally and the approximate shipment time and cost for each option.

- Provide a How to Order link for first-time buyers.

- Have a link to the order or checkout page on every product page so visitors don't get stranded or confused and abandon their order.

- Have a mailing-list page with a form customers can fill out to receive future information. Ask for their birthday (without the year) so you can send them an email card on that day.

- Offer a password log-in for fast repeat orders.

- Include a reorder number for fast repeat orders.

- Make the site's text large enough for senior citizens to read easily.

- Use swap or rollover images—put them on your homepage and other linked pages.

- Remind visitors that they can print out any copy and ideas to review later or share with others.

- Have a feedback link where you can receive comments.

- Give people a reason to stay awhile—offer interesting and informative articles and facts that will entice web surfers to go deeper into your site and stay longer.

- Have a What's New link if you regularly add new products, upgrades, or enhancements.

- Give people a reason to come back—change or add to your site weekly or monthly with items your visitors want to see or learn about.

- If applicable, offer printable coupons with barcodes for use in your store.

- If applicable, offer printable menus and email ordering for pickup or delivery orders.

Website Don'ts

You've spent your time and hard-earned money getting your website going, and now you want a million people a day to visit it. Well, as many as possible, anyway—and you want them to return often. Here are some things you *don't* want to do when creating and designing your site:

- Don't have an extremely long or hard-to-remember web address; make it easy to spell, say, and remember.

- Don't tell it all on your homepage; you want people to browse your site.

- Don't make first-time visitors to your site sign in or leave their email address just to enter; most will just leave and go to another site instead.

- Don't use misspelled words or incorrect grammar in your text; have two or three people review it before you use it.

- Don't make it difficult for visitors to contact you; have email links everywhere.

- Don't use pop-ups that interfere with what the visitor is reading. Most of us hate this and will exit the site quickly to avoid dealing with them.

- Don't use pages with tons of graphics that take a long time to load; some people just won't wait.

- Don't use flashing elements that are hard on the eyes or distracting.

- Don't have broken links; check them periodically.

- Don't forget to show and explain your products or services in an obvious place; don't hide them so deeply in your site that customers can't find them.

- Don't avoid showing your prices. Instead, show and explain them.

- Don't forget to have a secure site if you're accepting payments or personal information.

- Don't forget to include your phone and fax numbers for people who may be having trouble navigating your site. Specify the offline hours that you are available.

- Don't forget to get listed on search engines and in web directories and to use blogs.

- Don't forget to make an offer of some type to get people to take action.

- Don't wait too long to answer emails; always respond within 12 hours.

- Don't neglect to add new products as soon as they are available.

- Don't ignore Internet buyers and their concerns. They are your marketing goal of the future.

Most of these points are just common sense, but how many sites have you been to that didn't follow these simple guidelines? You probably didn't stay long...*click.*

Promoting Your Site

After you're open and ready for visitors and business, you want as many people as possible to come to your website. There are many ways to promote your site, and perhaps surprisingly, many do *not* involve the computer.

Not all website promotion involves the computer.

Put your URL on all business cards, stationery, product literature, invoices, and print advertising. If your address is short or easy to remember, there's no limit to where you can use it. Use it on promotional giveaways, signs, magnets, vehicle lettering, and shirts or uniforms. If you're a Chamber of Commerce member, make sure your web address is listed in their directory and on their website. Think of other places where your customers and prospects look or things they read and then make sure they find you there. If you sell locally, consider a billboard on a busy street with your URL in large letters and an offer of a gift or discount to visitors. You can also trade links with other companies that are after the same target market but are not competitors—do so by adding a link for your business on their site and their link on your site.

Another idea to drive visitors to your website is the use of traffic exchanges. They will help you trade links with other sites that are looking for a similar target market. Search the Internet until you find a traffic exchange that is close to your type of industry; check as many as you can before registering with any.

Social networking sites, such as LinkedIn, Facebook, YouTube, and Twitter, allow you to create a professional profile for others to see. You can also use their venues as a forum, blog, or bulletin board. Add new content to your site as often as you can and encourage visitors to come back regularly by reminding them on social networking sites.

You can also offer a free weekly or monthly online newsletter that pertains to your industry and contains facts and new information. Let visitors read and/or download it and encourage them to come back regularly to see the next issue. Have a sign-up link where customers can register to receive special offers and reorder reminders. That way, you can build an email list you can use for other purposes and promotions.

Don't have a great, informative, and fun website that nobody knows about. Find creative ways to drive traffic to it and make people want to come back. Several sites out there offer website promotion ideas that are free, so don't pay for them. Keep looking for new methods to get those visitors to stop by and see what you have to offer. Obviously, having more people visit your website will increase your chances for new sales.

Lure Visitors Back with Interesting Bait

Getting visitors to visit your site regularly is a challenge and an effort. Provide regular tips and post lead-ins on social networks and blogs. Try to pique people's curiosity so they will visit even without your nudge.

You can't do business online with people if they don't visit your site, return, and remember it. You want to offer some type of bait that keeps them checking your website because they know there will be something new. Here are some ideas you can use to lure repeat visits:

- Have a regular tip of the week (or month) that provides information and help for your target market.

- Offer a newsgroup with customer feedback, questions, and comments.

- Have advance notice of upcoming sales and what will be offered.

- Have Internet order discounts for purchases at your secure website. Or, offer a bonus or gift if customers order on your site.

- Have an email newsletter with free tips and ideas that change often. Register subscribers and encourage them to print out the newsletter.

- Include a FAQ section where visitors can quickly get answers to common questions.

- If possible, include comments and photos from satisfied customers.

- Have a coupon, special, or discount-of-the-week offer.

- Consider using a quote or joke section on your site that changes daily or weekly.

- Offer a monthly prize for the customer tip of the month.

- Have holiday greetings on your homepage, but be sure to change them when the holiday is over. Don't leave Happy New Year up until May.

- Have a Coming Soon section so visitors will anticipate news and come back to find out what's new.

- Have a Customer Requests link so people can tell you what they want to buy.

Order Follow-Up

If you're planning to take orders and accept credit cards, be sure your site is customer friendly. It goes without saying that you need a secure page when credit cards and/or personal information are used. But what about order follow-up that customers can do themselves—easily and 24/7/365?

If you order products from Amazon.com or BarnesandNoble.com, for example, you'll notice that both have customer-friendly sites that even a non-techie can understand and navigate. If you need to check on part of an order at any time of the day, any day of the week, you can do so with a few clicks or perhaps a quick email to the shipping department. Easy!

> Visit a major online retailer to get ideas for how to provide access to 24/7/365 follow-up service for your customers.

When customers have questions before or after a purchase, they need a quick and easy way to get a response. The whole idea behind your website is that customers can use it any time of day or night. But even if your site can handle most of the questions and give your customers their tracking numbers, you still need to have a way for them to contact you directly. Email is a good method, but a small business should also be able to handle a phone inquiry, which gives many customers a comfort level with the business. So it's a good idea to include a toll-free phone number at the end of the follow-up page for those who need more help. If you wish, you can forward the contact number to a cell phone so the customer doesn't have to wait for a response. Or, you can just let customers know on the site that phone service is available at certain hours of the day.

Above all, make it easy for customers to order, follow up, and track their shipment, and they will be back to your site. Repeat business always pays off big!

Getting Attention

When you have your website up and running, you'll want to attract the attention of your target market and others. Visitors won't come to your site if they don't know about it or they can't find it easily. Your small business likely doesn't have the megabucks that the big companies do, so use the least expensive methods first and then increase your exposure as funds permit. Here are some ideas to draw attention and visitors to your site:

> To maximize the effectiveness of your website, check out *Increase Your Web Traffic in a Weekend*, Sixth Edition (Course Technology PTR, 2010).

131

- Register with Internet directories and choose the category that will create interest with your target market. Just search for your type of industry followed by the word "directory" to find applicable directories. Many will let you include a listing at no cost or a nominal charge.

- Locate and use free new-site services that will create interest at little or no cost.

- Post messages and articles to newsgroups that are of interest to the audience you want to reach.

- Start by listing with your favorite search engine and add others as your advertising budget permits. Some search engines are free to be listed on, but specialized ones may charge a small fee to be included or to be on the first page of search results.

- Send press releases to the local media and offer something free at your new website.

- Send press releases to trade publications in your industry and make a unique offer.

- Trade links with another non-competitive site that has the same target market.

- Advertise a printout coupon that can be used at your site for the first 30 or 60 days.

- Encourage visitors to bookmark your site or send info to a friend.

- Be creative in your use of keywords for search engines, but use both ordinary and unusual words.

- Use blogs and forums to let people know who you are and allow them to leave comments.

- Email your new web address to friends, relatives, and everyone you know and ask them to spread the word to others.

- Sign guest books on other websites and list your site and who should visit.

- Use social media, such as Twitter and Facebook, to promote your site and business.

- Send emails to associations and organizations to which your target customer may belong.

Don't Let Your Site Get Stale

Once your website is up and running, you need to make periodic changes to keep visitors coming back. If you had a web designer create your site, try to put in your contract or agreement an automatic three- or four-month update to your site. You don't want to have to pay big rates or fees for the designer to come back, so plan in advance.

Make site updates frequently to keep people coming back to see what's new.

If you have a computer-savvy person on your staff, another alternative is to have the web designer show that person how to make site updates. Start collecting ideas right away for changes and additions. Keep a file of all your site ideas so you can review them when it's time to make changes. Set a schedule for regular updates and then make them. Just remember to update your links as needed when you do this.

Assign someone on your staff to monitor and suggest changes to your site and get them done.

Be Charitable

If you want to create compassion with your online customers, offer to support popular charities. You can donate a small percentage of each sale to a charity of your customer's choice. Select four or five different charities of interest to a large number of people. Let the customer select or check a box to indicate which one they would like to receive their order donation. Alert each charity you're using that they are listed on your site, and they may respond by giving you a mention or link on their site. You can also have a link to their site for further information.

Offering to support popular charities with a small donation for each sale made is a smart way to earn customer respect. Most people like to give back, so if they can do so by using your site, you may earn their repeat business and referrals.

This strategy is easy to accomplish because the donation money comes out of sales dollars after the sale is made. Just be sure to send or transfer the donations in a timely manner—at least monthly.

You might also encourage customers to email you with the names of other charities they're interested in. You can consider adding new charities for which you get a lot of requests.

This is a win-win-win situation because you make three people happy—you, the customer, and the charity. It's a good feeling to give a part of your success back to those in need. If you give a lot to these charities, you might have a note on your site saying, "$X donated so far." And you and your staff can volunteer your time for local charitable events.

Social Media

One of the fastest-growing areas of electronic communication is social media. And what started as a fad has quickly turned into a business tool to create value and a venue for marketing. The key

Find a way to connect your business with one or more social networks. Your smart competitors will use it to reach your customers if you ignore them.

part to successful social media marketing is to establish yourself and your business as an expert in your industry or field. Because you can't control social media, you can only hope to influence the exchanges between members. Over time, you can build a level of authority that can contribute to your marketing efforts.

Some of the more common social networks are:

- **Twitter.** This site offers social networking by allowing users to send and read messages called *tweets*. These tweets are text posts with a limit of 140 characters (letters, spaces, and punctuation). Users may read any message (unless it's protected by sender) and follow other users and see their tweets. Twitter was started in 2006 and has grown rapidly worldwide.

- **Facebook.** This site was started in 2004, and as of 2010, it has more than 500 million active users. Members must be a self-proclaimed 13 years old to join and use the network. Facebook users create a profile to inform friends about themselves. A popular feature is status updates, which allows users to post a short message mentioning what they're currently doing or thinking about. Users can also link to news or human-interest stories or other sites and post them as status updates. Facebook allows members to join networks, which are organized by schools or colleges, for example, to let students get to know each other and the school better. Businesses are now using the network for marketing and to keep their "friends" in touch with industry developments.

- **MySpace.** This was the first big social network where members could exchange messages with other users. It became the most popular social networking site in the U.S. in 2006, but it was overtaken in popularity by Facebook in 2008. MySpace is currently owned by the News Corp, a large media company.

- **YouTube.** On this network, users can upload videos for anyone to view. YouTube was created in 2005 by three former PayPal employees, and it has grown exponentially since. Users post amateur music videos and movies, TV clips, and other performances. Google purchased YouTube in November 2006, and it has become the number-two search engine behind Google.

- **LinkedIn.** This is a business-oriented social network launched in 2003. The number of LinkedIn users is approaching 100 million as of this writing. Users can enter their profile, including their business skills and talents. The network is used for job searching, professional networking, and exchanging professional opportunities. Members can follow companies and join specialized groups.

Some other, lesser-known network sites include:

- **AsianAve.** Targeted for the Asian-American community.
- **Friends Reunited.** A UK-based site designed to connect neighbors and friends from school, work, and the armed forces.
- **Classmates.** Designed for users to find and communicate with past school friends and faculty.
- **Last.fm.** A music networking site.
- **Stickam.** A live video steaming and chat network.
- **Bebo.** A general social network.
- **Flickr.** A photography-related social network.
- **Habbo.** A worldwide general network aimed at teens.
- **weRead.** Network that allows users to rate and review books they're reading.
- **WAYN.** A network about travel and lifestyles.
- **XING.** A business network for Europe.
- **deviantART.** An art-related network and community.
- **MyHeritage.** A genealogy-oriented social network.
- **Flixster.** A network that allows users to share movie reviews and ratings.
- **BlackPlanet.** The largest African-American online community.
- **StumbleUpon.** A network that allows you to find websites that match your interests.

Blogs

A blog is supported or maintained by an individual or a business. The blogger makes regular entries providing information, specific news, commentary, or events. Bloggers can add video or graphics to enhance their commentary or entertain visitors.

Have a business blog and post at least twice a week. It's even okay to even give away your secret ideas, but always leave readers asking for more. The "more" can be found at your website.

You can use blogs for marketing by getting more personal with visitors with regard to products or services, or you can use your blog to drive visitors to your website. Blogs are interactive and allow visitors to leave comments or suggestions.

Readers can find blogs that interest them by using blog search engines, such as Bloglines, BlogScope, IceRocket, and Technorati. Blogs have been gaining popularity over the past 10 years, and these days even news broadcasts often refer to information found in the "blogosphere."

Don't Quit Your Day Job

The Internet is a big part of the future of retailing, and to grow and prosper in most businesses, you need to have a presence there and conduct some business online. But just because you now sell through your website, that doesn't mean you can or should abandon your office, mail-order, or brick-and-mortar store. The Internet marketing and sales you now do should likely be in addition to other ways of doing business, not in place of them.

So don't close your physical store or office just yet and rely only on the Internet sales. Many local customers still enjoy browsing a store and handling the products they buy. They may visit your site to see what's new but come to the store to buy it. Internet sales are growing all the time, but it will be a while before they begin to approach 100 percent of purchases. So get excited about your website, but don't neglect the parts of your business that helped you get there. Personal contact with customers still offers a comfort level you can't get on your computer screen.

Although marketing to overseas countries might *seem* simple when you have an Internet presence, be sure you consider all the factors affecting overseas business before you jump into it.

Further, although the Internet opens doors for selling and marketing all over the world, can you really provide service outside the U.S.? Most small businesses can't afford to. The longer your website is active, the more you'll learn whether there is actually a profitable market across the ocean. Will foreign customers be willing to pay the necessary additional shipping charges to receive your products? And how will you communicate with people in time zones that are 5, 8, or 12 hours different from yours?

Asking Permission First

Last but not least, if you want to email offers and information to prospects and customers, ask first. Let them register or subscribe to receive email from you so they won't consider your email as spam. Let them sign up, but also provide a way for them to unsubscribe. You don't want to lose any visitors or orders because people are afraid of excessive emails when they visit your website. By letting them control the number of emails they receive, you will make them more receptive to your online business. And don't flood people with emails, because they will eventually just delete them without reading them.

People will be more receptive to receiving your email if they know that it will be informative and useful.

Action Plan

✓ Decide what your website's purpose will be.

✓ Make changes often to your home page.

✓ Make your site easy to navigate.

✓ List your site address or include a link everywhere you can.

"If you buy the latest business software today, tomorrow it won't be."

—BT

Chapter 9

Pricing Strategies

- Pricing Headaches
- Higher Prices!
- Raising Prices
- Lowering Prices
- Pricing Strategies
- Offer Platinum, Gold, and Silver Levels
- Being the High-Priced Brand
- Loss Leaders
- Customer Quotes
- Price and Quality
- Prices on Window Items?

There's an old saying: "If you live by price, you may die by price—unless you're the market leader." Chances are if you're a small business selling commodity-type products, you won't be the market leader. Do you really want to go head-to-head against the massive discount stores and low-cost service companies on price alone? The low-price leader must make up the lower cost and potential lost profit with a higher sales volume, but what if that volume is not there? Once you've reduced prices to be or match the lowest price, it's difficult to raise prices again if the volume is not what you expected.

By offering products at a super-low price, you also run the risk that another merchant or middleman will buy a large quantity from you and resell the product at his or her business with a high markup. If you're paying the shipping, stocking, and display costs, why should someone else profit? Fortunately, you can help avoid this by limiting the number of items that a single person or group can purchase at one time. But people can get around this restriction by coming back on multiple occasions or ordering several times and having associates purchase for them.

And prices on some things never stay the same for very long; they're constantly changing based on various market factors. Look at the price of bananas or gas for your car—those prices sometimes change daily or weekly! And these aren't products people can stock up on, either, because bananas will spoil, and it's not exactly easy to store extra gas. Trying to build a business based on price is not only risky, but it's also very stressful for the owner.

Fighting the price war is a frustrating and many times a losing battle, and it is not for most small businesses. So, don't start it— and don't be lured into it unless you're sure you can succeed. Chances are you will see more frustration than success.

Pricing Headaches

Pricing products or services can be a real challenge for a small-business person because there is no real set of rules. So many variables go into a pricing decision that it's very difficult to use the same pricing strategy all the time. And if you *do* use the same pricing strategy repeatedly, your competition will figure it out and beat you at your own game.

As mentioned earlier, if you're competing with a major discount chain on the same or similar products, forget about being the lowest price—it won't happen. You must add some value to make it worth the customer's while to purchase from you.

When new technology comes on the market (iPods, HD televisions, digital cameras, and so on), prices initially are very high to try to cover the research and development costs before the competition jumps in and sells a similar product at a lower price. So often trial and error is the only way to test prices on new products. Here are some things to consider when you're trying to decide how to price your products or services:

If you're selling a common product, the chances of you being the low-price leader are slim to none. Instead, try to add extra value to make it worth customers' while to deal with your company.

- What the market will bear
- The actual cost to acquire or manufacture the product
- Service and backup costs
- Display costs and promotion
- Brochure and direct-mail costs
- Advertising and marketing costs
- Personnel costs to sell the product or service
- Your total overhead
- Your profit goals
- Your volume goals
- Your value-added services
- Your costs to market the product
- Your expected sales volume
- What your competitors are doing
- Your position in the market
- Whether competitors will follow your lead
- Seasonal changes
- Large-quantity discounts
- Delivery costs
- Payment terms offered
- Free trial offers and giveaways
- Whether the product is in stock or is a custom order
- Whether it's a discontinued item or service
- Consumer/business demand

You should always have set prices unless you are selling at a flea market, a garage sale, or a used-car lot. Although in some countries bargaining is the norm, that is not the case in the U.S. Discounts, coupons, or special sales are fine, but don't haggle price with a buyer.

Take all these factors, throw them into a blender, and see what comes out. You must come up with prices that you and your customers can feel comfortable with—and it's a challenge! But challenge or not, it has to be done.

Higher Prices!

Why will people pay more money for a product or service at a different store or company? It happens all the time, so there must be a reason for it. Perhaps a customer needs a tube of toothpaste, sees it in a store he or she is shopping at, and says, "I can get that for 30 cents less at the discount store." But the customer is not at the discount store, so instead he or she purchases it now. Convenience can be a big motivator.

One way to look at pricing is to say that giving customers more will make them willing to pay more. But customers must know that they are getting more and consider it an added value.

Chances are you can't beat the giant discount stores at the price game anyway, so you need to find other reasons for customers to buy your products or services at higher prices. Customers need a feeling of added value to feel comfortable buying a product now regardless of price. For example, some people will pay a little more at a smaller store because they get personal attention and eliminate the hassle of long checkout lines. The time saved is the added value that makes the product worth the higher price. As another example, people getting takeout food at lunch usually hate to wait, because they have limited time available and they don't want to waste it standing in line.

To justify higher price, you must offer added value that the customer wants.

If you want customers to ignore the fact that your price is a little higher, you need to show them the value. Here are some ideas for how to do so:

- Offer a better quality or brand
- Offer a better guarantee
- Have a better or bigger selection
- Have a well-informed staff
- Offer free installation
- Offer free shipping or delivery
- Have a closer location for your target market
- Offer a free product or service
- Have a good return and exchange policy
- Cultivate a strong reputation
- Offer great customer service and customer relations

- Offer the prestige of owning a high-priced product
- Feature the latest state-of-the-art technology
- Have a beautiful store
- Offer easy/free parking
- Hire likable salespeople
- Offer products that are worry-free for the long term
- Feature faster checkout and/or delivery
- Have longer store hours
- Offer a unique product
- Be the only supplier of the product or service in the close vicinity
- Offer more specialty products
- Have a free help line (an 800 number)

Some of these factors are difficult to control, such as having a closer location, but others are more easily controlled. Work on the factors you *can* control so that price is not the main buying factor in your business. When your prices are fair in your mind *and* in your customers' minds, you'll reach a position where you can create repeat business. When your customers feel confident about your prices, it won't be an issue every time they buy from you. You need to generate that comfort zone on the very first sale so that it won't come up again in the future. You don't want to have price be an issue on any repeat orders.

Raising Prices

When you have finally reached a common ground where both you and your customers can live with your current prices, something will rock the boat. For a variety of reasons, you may find that you can no longer make a fair profit at the prices you have. You have to raise prices! So you think about how you're going to do it without losing all your customers. As the sweat builds on your forehead, you realize that you just have to do it, and that's it.

When you raise prices, have a 30-second response ready for anyone who questions the increase. Don't just snap back with a quick answer; try to explain briefly your reasons to them. The way you respond will make it easier for people to buy at a higher price.

Most of your customers will expect prices to increase from time to time, if for no other reason than inflation. A few customers may ask why you raised prices, and for those customers a short simple explanation should suffice. Being upfront and out in the open with your customers is always the best approach. Chances are you'll have very little, if any, lost business, so relax and do what's necessary. Your competitors may be considering price increases and will follow as soon as they see yours.

Raising prices doesn't have to be a big deal. Most customers will understand that it's a periodic necessity in the business world.

Here are some reasons why you may need to raise prices:

- Increased manufacturing costs
- Higher payroll costs and employee raises
- A raise or bonus for yourself
- Desire to increase your profit margin
- Rent increase
- Higher delivery costs
- Increased utility costs
- Higher cost of raw materials
- Higher advertising rates
- Increased postage rates
- Increased insurance costs
- Increased selling costs
- Increased supplier costs
- Increased cost of employee benefits
- Necessary renovations to your office or store
- Increased prices from your competitors
- Increased taxes and licenses
- Higher food costs (applicable to restaurants and food-service establishments)
- Necessity of hiring additional staff
- Necessity of adding new displays
- Increased interest rates on working capital loans
- Product upgrades or enhancements
- Addition of more services
- Offering a better guarantee
- Excessive returns or spoilage

Now that I've stimulated your mind, you can probably think of several other reasons to increase your prices. Have you overlooked some of the above motives, and should you start working on your new prices today?

When you decide the time has come to raise prices, consider what other costs will increase within the next six months. It's better to have a bigger boost now and then wait at least six months before the next one than it is to do two smaller increases. Too many smaller increases done too often tend to irritate buyers and stick in their minds. If you increase your prices only twice a year or less often, people tend to forget about the first increase by the time the second one comes around. Your increased price will soon become your regular price in their mind. You may even consider adding 2 to 5 percent extra to your increase to cover short-term future cost escalations. This might allow you to wait longer before you need to increase your prices again.

Before you start charging your new prices, plan ahead. Have new menus, literature, price lists, or catalogs printed and ready to use, and don't forget to update your website. Don't worry about using up all the old literature; just recycle it. You don't want to distribute anything with the old prices after the effective date of the new prices—doing so will only serve to remind your customers that you just raised prices.

You may want to consider printing catalogs without prices and then inserting a separate price list that you can change easily. This will save you from wasting all those expensive unused catalogs when you change prices.

If you have a lot of stock on hand or it's a slow period, you can promote or advertise that a price increase is coming to promote some quick sales now. Give the effective date for the new prices and notify all of your regular customers so they will have the opportunity to buy at current prices. Once the new prices take effect, there should be little or no resistance from customers because you gave them ample notice and a chance to stock up before the increase.

> Do not increase your prices more often than twice a year, at most. Frequent price increases can irritate buyers. It's better to have a bigger increase one time and hold the price there for as long as you can.

Lowering Prices

There may come a time when the market can no longer support your current prices. Sales may be dwindling, and you may see potential customers looking at your products or calling for quotes, but sales and orders don't result. If you can, ask customers why they're not buying to see whether they feel your price is too high or they saw the same thing for less elsewhere. Some people will be happy to tell you if you ask in a friendly manner.

This is also the time to sell the benefits of your product or service—better selection, guarantee, service, or delivery than your competitors—but some people will still prefer the lower price.

> Lowering prices is sometimes a necessity. Just be sure you're still making enough profit to survive and you don't draw competitors into a price war.

When you're reducing permanent prices, don't make a big deal about it. You don't want customers asking why you charged them more the last time. You may have good reasons for why prices were higher before and have now come down, but why even get into a discussion?

Have you looked at your price on the products in question to make sure you're up with the current trends? Some products get better while the price drops at the same time. Look at computers and other electronics—you get much more for less than you did five years ago. Can you reduce any prices to pick up sales and market share while still making a good profit?

Here are some reasons why you might lower prices:

- Supplier cost is less now.
- You're getting larger quantity discounts.
- You're offering larger quantity discounts.
- You've found a new lower-cost supplier.
- Manufacturing costs have been reduced.
- You're taking prompt-payment discounts from suppliers.
- Sales have increased, so you can accept a lower profit per item.
- You want to meet competitors' prices.
- You want to gain more market share.
- Your products are becoming a commodity.
- You want to use a product as a loss leader.
- You want to move excessive inventory quickly.
- You've downsized your staff.
- You want to increase sales to sell the business.
- Technology has forced prices lower.
- You want to clear out soon-to-be obsolete products.
- You want to use lower prices for an advertising campaign.
- You are outsourcing some work at a lower cost.

Keep in mind that by pricing your products or services too low, you'll force competitors to react. If they go lower than you, do you want to lower prices again? This can be financially dangerous because no one wins, and it can be even more harmful to your business growth. You don't want to be lured into prices so low that you don't make a profit.

If you're competing against a large company with commodity products, you can follow their lead in pricing, but sell a little higher if you have value-added service. Normally, large outlets have an impersonal sales staff or none at all, and as a small business, you can provide an informed staff. Great customer service can add value to even the most basic commodity items; we'll discuss this more in Chapter 16, "Customer Service."

As a matter of practice, when you're lowering prices, don't go below your bottom line and give away the farm. You won't stay in business very long if you're selling below your cost.

Pricing Strategies

The most common way to determine your selling prices is usually the *cost plus* strategy. You calculate exactly what a product costs and add your profit to it, which results in your average selling price. The only shortfall with this method is that if you don't include *all* your costs, the net profit is really lower than you think it is. Sometimes it's a good idea to add a few extra percentage points to the cost for unexpected expenses or things you've forgotten. When considering your total cost per product, here are some factors to consider:

The *cost plus* strategy is the most common way to determine selling price.

- Manufacturing or supplier costs
- Packaging or repackaging costs
- Staff selling expenses
- Advertising, direct mail, and promotion costs
- Administrative staff expenses
- Maintenance and repairs
- Rent and office expenses
- Shipping and receiving costs
- Costs for physical selling aids and displays
- Distribution costs
- Collection and loan interest costs
- Bad-debt losses and collection costs
- Return and exchange expenses
- Interest on borrowed capital

Add all these costs together and divide the result by the number of actual products or units to get your approximate cost per unit or package. Now you can add to your cost the percentage profit you need or want to make. It's a good idea to stay within the range for your industry so that you will be competitive. You should review what your competitors' prices are and decide whether you want to be higher, lower, or about the same. If you're selling to other businesses, you'll need to have a comfort zone where you can offer quantity discounts, which is generally expected for large orders.

Should price determine your positioning in your target market, or should the position you choose dictate the price? Marketers have gone back and forth on this topic, and it comes out even. But the more premium or luxury the product, the higher the price should be. That's common sense, and customers expect it.

Another pricing strategy is to determine your selling price first and work backward to your cost. This method is generally used if you want to meet or beat your competition or establish a high-quality, new product in the market.

If your prices are low, you need to find ways to reduce or control your supplier or manufacturing costs. Look for and evaluate new suppliers that can offer similar products at a lower cost or better quantity discounts. If you need to sell at a specific price point and you just can't get your manufacturing costs any lower, you might want to consider outsourcing production to a separate company. Once you find a manufacturing company with the correct equipment and cost, you can also eliminate some of your payroll and benefits expenses, as you'll be trimming your workforce. The manufacturer can sell to you, a dealer, for less because they have little or no advertising, sales, and promotion expenses.

The bottom line is that if your selling price is predetermined, you *must* get your cost to a point where you will make a profit.

A longtime friend in the Chicago area built his entire business by selling at prices the buyer couldn't resist. He was a distributor of loose gun nails, automatic staples, and construction supplies for use in home building and manufacturing. He studied his market, found what customers were paying, and offered a lower price for a larger minimum order. Unlike other suppliers, who cut services when they cut prices, he didn't. He offered free delivery to construction sites early in the morning, which no one was doing—especially *very* early in the morning. He also supplied the automatic "guns" for nails and staples free of charge for those buying his products. He included prompt repairs or replacement gun machines when breakdowns occurred. It was difficult for his customers to change suppliers because they would have to return all the free equipment.

To sell at the lower prices, he called every manufacturer in the U.S. and some around the world and attempted to get the best prices if he guaranteed a certain quantity of purchases and quick payment. He's currently buying a majority of his nails from Far East and European countries and finds the quality is excellent. Because his orders are for big container loads, he gets the suppliers' very best prices.

In the beginning, he used his home equity to finance these larger purchases, and later banks gave him substantial lines of credit. Today, his business is going strong with about $18 million in sales, and he is still using the same pricing strategy. He has added a few additional products with higher margins that many of his customers purchase without comparison. I have always admired his ability to judge his target market.

Offer Platinum, Gold, and Silver Levels

Not everyone is interested in buying top-of-the-line products or services. Some people use a hammer once or twice a year, so why should they buy the $25 model when the $5.99 model will suffice for their purposes? The same is true for a car wash, a computer, a lawnmower, or nearly any other product or service, so offer choices. The professional who uses your product will usually want the best available, but the casual user doesn't need the top of the line and likely will want to save the extra cost. Give people choices and make the sale fit the buyer.

> Give people buying choices so they can find the option that best fits their needs and their budget.

Can you offer products that vary in quality and cost? If so, you'll have a larger customer base because you'll be able to satisfy more levels of buyers. Consider offering three levels, because the consumer's mind usually thinks of good, better, and best. Offer some type of sign or explanation of the different levels available. And always be sure that your lowest-level product will still do an acceptable job.

- **Silver.** This product is guaranteed to be very good.
- **Gold.** This product has added features and increased durability.
- **Platinum.** This product has all the bells and whistles.

Be able to explain the differences in level to your customers in easy-to-understand terminology. And don't try to sell customers more than they need, because they'll know you're being insincere. Usually with a few questions, you can determine the level of product or service the customer needs. After using your product, customers may return for the next higher level—especially if their needs change.

Being the High-Priced Brand

You can, of course, price your products and services above the average price in your industry. Auto dealers sell cars with prestigious names and designs for double or more than the price of an average car. They have created a higher perceived value in which the buying public believes. But disassemble all the parts in a high-priced car and spread them out on the ground. Where's the value now? Sure, some of the parts may be better quality than what you'll find in the lower-priced car, but they probably don't really cost double. Only when you see the finished product do you associate the higher value. Some people want the higher-priced model just because it is the higher-priced model.

To be the high-priced brand, you need to create a high perceived value for your company, backed by exceptional service.

If you're going to be the high-priced brand in a small business, you must create a higher perceived value for your company. Why is your product or service worth more? List your reasons and then sell them to your customers. Maybe it's your experience, your guarantee, your unique style, or just your professionalism. Whatever the reason, you need to sell it.

You will probably appeal to a smaller market and have fewer customers, but your profit margin will be higher. If you can find a niche market, and it becomes popular, you can likely demand a high price. But always be aware of competitors who will see your profit level and want a part of it. The longer you can hold your higher-profit niche market, the harder it will be for your competition to break in. So, before you take the high-price plunge, have a plan to hold your customers as long as you can.

Above all, don't take a common item that can be found anywhere and price it high. This will turn off customers, and you'll lose most of them. If you're going to price high, it needs to be to fulfill a need or desire that people can't get filled elsewhere.

Loss Leaders

We've all seen the big ads for common products with prices that are much lower than normal—these are called *loss leaders*. Supermarkets, liquor stores, and big discount stores are notorious for offering this type of promotion on a regular basis. But how can a small business use this tactic?

Loss leaders are only profitable if you have some related product that you can sell to the customer at its regular price.

The main purpose of loss leaders is to get the consumer in the store or calling to order the low-priced items, so that they then purchase upgrades or other products at the regular price. The question for a small business is, do you have enough other products to make this worthwhile? Or will customers just purchase the loss leader and nothing else? Can you upsell or offer add-ons or accessories?

If you have nothing else to entice the customer to buy in addition to the sale item, then this strategy is not for your business. The people who buy from these sales are not doing it out of loyalty, and they are likely to be only one-time customers. You need to make additional sales while you have them there in person or on the phone. You may not have a second chance.

If you decide you want to attempt a loss-leader strategy, contact your big suppliers to negotiate a deal for lower prices on a bigger order. Explain your plan to them, and they should be able to help you with lower costs. You may even be able to get them to deliver some items on consignment, just for your promotion. You probably don't want to use items that will spoil or have expiration dates on them, though—if you don't sell them all, what will you do with them? Also, you shouldn't use the same product or service as a loss leader too often, or your regular price will mean nothing. Offer and test different items to see which ones bring the biggest crowds and then use those twice a year.

> Big-box stores and grocery chains are always luring shoppers with below-cost items, called *loss leaders*. This is not something a small or medium-sized business should usually try to compete against. Taking a loss on sales won't get you anywhere. These price reductions don't usually last long, so just wait it out, and business will come back.

Customer Quotes

If your business sells specialty or custom-made products, there is usually no set price, because they are not stock items. Contractors building an addition onto your house don't pull out a price list and hand it to you. They can't—every situation is different and must be quoted or estimated after the contractor inspects or analyzes the entire project. The contractor may have a percentage markup in mind to add to his cost, but he isn't likely to reveal it.

The printing industry is the same—each job or project is unique and is priced accordingly. The price for 5,000 #10 envelopes might be set, but when you use a different color or multiple colors, the price is usually different. The same goes for brochures, direct-mail pieces, and business forms. The custom order gets custom pricing based on its specifications.

A good salesperson can determine what the customer will pay and whether there are competitors in the picture. If there are four people bidding, you'll probably need to be one of the lowest unless you can show additional value.

> Try to determine what the customer will pay and whether competitors are in the picture.

Try to itemize as much as you can in your quote—it helps customers realize how much they're getting for their money.

My favorite type of customer is the one who says, "I don't know anything about this. Can you handle the entire project for me?" Right there, you know that it's unlikely that there are any competitors, and if you put the customer in his or her comfort zone, there won't be any. You can then quote a higher price (and resulting profit), which should be accepted because you're offering more than just dropping a product on the customer's doorstep.

If you're presenting a quote to a business, address it to the decision maker, not the secretary or an associate. Also, when quoting for a business, you have to weigh the credit risk with the prospect and whether you will request a deposit.

Always get a signed quote or purchase order when accepting an order in case the buyer leaves the company and you need proof that the products or services were actually ordered.

Although perhaps more time consuming than flat pricing, custom quotes offer the opportunity to make a higher profit if you know your customer and can supply something to meet that customer's unique situation.

Price and Quality

When customers notice that your price is a little higher, but you know and believe that the price is fair because of the quality, you need to convey the reasons why. You're better off explaining the price in the beginning and showing customers the value than you are lowering your prices and trying to come up with excuses and defenses for poor quality over the long term. Once the customer agrees and pays the price, it will soon be forgotten. But poor quality and problems with your product or service will last a long time, and that's what customers will remember.

What does the product really cost them over the course of using it, taking into account lost time and aggravation? If your product or service costs 15 percent more than a competitor's but lasts 25 percent longer, it's really less expensive in the long run. These are the things you need to stress during your sales presentation. If you cover this up front, it won't come up later. When you look at price from that perspective, it doesn't look so high after all. Explain this to your customers and get the order (and referrals).

Prices on Window Items?

Should you put prices on window items? The jury is still out on this one because it depends on your type of business and the image you want to project. One reason to put price tags on window display items is to let shoppers know what's on sale or what special items are featured. If the prices are on the high end, it projects the image of an upscale store, which appeals to more affluent customers.

Another approach is to not include prices in the window so you can lure shoppers into the store and have experienced salespeople close the sale. If people like an item they see in the window, but they don't see a price tag, they're likely to step in the store to find out how much it costs. Further, if prices are negotiable, you don't want to display them and risk them being too high or too low.

So, whether to use window pricing is really up to you and how you want to sell. You can always go by the old adage that if someone has to ask the price, he or she can't afford it.

In the end, you want your window display to entice your target customers to enter the store, where you have more control. Your window design should be the showcase of your products, but it should not be for price comparison.

Whether you should use window pricing depends ultimately on your sales strategy.

Action Plan

✓ Decide whether you want to be the low, medium, or high price.

✓ Determine your cost, including the selling cost.

"When price becomes an issue, something suffers."

—BT

Chapter 10

Face-to-Face Selling

- What Is a Sales Professional?
- The Decision Maker
- Ears before Mouth
- Some Good Things to Know
- Don't Ignore the Advisors
- Closing Signals
- Make Lunch Pay Off
- The Honeymoon Is Over?
- Should You Take the Small Order?
- Ready to Buy?
- Your Personal Billboard
- Break the Ice
- Play Your Cards Right
- Dress for a Sale
- Qualify the Buyer
- Sales Rejection
- I'm Still Waiting…
- Ace in the Hole
- Don't Lose More Than the Sale
- No Ceiling on Commission
- Reduce Your Sales Staff
- Be a Yankee Peddler

S mall businesses have the same dilemmas as larger companies when it comes to sales reps—finding good ones, motivating them, and keeping the top performers. There have been many books written on how to hire and train the best salespeople, and they're probably all correct about one thing—it's very difficult. You can have all the hiring guidelines and requirements you feel are necessary, but the only true factors are time and results.

Good sales reps go into every sales presentation feeling as if they will get the order but accepting the fact that they will lose some. After every presentation/interview, a sale is made by someone: Either the prospect buys the product or service, or the salesperson buys the prospect's excuse about why he won't purchase.

Many people love the freedom and rewards of sales and get an ego boost from every closed sale. After 35 years in sales-related positions, I still get excited when we get a new customer. And what other occupation allows you to do your job while eating lunch or driving in your convertible with the radio on? What other job lets you earn as much as you're able to, with no ceiling, and allows you the freedom to motivate yourself? It's a career where your attitude and perseverance are your greatest tools.

So, where do you find excellent salespeople? If you have a home business, it's probably just you. But if you have a small business with more than just one employee, you may have a designated salesperson. What qualities make a person excel in sales? Is a great salesperson born with the ability to sell, or is it learned? Let's start there.

What Is a Sales Professional?

Doing and earning the minimum does not make you a true professional in the sales world.

Anyone can be a salesperson—you see them every day and everywhere—but it takes desire, perseverance, and hard work to be a true professional. Many people in sales get by selling the minimum and earning the minimum, but these are not the true professionals. A select few are the top producers and top earners, and these are the true professionals.

Why are there only a few true professionals, and what does it take to be one? Why can two different salespeople sell the same products or services in the same market, but one sells five or ten times more than the other? Being a true professional and rising above the ordinary is the answer. These professionals are constantly seeking a better way to achieve their goals and honing their skills. Here are some qualities necessary to be a true sales professional:

■ **Desire.** You have to have a burning need to succeed and be the absolute best you can be. Some people are born with this, and others acquire it. The desire to win makes everything else easier because there is no second choice.

■ **Ethics.** Being honest and truthful in today's world will help you build a long-term reputation. Even one dishonest or unethical act can follow you through your career. And there's a very true old saying that says, "It takes five more lies to cover up just one lie."

■ **Optimism.** You have to always look for the pot of gold at the end of the rainbow because you know it's there. You need to know that rejection is only part of the journey and must be endured to reach your destination. Start every day with a smile and great expectations.

■ **Empathy.** You must understand the prospect or customer's feelings and motives even if you don't agree with them. You must be able to find their needs, desires, and reasons why they will buy and when.

■ **Preparedness.** You must get to know the prospect and the company before the sales appointment. Do research at the library or on the Internet so you know their type of business and how they can use the product or service most effectively. Make your presentation fit the mold of the prospect.

■ **Conscientiousness.** You need to have a stick-to-it attitude and not be easily distracted. You can't be at the ballgame or playing golf when you should be making sales calls. Make a plan and keep at it until you achieve your desired results. Schedule fun and personal activities only for non-selling hours.

■ **Good listening skills.** Listening to a prospect or customer gives you an edge in making the sale. Doesn't interrupt, and makes notes on critical points that will be helpful later. You must have the mental fortitude to keep quiet and learn from each situation.

■ **Focus.** Set goals and monitor your progress on the way to achieving them. Keep your mind on the end result and do what's necessary to get there. Make necessary adjustments along the way and keep an eye on the light at the end of the tunnel.

■ **Energy.** You must be tireless to keep going when the going gets tough. Don't quit, because the next presentation could be the big sale you've been striving for. Keep yourself in good physical condition and mentally ready for the next challenge.

- **Experience.** This will come when you've been in the sales profession for long enough to fine-tune your skills. You won't be afraid of new challenges, because you'll be able to draw on your past successes and failures. Log each new success or failure in your memory bank for future reference.

- **Tact.** Don't say things that can kill a sale, and think before you speak. Be able to change directions during a sales presentation as needed based on a customer's responses. You also need to have the common sense to know the right thing to say or do at a given time.

- **Creativity.** Use new ideas to benefit the overall sales procedure and share those ideas with others. Have an open mind regarding new solutions to old problems—don't be afraid to try them. Use your creativity and imagination to stimulate new ideas.

- **Persuasiveness.** You must have the ability to turn objections into benefits without the prospect feeling pressure. You should be able to convince the prospect that the sale will make his or her job or life better. Keep the sales interview going in the direction of a close at all times.

- **Concern.** You should have a sincere interest in providing a great service to the customer—and then follow up to make sure it's done. Handle any problems with an order in a timely and caring manner, to the satisfaction of the customer.

- **Professional attitude.** Act and dress in a way that gives confidence to the prospect or customer. Practice good manners and efficiency in words, actions, and deeds.

- **Interesting presentation.** Keep prospects' interest and attention by getting them involved in the sales presentation. Never sound as if you're reading a script or using a canned approach.

- **Savvy.** You need to be able to sell the value rather than the price. Be clever enough to understand the customer's objectives rather than your own. And you need to know whether you are meeting with the decision maker or just a messenger.

- **Wisdom.** Know that it's time to stop talking when the sale is made. Don't talk yourself out of a sale by bringing up previously unmentioned features when the prospect has already decided to buy. Recognize closing signals at any time during the presentation and do a sincere follow-up after the sale.

- **Customer-oriented attitude.** You should have the ability to know what the customer needs to know or how they feel so they can make the purchase without remorse. Use all the company's resources to satisfy the customer.

- **Enthusiasm.** Be excited about what you're selling every day, so that it's contagious to the prospect and others in his or her company. Start every morning with a positive attitude, a plan, and a smile.

- **Persistence.** You must have the ability to keep going at full speed when rejections are high and sales are low. You can't give up in the face of opposition or objections.

- **Loyalty.** You should be faithful and devoted to your company and all of its products and services. Be a believer that your sale will benefit the customer, and be backed by an honest and truthful guarantee. Always give 100 percent effort during working hours.

- **Confidence.** You must believe that you'll be successful. Trust your abilities and your company. You should feel as if you have a chance to close every sale before you even start. You should never worry about making your quota, because it's a shoo-in!

Do these qualities describe you or most of your sales force? Are there any reps who need some reinforcement or strengthening? Think about them one by one when you're driving in your car, eating lunch, or conversing at a sales meeting. Knowing your strong and weak points is half the battle to being the sales professional you really want to be. When you master most of these qualities, you'll be a winner, not a wisher.

The Decision Maker

If you're selling saddles, make sure you're not talking to the horse! You need to be speaking to the decision maker—not someone else who isn't qualified to make purchasing decisions. Suppose you've just made one of your best sales presentations ever, and when you ask for the order, your prospect says, "I'll have to give all this information to Mr. Big; he makes the final decisions." You've just spent all your time with the messenger! When it's presented to Mr. Big, it won't have the same impact that you can give it.

Don't waste your time presenting only to someone who can't make buying decisions. Be courteous, but ask to have the decision maker present.

So why not find out early in the meeting whether the person you're talking to can make a decision? If he can't, you can suggest that he bring in Mr. Big halfway through if he likes your presentation up to that point. At that point, you can give a short recap of what you've already presented and ask for any questions right away. Then proceed to close the sale with the person who *can* make the purchasing decision.

Always ask early in the presentation or when you're setting the appointment whether the person you're talking to can place an order. If the decision maker is not available, you can suggest that you set up another meeting when he *can* be a part of the discussion. Leave some literature (but not everything) for them to review before the next meeting. Always leave people wanting or needing more information, so that they can't make a negative decision without you present. If you leave some basic literature, they should have questions ready for you at your next appointment, which will show interest in your product or service.

Having the decision maker present removes the guessing of what people will talk about after you leave. Often if you have the decision maker present, you'll get a quicker answer or maybe even a sale on the spot.

Ears before Mouth

Listen for clues about what features or benefits your prospects are most interested in so that you can customize your presentation accordingly. A smart salesperson will change midstream after picking up buying signals from the prospect.

When you're making a sales presentation to a new prospect or to a company you've never worked with, use your ears first. Preparation and approach can mean everything in getting that first yes. Ask general questions about how they will use your product or service; then keep quiet and listen to the answers.

Try to pick up little clues or keys in what people say so that you can customize your presentation to emphasize the benefits in which they are most interested. Before you even arrive, you should know something about the company and/or the person with whom you are meeting. Search the library or the web for information, and be sure to know what the company does and their position in their industry. Have the people you're seeing written any papers or published articles that will give you valuable clues to their views and personality?

Great salespeople listen more than 50 percent of the time instead of talking. Ask questions that require something more than a yes or no answer and then stop talking. In most cases, people will tell you what they want.

The larger the account, the more preparation you'll need to do. You'll only get one chance at a first meeting, after all.

When you're face to face, it takes more restraint to listen than to talk. Ask questions that require more than a yes or no answer and then sit there and really listen to the responses. Customers like to feel as if you're really listening to them—and it's hard to get your foot into a closed mouth.

Plan your questions in advance and be prepared to deviate from your original approach based on the responses you're getting. You may need to come up with new questions on the spot to keep going in the right direction. Make sure that you look and act interested and try your best to remember their responses. You likely won't remember everything, but do take note of the important points the customer makes. Write down the high points and keep your notes in front of you so you can refer back to them as needed.

Take notes on the important points your customer makes. It will help you remember the overall direction of the conversation.

Some people get right to the point, while others take a little longer. Give your prospects and customers whatever time they require. Don't let silence scare you—wait for an answer. Sometimes 10 seconds seems like forever, but don't give in. If you feel the silence has gone on for too long, just remind the person of the question, courteously. Above all, never talk down to a prospect or make him or her feel inferior. You want the prospect on your side, not against you.

Listening is an art that sometimes needs to be acquired through practice and patience. Many sales reps are Type-A personalities, and listening can be a nuisance—they want to get on with things. But your prospect may be the opposite personality type and may not want to be rushed, so you must listen and understand. Try this with your spouse or friends until it becomes a regular habit. You'll find your prospects are more comfortable when *they* are doing the talking, and you'll learn the secrets of closing the sale from what they are saying.

Some Good Things to Know

During your sales interview and presentation, ask questions to guide you in the right direction. After you ask the question, stop talking and give the customer time to answer. Asking the correct questions will give you that little extra advantage you need to finalize the sale. The more you know about your prospect, the closer you'll get to the *yes*. Stay focused on what the customer wants to buy, not what you want to sell. You don't want to be pushing apples when your customer wants to buy oranges.

Always remain focused on what the customer wants to buy, not what you want to sell.

In addition to focusing on your customers' wants, there are some other important factors you should consider when selling. Here are a few general questions to ask your customers that can give you a step in the right direction. Add a few more of your own that can help in your specific industry.

- Are you the person who will make the final buying decision?
- How soon do you plan to purchase?
- What quantity do you usually purchase?
- How often do you reorder?
- How soon do you want delivery?
- Have you ever purchased this product or service before?
- How long have you been buying from your current supplier?
- Have there been any problems you would like to eliminate?
- What's your most important consideration when selecting a supplier (quality, price, delivery, reputation, and so on)?
- What kind of budget do you have for this purchase?
- Are you also looking at any other products or services?

You can ask these questions in any order. If your prospect hesitates about answering one, skip it and go on to the next one. Either mentally remember the customer's answers or quickly jot them down for future reference. In the course of answering, the customer may even give you a little more information than you asked for. Be ready for it, and let him keep talking. When you know what's most important to the customer, you can guide your presentation in that direction.

Don't Ignore the Advisors

For weeks, you've been trying to get an appointment with the decision maker, and now you finally have it. You plan your presentation; gather all the literature, visuals, and order forms; and arrive 10 minutes early. You're ushered into a conference room, and you eagerly await your next big sale. After what seems like an eternity (but is really about five minutes), the door opens, and in walks the person you've been waiting to see. But wait! Someone else—no, two more people—are entering. Your one-on-one meeting is now a three-on-one. What do you do? You weren't informed of anyone else being in the meeting, so why are they there? To take apart your presentation and ruin the sale? Help! You didn't plan for this.

This happens more often than you might think, especially when a larger-dollar sale is involved. The decision maker may have the authority but not all the knowledge necessary to make a purchase that's in the best interest of the company. That's why they bring advisors and aides to the sales meeting. You should not feel offended; rather, you should feel inspired that there is so much interest in what you have to say. The customer is likely to make a buying decision now because the extra people are there to find out whether your product or service will fill their needs. The stall tactic of checking with someone else may not come into play—you may be able to make the sale now, today. These advisors can give the decision maker support when the sale is going in a positive direction.

Before you ruin your chances for the sale you've been waiting for, let's think about why the advisors are there—to provide support and information to the decision maker. They can be your allies or your enemies, so don't ignore them. Sell the benefits to the decision maker and the features and technical data to the advisors. Hopefully, you know your product or service well enough to answer all the technical questions.

If you knew in advance there would be additional people at the meeting, you might have brought a technical associate from your company with you. But you're here now, and the prospects are ready, so go for it. If a question comes up that you can't answer, you could consider calling your office on your cell phone and letting your technical support answer it on the spot. You could even let the advisor talk to that person on your cell phone to get the answer firsthand.

You want to satisfy the advisors and answer all their questions so they will give the decision maker the go-ahead from their point of view. The worst thing you can do is concentrate only on the decision maker and downplay the advisors' questions and opinions. You want them on your side to make it comfortable for the decision maker to say yes. So be a professional and don't show any negative reaction if several extra people are included in your sales meeting. In most cases, it will give you an even better chance of closing the sale right away.

> Advisors can be your allies or your enemies, so treat them with respect.

Closing Signals

During your sales presentation, you need to keep observing your prospect for signals of ready-to-buy interest. Some prospects can make a decision to buy faster than others, and you need to watch for the signs. If the customer has decided to buy, you don't even

The first rule in sales is to stop talking when prospects say that they want to buy. Don't give them any reason to change their mind. Many a sale has been lost because the salesperson rambled on, and the buyer either got tired of it or heard new information that he didn't want to hear.

need to finish your sales presentation. At that point, go right to your closing procedure and write up the order. Here are some things to look and listen for with customers:

- They tell you they are ready to buy.
- They ask about the guarantee.
- They ask about the terms.
- Their voice and attitude become friendlier.
- They start looking at your order form.
- They want to know about delivery time.
- They start handling or inspecting the product.
- They show the product to their associate or spouse.
- They want to know who else is using the product.
- They state that the demo model will handle their needs.
- They ask about a larger model or package.
- They ask about accessories or add-ons.
- They ask other in-depth questions.
- They ask for your best price.
- They compliment the product or your company.
- They start writing the deposit check (a salesperson's dream).

These are just a few signals. Write your own list, carry it with you, and remind yourself of them before you walk in the prospect's door. You always want to close the sale as quickly as you can. Like my sales-trainer friend, Ben Gay III, says, "Strike while the iron is hot."

Make Lunch Pay Off

Take your customers and prospects to lunch and bond with them in a pleasant, non-office atmosphere. A lot of customers enjoy getting out of the office for lunch without going to a fast-food joint. Getting to know buyers does wonders for repeat business and many first-time orders. They may let down their guard and give you hints for how to get more business from their company. Networking is the name of the game. Here are some ideas to make your business lunch a winner:

- Select a restaurant where other businesspeople go (not a truck stop, for example, although the food might be better there).

- Invite your guests a couple of days in advance so they can get it on their schedules.

- Make a reservation, preferably a little before noon so you'll miss the crowd.

- Offer to pick up your guests or meet them there—let them decide.

- Leave your cell phone in the car so you can give your guests your full attention.

- Let your guests be the first to order and then follow with a similar type of item.

- If your guests ask what you recommend, suggest a medium-priced item.

- Don't order messy foods, such as barbecued ribs or fried chicken.

- Don't let your guests eat alone—order something even if you're not hungry.

- Limit alcohol to one drink or none.

- Don't argue with your server if your order is not perfect—it makes the experience tense.

- Make sure your table manners are faultless.

- Talk about personal things first and get to know your guests. You may find out some things that will help you later.

- Bring up products and sales near the end of the meal, when your guests are feeling comfortable and know that they will be leaving soon.

- Don't make your guests feel as if they owe you an order just because you bought lunch.

- As you're leaving, ask your guests when you can get back to them in reference to your products or services or an order.

- Try to set up another business meeting before you leave them.

- Write down when they want you to call or stop in next and do it at exactly that time, and you might open a few doors to getting their business.

You're probably going to eat anyway, so why not give your lunch a chance to be profitable? You will enjoy some people more than others, so invite those you enjoy more frequently if your budget can afford it.

Breakfast is also a good time for a meal with most customers and prospects, because they won't have anything come up before they meet you, and they're less likely to cancel. A pleasant restaurant near their office is best and easiest for them. Networking and friendly encounters such as these with buyers can lead to referrals and ensure repeat business.

The Honeymoon Is Over?

You have a hot prospect! He's ready to order, and you want this order. You've worked hard to get this customer, and now he's ready. You returned all his calls promptly, answered all of his questions, took him to lunch, and filled his desk with samples. You always acted courteous, staying in constant touch without being a nuisance. You missed your kid's soccer game so you could bring him the additional information he needed—you earned this order! So he calls you and places the order—WOW! All your hard work paid off. You also know that he needs to reorder every three or four months. In three months, he reorders again, and again in another three months. You now have this customer for life!

Stay in touch with your customers, or your competitors will!

But then four months go by, and there's no reorder. You don't really pay attention, assuming he's not ready yet. Another month passes, and another—no reorder. You start to think that you should call and see whether there's a problem, but you're too busy now—you'll wait a couple more weeks. But while you were waiting and doing other things because you *knew* you'd get the reorders, another sales rep was trying to get your customer. You didn't call or follow up, so your competitor had your customer's complete attention. You then find out that the last two orders went to this new sales rep. The divorce is final—sorry.

There's always someone waiting to take your best customers. They're just waiting for you to slack off so that they can jump in. Isn't there a customer you want to call back right now? Stay in touch, or your competitors will.

Should You Take the Small Order?

There is no set answer to this question; it depends on the long-term potential of the customer. If the company is small and has been the same size for many years, chances are there won't be too much more business from them—perhaps just other small orders. As a salesperson, can you invest the time needed and still make a fair profit? Probably not, if sales calls and order maintenance are always requested. You have two choices: one, refer them to a catalog or other vendor, or two, have your customer service department handle the order over the phone.

The other type of small order is from a bigger company that allows you to get your foot in the door. This is worth the low profit because it gets you on their vendor list. When you're an approved vendor and listed in their computer, other company buyers will find you, and anything can happen. Bigger and more profitable orders may be on the horizon.

> A small order from a large company will allow you to get your foot in the door.

Process and handle the small orders in the same prompt and professional manner you would if they were much larger. Buyers will remember who did a good job for them and who caused them the least problems. The company may also have a vendor rating system that they use to score your performance and service.

> Small customers can grow quickly and turn into big customers in a short time. They will remember how you treated them when they gave you only minimum orders. Also, some larger companies will test you with a few small orders before trusting you with larger ones.

Here's a case that happened in our plastic card and printing company. We'd been trying to break into the Las Vegas hotel and casino market for a couple of years, and you can't even talk to many of the buyers for the large properties. They all have direct lines that are guarded like gold. So we just kept sending direct mail (refer to Chapter 6) to their purchasing and marketing departments and their casino managers every two to three months, hoping for a break. One day, we got a fax from a buyer requesting a price for 2,000 labels for a large hotel/casino. Our first thought was that this hotel uses much more, so why was the possible order so small? We just quoted a fair price, got the order, and gave them our usual good service.

About a month later, we received a repeat order for the same quantity. We processed the order quickly, and they were satisfied. We were only making $25 to $30 profit on these small orders, but they paid quickly, and we could say that the big hotel was our customer! We were also put on their approved vendor list.

Six weeks later, we received another order for 5,000 of a similar label, and the profit was about $60—nothing to rave about. As it turned out, they kept ordering these labels on and off for about a year, and then we received a price request for 15,000 Do Not Disturb door hangers. We got that order partly because of our good service on the labels, and we made a much better profit. Shortly after that order, we were the final stages of an order for 300,000 plastic door keys for a sister hotel in Las Vegas. We saw the potential of the company and treated the small orders the same as larger ones. You just never know how or when the door will open to a large customer.

Ready to Buy?

When the customer is ready to order, be there and ready.

If customers are not ready to buy your type of products or services now, all the advertising and promotion in the world won't change their mind. But when they *do* have a need or want for your type of products or services, are you the company they'll think of? You have to leave the door open and the light on, because you never can be sure when that time will come.

Is your contact information in their face so they think of you first? Are you easy to find and eager for their business? Isn't this why you've been advertising and promoting all year? When the customer is ready, be there. Here are some ideas you can consider so that you'll be their first choice:

- **Business cards.** Is your card in every prospect's business card file? Do you give your cards to everyone and always carry a supply with you?

- **Phonebook listing/ad.** If applicable, are you easy to find in the phonebook? Can you be listed under more than one heading? Are you in the online directory?

- **Billboard/road signs.** Can your product, service, or location be seen by many drivers? Think about the number of potential buyers that pass by every day.

- **Location, location, location.** Is your retail store on a main street that most people pass every day? If not, can you put a sign on the main street with directions to your store?

- **Reorder cards.** Do you send reorder cards to customers when they should need to purchase your products again?

- **Giveaways.** Do your prospects have letter openers, cups, calendars, pens, and so on with your phone number on them?

- **Telemarketing.** Do you make brief calls regularly to remind buyers of who you are and what you offer? Have something new and exciting to tell them when you call.

- **Labels/stickers.** Are these on your products with a phone number to call for supplies, service, or repairs?

- **Target ads.** Do you regularly advertise in newspapers, magazines, or trade journals or online where your buyers generally look? Do you know your response rate?

- **Moving signs.** Do you have your logo, name, and phone number on all delivery trucks and vehicles?

- **Tradeshows.** Do you have exposure in tradeshows where buyers look for ideas and new vendors? Do you mail to lists of show attendees?

- **Direct mail.** Do you regularly send new information and literature?

- **Magnets.** Are these on your customers' and buyers' filing cabinets, computers, or refrigerators?

- **Hours of operation.** Is your business open when prospects/customers are available? Do you ask your customers and prospects whether your hours are convenient for them?

If you're not available and easily accessible when buyers are ready to purchase, they may just spend their money with your competitor. Don't think that because you have contacted them once, it's enough. You don't know what other information they're seeing or receiving from your competitors. Make yourself available and easy to find at all times.

Your Personal Billboard

If prospects are going to save *anything* about you and your company, a business card is the easiest and usually the first choice. Most buyers have card files or scan cards into their computer so they can find them easily if needed. This can be your least expensive marketing tool and may be saved by your customers and prospects for years.

Have a supply of your business cards in your pocket or purse at all times. Give them out to anyone who will take them.

Your business card should have enough information but not be cluttered and difficult to read. Here are some ideas for making an impressive card:

- Use standard size, weight, and shape cards for easy filing.

- Choose bright white or a light-colored stock.

- Linen or rag-bond stock is the best choice.

- One or two ink colors are the norm (unless you're in the real estate or insurance business and you want a color photo of yourself on the card).

- Use a street address, not a PO box (unless you have a home business).

- Don't clutter your card with needless information.

- Use your *full* name—no initials.

- Use your logo or special type style.
- Use a short slogan to describe your business.
- Gold foil adds a lot of class but also costs much more.
- Make sure all type is large enough to be read easily. Customers can't call you if they can't read your phone number.
- Always include your area code with your phone and fax numbers.
- If you're a retail business, you can put a map to your store or a list of your locations on the back.
- Fold-over cards give you more room for information, but they are a nuisance to carry and store.
- Odd-size cards attract attention but don't fit in card files.
- Include your company name, your name and title, your address, your phone numbers (including toll-free if you have one), your email address, and your website.
- Don't put all your products on your card, but use a general product term.

When you have your business cards just the way you want them, order a lot. Forget the 500 or 1,000 orders—order 5,000 or 10,000. The price is minimal for larger quantities, and you should be leaving them everywhere you go. You never know who will need your products or services.

Some stores and carwashes have bulletin boards where you can put your card—leave two or three at every one. And, of course, you should have several with you at all times. Keep a supply in your car to replenish the ones you give out.

Break the Ice!

When making residential sales calls, it's important to put your prospects at ease and take away some of the on-guard feelings. You're going into someone's private home. Very few non-friends or relatives are even invited in, so consider it a privilege. Always dress neatly, arrive on time, and offer to take off your shoes. Once you're inside, you need to break the ice. Why not offer a token gift right away, before you give your sales presentation, to make every-one relax a little?

One idea is a $5 gift certificate to a local fast-food place or an ice cream store. If you purchase such certificates often, sometimes you can make a deal with the local owner to buy a certain number for a discounted price—perhaps 20 $5 gift certificates for $90, for example.

When you first arrive at the customer's home, hand the gift certificate to them and say, "I just wanted to thank you for letting me come and talk to you today." With any luck, you'll see a little smile, and you can get on with your business. There are no guarantees of success, of course, but a less defensive prospect is always easier to sell.

Try to set your customers at ease—a less defensive prospect is easier to sell.

When you're selling to consumers at home, you may hear, "We want to think it over." If you can, make them feel the need and desire to buy now—you'll eliminate any competition. Offer to leave the room while they discuss your offer. Or, tell them you'll go out for coffee and come back in an hour and answer any further questions. You're taking off the pressure of a right-now decision but not letting it go until tomorrow.

Play Your Cards Right

In poker games, the best hand doesn't always win—the best player does. Great players make you believe they have a strong hand regardless of whether they actually do. They can also read their opponents and spot their weaknesses. The same strategy can work in business and sales if you play your cards right. Giving your customers and prospects the confidence that you and your company are the best will close more sales and make your business grow.

A customer's weakness may be that they need a quick delivery, so play your strong hand by providing speedy delivery and make it the main issue in your presentation. Your objective is to win the sale, so watch and listen for other clues that will give you a strong hand. Be careful and watch for the bluff if customers say they are getting other quotes. Is the quote what they really want, or is it a stall? What's their actual need? You want to make the prospect believe that you have the best product, the best delivery, and the best service, so they need to act now. Play your cards like a winner from the start, and you'll win.

Dress for a Sale

It's your business, and you can wear anything you want, right? Who cares? Well, your business cares, even though it won't tell you. It won't have to tell you, because the result will show up in your bottom line.

Be sure you're always neat, clean, and well groomed. After all, you're representing your business.

Being a business owner gives you a status position with your customers, and you should look the part. That doesn't mean always wearing a suit if you own a tire store, but your uniform and shirt should be clean every day. Your staff should follow your example and be neat and clean, especially if they might meet customers. Personal grooming must be impeccable. That means fresh breath, clean hands, neat hair, and a daily shower.

All of your employees should know what you expect. Discuss it openly or at least post a general dress code and grooming requirements on company letterhead. Most people will take the hint, but don't hesitate to talk to those who need it. This is your company's image and what your customers will see when they visit. Taking care in personal grooming gives your customers and prospects a feeling of confidence in you and your company.

When selling to other businesses, I'm from the old school that believes a man should wear a tie and dress shoes and a woman should wear appropriate business attire. Be careful not to overdo jewelry; save it for your personal time. In general, being well dressed usually gives you a belief that you are a professional, and it will help you close more sales.

Qualify the Buyer

Don't waste your time with your sales presentation before you know whether the person is a qualified prospect.

You can be the best salesperson in the world, but if you're not talking to a qualified buyer, all your efforts will be for naught. So before you even attempt to make the presentation of your life, be sure you're speaking to a real prospect.

There are three levels of people a salesperson can be involved with—a suspect, a prospect, or a customer. Suspects need to be further qualified to see whether they really are prospects who can actually buy your product or service. Some things you need to find out before you have a bona-fide prospect include:

- Does the person have a real need for your product?
- Has the person expressed a want for your type of product?

- Does the person need or want your product *now*?
- Can the person afford to pay for it?
- Will your product fill the person's needs?
- Does the person have the authority to buy?
- Is the person creditworthy if payments are involved?
- Has the person ever purchased this type of product before?

If you can answer yes to most or all of these questions, you're ready to go on the sales presentation and make the sale. When you know you're speaking to a real prospect, you can forge ahead, knowing you're not wasting valuable time with someone who will never buy.

Qualifying a buyer can be done by you or by telemarketing (see Chapter 14, "Telemarketing"), but it should be accomplished before you make a serious sales effort. Spending your precious sales time in front of a bona-fide prospect will obviously increase your sales and profits. But just because someone isn't a prospect today, that doesn't mean he or she won't be in the future. Check back periodically to see whether the situation has changed. Your suspect may not be buying a new car or house now, but he might be buying next spring. Don't delete him from your files forever; just future-date him. It's hard to sell Christmas trees in June, but everyone's a prospect in December.

Sales Rejection

I don't want to dwell on this subject for too long, but as with any rejection, you should deal with a sales rejection quickly and then forget it. Don't let it affect your next presentation, which may result in exactly the opposite response. There's an old adage worth heeding: "Learn from it and turn from it."

Here are some points to consider about sales rejection:

- It's generally not personal.
- It may not have been a qualified prospect.
- The timing for the purchase may not be right.
- The prospect may not have been able to afford your product or service.
- The prospect may have a relative or spouse selling the same thing.
- The prospect may not have a real need.

If you can pick up a tip or idea from every lost sale, you'll be a wiser salesperson.

- You may have left out important benefits the prospect wants.
- It's possible the prospect just didn't like your product or service.

If you made a sale on every presentation, you'd be the richest salesperson ever, and I'd be buying *your* book. Rejection is part of the sales game, and there's no way around it—it's going to happen. You've probably done it many times to other salespeople. But if you can pick up one little tip or idea from every lost sale, you'll be a much wiser salesperson. This is an education you don't get in school; you have to experience it firsthand. Remember, Babe Ruth not only had the most homeruns; he also had the most strikeouts on the team.

I'm Still Waiting…

Suppose you're in business-to-business sales, and a prospect contacts you for information or a quote. You want to put your best foot forward, so you take the time to fulfill all the prospect's requests in a timely manner. A little time goes by, and you call to follow up, but the prospect isn't available. That's okay—you leave a message and expect a call back shortly. Two days go by, and no return call; maybe they didn't get the message. You try again, but you have to leave another message. This goes on several more times, and for some reason you just can't get the prospect to respond.

What's going on here? The prospect called or contacted you initially, didn't he? You did all your work and can't even get a response.

You can't expect an order each time, but you can expect the courtesy of a response. The types of people who don't respond to your calls will not be your best customers even if they *do* order in the future. Complete disrespect for another person is not what I look for in a valuable customer. A simple call or email saying they are not interested and why is not too much to ask.

Ace in the Hole

When you're selling face to face, whether to a business customer or a consumer, don't put all your cards on the table right away. If you have nothing left, and your prospect is still hesitant to buy, you might as well pack up and leave.

If you've asked the correct questions during the sales interview and paid attention to your prospect's responses, you should know the person reasonably well by closing time. Save some bit of information or selling point that you know the prospect will be very interested in hearing. After several unsuccessful attempts at closing the sale, jump in with your ace in the hole to overcome that final resistance. The prospect may forget his objection in favor of the new benefit you just told him about.

However, if you can close the sale before you need to use your ace, then hold it back and get the sale completed as quickly and professionally as possible. There's no sense in rocking the boat with any additional selling points if they're not necessary.

Don't Lose More Than the Sale

You're not going to make every sale, and you're not going to win the lottery every time you buy a ticket. So get used to losing a sale every now and then, live with it, and use it as an opportunity. Don't slam the door and huff your way out; leave the door ajar so it's easier to get back in.

There are many reasons why you may not get a sale, some beyond your control. But the person or company that beat you out may not deliver or perform to the customer's satisfaction, and they may not get the next order or reorder purchase. So who is the customer going to turn to next time? They will probably review the reasons why they didn't buy from you or others before they start looking at new or unknown suppliers. The only reason why they wouldn't reconsider your product or company is if the reason they didn't buy the first time is *you*. Don't let that happen; be cordial in accepting defeat, so there can be another chance later.

Don't slam the door when you lose a sale; leave it ajar so it's easier to get back in later.

It's also a good idea to check back with your prospect after they've had a chance to receive and use the competitor's product or service. You might call or stop by with any new literature or products you have to offer and casually ask about the previous lost order. Are they satisfied with their purchase, and will you have another chance when they reorder?

Do you ever inquire why you haven't gotten an original order? If you don't, how will you know what it takes to get the order the next time around? It may take several contacts over a period of time to have a solid chance at the order you lost. Don't give up, but don't be a pest either. Always have something new or special to start out with. If the prospect talks or meets with you on subsequent calls, it means you will be given some opportunity in the future. So hang in there and always be professional—it could pay off in the long run.

175

No Ceiling on Sales Commission

Don't cap your salespeople's commissions, or they won't stay with your company for long.

If you have salespeople who really sell, not just manage accounts, they need an open-ended commission plan. Whether they are on salary plus commission or straight commission, the best ones need to know that their earnings are unlimited. The real pros will want less salary and a higher commission structure because they know they will earn more that way. If they feel restricted and that their plan is unfair, they won't stay around for very long. As long as they follow the general policies of your company, turn them loose with a long leash.

Most great salespeople don't really want to own the company; they love their freedom too much. So if they are allowed to make big money without a ceiling, they are likely to stay with you for the long term. But try to put a limit on what they can earn if they bring in profitable sales, and you've violated the one unwritten rule of super salespeople. If you're ever lucky to have one or more super salespeople, take the roof off the commission plan.

A great salesperson should easily make more than his or her sales manager. These are actually two different positions and really shouldn't be compared. And in some cases, the super seller will even approach or pass the earnings of the company's owner. And why not, if he or she earned it? Who really cares if the commission goes to one person or to several? You're still paying out the same amount. Imagine all the good that seller has brought to the company and all the new customers. How many other people added together would it take to achieve that person's sales numbers?

If salespeople are bringing in the big sales figures, they obviously need less supervision and a few perks to make them feel appreciated. The challenge of making the sale and their compensation is usually all they need. Most of them will dislike sales meetings if they eat into their selling time, so schedule them early or late. Super salespeople can easily motivate themselves and don't need the continual supervision to perform well.

The thrill of the hunt for new customers is what really feeds these super sellers, so you may want to offer a two-step commission plan: a higher percentage for new sales or customers who haven't purchased for two years or more and a secondary or lower percentage for repeat customers who need little or no selling. You can assign an inside customer service person to handle these routine orders. The salesperson should have regular contact with the customer, though, and jump in if any problems or questions arise.

It takes little more than freedom and fair compensation to keep these valuable assets to your company happy. Super sellers are very self-motivated, so contests and pep talks are usually unnecessary. And most won't like to help train or motivate the rest of your sales staff, either. So give them a good commission plan and then back off and let them do what they do best. You will reap the big rewards along with them.

> Give super sellers a good commission plan and then step back and let them do their job.

If they're happy, your sales staff will make you more than you'll ever pay them, as long as they're producing above average. It doesn't matter if you have only one or twenty salespeople, encourage them and pay top commission. You'll save on replacement and training costs, and your customers will show more loyalty.

Reduce Your Sales Staff

I'm going to state an opinion that your sales staff may not agree with: You can eliminate 20 to 50 percent of your sales reps. Really, think about it. Remember the old 80-20 rule that says that 80 percent of your sales come from 20 percent of your sales reps? If this is true, then why are the underperforming 80 percent still on your payroll? Are they all relatives that you have to keep to eliminate friction in the family?

> Remember the old adage that 20 percent of the salespeople make 80 percent of the sales. Not only is it true, but it's also a fact that in most companies that have five or more salespeople, one out of every five will be a star and will provide the foundation for a growing company.

How many are actually bringing in more money than they are costing you? How many are just making social calls to your friendliest customers and an occasional attempt to get a new customer? Can some of your regular customers be handled professionally by your best inside customer service people? You can use the money you save on salaries, benefits, and expenses for these underperforming sales reps for more advertising, direct mail, literature—and, ultimately, profit. If the under-producers have been with your business for more than a year and are not carrying their weight, they never will. If they are not making the company money, then it's time to say, "Adios, amigo"—*now*.

When you eliminate some of your sales reps, the others should do even better because they won't want to be next on the bottom of the sales-rep list. If you have a sales rep who is great at servicing existing customers but not at selling new customers, consider moving that rep to customer service and review your least effective people there. Good people are hard to find and keep, especially sales reps, so feed your best ones and say farewell to your lowest producers. Unfortunately, downsizing is the way of business these days—but it should be to the benefit of your sales.

> If your industry needs face-to-face selling, always send your best sales rep to your best leads.

Be a Yankee Peddler

About 200 years ago, as our new nation was growing, people in remote areas didn't get the benefits of all the product choices that people in the populous cities did. So wise salesmen called Yankee Peddlers gathered up wagons of goods and visited these remote areas, where the products were all eagerly bought. They were like a traveling store, and everything sold quickly because there was no competition. The peddlers would go back to the bigger cities and towns, fill up, and go back out again. They may have added a little extra to the price for their traveling expense, but the new consumers didn't mind because of the convenience. What other choice did they have except ride to town themselves? The Yankee Peddler did very well and was always welcomed by the homesteaders.

It's always easier to go door to door when the doors are only a few yards apart, but what about where they're miles apart? The people and companies that are far from big cities need the same goods and services that everyone else does, so why not be a Yankee Peddler and go where your customers are? Chances are you won't be walking in a door that your competitor did an hour ago. Also, small towns and remote areas are usually more receptive and friendly to salespeople because they don't see as many. If you're selling items that need to be delivered by truck, schedule a day or two each week to a certain direction to save costs. By going that extra mile, you may get a whole new group of customers that your competitors forgot about.

Action Plan

✓ Find and hire the best salespeople you can.

✓ Always try to talk to the decision maker.

✓ Watch for closing signals and stop selling when you pick up on them.

✓ Don't take rejection personally; it's only business.

"A sale is not a sale until you get paid."

—BT

Chapter 11

Retail Sales

- Why Should Customers Shop at a Small Store?
- Finding Retail Employees
- Hiring Part-Time Employees
- Entice Customers to Visit the Store
- Be Customer Friendly
- Customer Satisfaction
- So You Want to Have a Sale
- Overstock, Deals, and Consignments
- When Goliath Moves into Town
- Why Offer a Discount?
- Use Gift Cards
- Offer a Big Selection
- Senior Sales
- The Unfriendly Customer
- The Indecisive Customer
- Impulse Buyers
- Slow-Day Marketing Ideas
- Outdoor Temporary Displays
- Hey, I've Got a Coupon!
- Get Visitors' Business
- Retail Payment Choices
- Let Their Fingers Do the Walking
- Store Within a Store
- Keep It Clean
- Free Displays and Signs

Whoever said that it's a jungle out there must have been talking about retail sales. It can be a ruthless and cutthroat business, fighting for consumers' dollars. It's also usually expensive to open a retail store, with build-out, inventory, and fixture costs, but the rewards are there if you plan and execute correctly. The retail business is fun for some people and a nightmare for others, so you must decide which type of person you are. When you're having fun, it's always easier to make profits.

Many people open retail stores when they leave corporate positions and want to have more control over their future. In the case of corporate layoffs, these can be abrupt decisions with little or no planning, and that's one reason why the failure rate for new retail ventures is so high. You might be jumping feet first into a market where your competitors have much more experience and have already established a position.

This is not to say that your retail venture won't work and be a success, but you need to plan a strategy. You created a job for yourself by investing much of your savings, and you want it to pay off. You need to offer the consumer—the public—new and better products and services; otherwise, why should they buy from you? Should they risk their money and time on an unproven store just because it's now open and has an attractive sign? No, they shouldn't.

Getting and keeping retail customers is kind of like chasing a fly around the room; soon after they settle in one spot, they're off again. Retail customers are capricious and fickle; it's just part of the business. What they loved yesterday is no longer their first choice today. They will try new stores and respond to advertising, but if the store doesn't measure up, they will go back to their old favorite. You want to be that old favorite regardless of how big or small you are.

I know a jeweler in our city who never advertises anymore. He only gets new customers by referrals, and he keeps 90 percent of his existing customers. He's *not* the lowest priced jeweler in town, but people love the personal attention he gives them. I took a ring to him that needed to be sized down, and he did it in 10 minutes at *no charge*. I didn't even buy this ring from him, although I had bought several other items from him in the past. He had the time, and it didn't really cost him anything—and in providing that service for me, he made me a long-term customer. He could grow and get bigger with advertising, but he's content with his business the way it is.

An owner can't always be there when situations like this come up, but as an owner you should hire only employees that provide the same excellent service you would. Train your employees to react the way you would under similar circumstances. If you like retail work, serving customers, hiring and training employees, and sometimes putting in long hours, let's look at some ways to maximize your profits.

Why Should Customers Shop at a Small Store?

Do you ever wonder why a customer would come to a smaller store instead of going to a larger chain store where the prices may be lower? They do it, every day—just drive around your local shopping centers and look at all the small stores. The ones that have been there a long time or have opened other locations are doing something right, so what is it?

Here are some ideas to make your store the preferred destination over the larger chain stores:

To make customers frequent your store instead of the local big-box competitor, you need to set yourself apart from the competition by providing superior service.

- **Provide better customer service.** With the owner present more often, customers expect to receive more attention. As a small-business owner, you can train your employees better so they are happier in their jobs, which will show in their actions.

- **Have an informed sales staff.** Staff members at a small store tend to have better merchandise knowledge, training, and supervision, so they are better able to help customers decide on the correct items. That also means fewer returns and complaints, as well as happier customers.

- **Have the owner on the premises.** Customers love to see and talk to the top person at a business; it gives them a feeling of importance. Saying hello and thanking customers in your store goes a long way in building loyalty.

- **View every sale as important.** A small store needs every sale and every customer, and that need is usually conveyed across the counter. Without repeat business, how can a small business survive?

- **Get to know your customers and your employees.** Employees usually stay longer at smaller stores because they are treated well, and customers feel comfortable knowing the staff. Nothing makes a customer feel more important or comfortable than a greeting by name: "Hello, Mrs. Mitchell."

- **Offer specialty items.** These are things customers can't find elsewhere and chain stores don't carry because of lower demand. This might include different items for special occasions. Customers will visit more often to see what's new.

- **Stock quality products.** A small store can't take the chance of selling inferior or poorly made products. Products that perform well will build loyalty and encourage repeat customers.

- **Offer faster checkout.** Most customers want shorter waiting times. When they've made their selections, customers want to pay for them and move on to something else; waiting in line is wasted time. If you see a checkout line building up, you can jump in and help.

- **Provide customer education.** An informed staff can advise customers on how to complete a project, how to select a color scheme, how to use special features of products, and so on. Time spent helping a customer cements a relationship and keeps customers coming back.

- **Feature a comfortable store layout.** Have more interesting and pleasing displays with related and complementary items grouped together. It makes a pleasant shopping experience.

- **Offer easier returns and exchanges.** Show that you value your customers' time by trying to efficiently resolve returns or exchanges of merchandise.

- **Allow special orders.** As a small store, you can order items that customers request and know that the customers will be back in to purchase them.

- **Have consistent quality and prices.** This way, customers are secure in the knowledge that there won't be any surprises, such as higher prices or poorer quality, when they come back to the store. They feel there is fair value in their purchases.

Are these the things that customers feel about your store? Can you implement the ones you're missing? Doing so will make customers forego the hassle of the big stores and will keep your cash register ringing. A small store not only can stay in business; it can prosper in spite of big discount competition. Price only comes into play when you don't have much else to offer.

Finding Retail Employees

If you're opening or operating a retail store, finding good employees can be a real challenge. You'll need to find people who will fit your type of store and who will be able to work the hours you need to fill. Retail positions usually don't pay terrifically well, so you'll need to look at a mix of applicants—cream-of-the-crop employees are probably working in fields other than retail.

The two most important characteristics to look for in potential retail employees are attitude and common sense. You can teach the other skills necessary to do the job, but you can't teach attitude and common sense. Additional characteristics of great employees are the ability to communicate well and an enjoyment in dealing with people. Product knowledge and service ability will come easily to those applicants who have these four key characteristics.

> Good retail employees should enjoy dealing with people and have a positive attitude, common sense, and good communication skills.

So where do you discover these wonderful people to help you run your store? Placing an ad in the newspaper or online are possibilities, but you'll be covering areas that are too far for people to travel and wasting some of your advertising dollars. A local or community paper may be a better choice, because everyone who reads your ad likely lives close enough.

If you don't want to use newspapers, here are a few other ideas:

- **Employee referrals.** Current associates may know other people looking for jobs, and they know what you expect. Current employees can prequalify applicants and tell you what they're like before you interview them. As an incentive, you can offer the employee a gift or bonus if you hire a referral and the referral stays for at least three months.

- **Online bulletin boards.** There are sites where you can list your open positions at little or no cost. Be sure to include specific needs, required qualifications, and a method to contact you.

- **High schools.** If you're looking for low-cost help, send a letter to the local high schools with the qualifications, hours, and pay. Most will post your notice on a bulletin board for students to see.

- **Internet help-wanted sites.** These reach a large audience and are generally less expensive than newspaper ads. I have found that Craigslist often brings a big response for local help-wanted ads.

- **Colleges.** As you would for high schools, send a letter to colleges. Just be mindful that these students will want a higher hourly wage than high-school students make. College students have classes at all different times of the day, so their working schedules may be more flexible than those of high-school students.

- **Customer referrals.** Let shoppers know you're hiring— many may be aware of someone looking for work. You can put a little sign near the cash register or on the front door listing positions available.

- **Churches.** Some larger churches will have an employment coordinator who you can contact with job information. They may put a notice on their bulletin board or in the church bulletin.

- **Store signs.** You can put a few signs in your store, but be sure to list specific qualifications. You may get a lot of under-qualified walk-ins, so be prepared for this. Look at a resume or application before you spend a lot of time with someone.

- **Local employment office.** They know people who are out of work and may have someone for you. When submitting job specifications be explicit, because you'll probably have to interview everyone who fits them and give a reason for not hiring a specific person.

When you find suitable candidates, you need to interview them and discuss what you're looking for and what you will expect. Does this sound like the type of position the person would be happy with? If the applicant seems hesitant or doubtful, it may be time to stop there and thank the person for his or her time.

If you continue the interview, ask the applicant what he liked most and least about his previous job. Make a list of questions you will ask each person and take notes. It's also a good idea to go over your company's goals and see whether applicants also believe in them.

It's smart to keep an open mind until you're finished with all the interviews and can compare notes to make a final decision. You also might have a trusted employee spend five or ten minutes with each applicant and offer her opinion at the end of the interview process.

Hiring Part-Time Employees

After you have selected applicants to interview, it's a good idea to analyze their actions prior to and during the interview. There's an old saying that actions speak louder than words. Most of these potential employees will be part time, and they may value the job less than full-time employees, so you need to qualify them in advance to avoid any problems.

Here are some things to look for that could spell difficulties later:

- Someone (a friend or parent) comes to pick up an application for the applicant.

- The applicant shows up for the interview with a parent or friend who wants to sit in.

- The applicant doesn't have a pen or pencil with him.

- The applicant forgets important information, such as her Social Security number.

- The applicant has too many short-terms jobs on his application.

- The applicant lists the reason for leaving a previous job as not caring for the management.

- The applicant can't find your address and doesn't ask for directions in advance.

- The applicant is inappropriately dressed for an interview or has a noticeable body odor.

- The applicant fills out the application sloppily—it's hard to read, has a lot of cross-outs, or has a lot of omissions.

- The applicant arrives late for the interview and doesn't call when she's on the way.

- The applicant doesn't have a phone number or a way to contact him quickly.

- The applicant tells you during the interview that she needs a lot of days off for vacations, appointments, weddings, and so on.

- The applicant is vague when answering questions about a previous job.

- The applicant has another job and wants to fill in with more hours to pay for unexpected expenses.

- The applicant wanted more money but will take your job anyway. (He won't stay with you for long.)

- The applicant can't decide whether to take your job until she sees other companies. (In other words, she's not really interested.)

- The applicant's parents want to decide when he will work and tell you what hours he's available.

- The applicant brings a pet to the interview. (Oh yes, it has happened.)

It's best to check your state regulations for things that you can and cannot say to or ask prospective employees. Once you know the law, you can go to step two—hiring the best, or at least good, employees for your business. If you own a retail store, you're probably going to trust these employees to use your cash register. Make sure you feel comfortable with them and can give them that trust *before* you hire them.

Entice Customers to Visit the Store

Offer free classes or seminars at different times of day to encourage people to visit your store.

If you have a retail brick-and-mortar store rather a phone-based or Internet-based one, you need to get people into your store before you can sell to them. One way to do this is by offering free classes or seminars related to your business. You'll want to reach both potential customers and regular customers. Most people want to learn new things, and who's a better teacher than the person who runs the store?

You need the class or seminar to be convenient for many people to attend. Offer several different times to accommodate everyone's schedules—days, evenings, and weekends. Plan this well in advance so people can get it on their calendar. Don't forget to let people know about such classes or seminars by advertisement, direct mail, signs in your store, and so on.

It's always nice to give a free sample of your product or a discount coupon to all who attend. You can also have someone who attends actually use the product in front of the class to show how easy it is.

If the seminar works well, you may want to consider holding it monthly or quarterly. It's a way to pick up new customers at a low cost. Following are some seminar ideas you can consider for different types of business. If your business type is not listed, try to think of something similar that your customers would have an interest in:

- **Florist.** Simple flower arranging.
- **Restaurant.** How to make a unique dish or appetizer.
- **Gas station.** How to check oil, coolant, and washer fluid.
- **Flooring store.** How to lay tile, carpet, grout, and so on.
- **Auto parts store.** How to change oil, hoses, and spark plugs.

- **Employment agency.** How to write a professional resume.
- **Sporting goods store.** Tips on golf, tennis, or bodybuilding.
- **Gift shop.** Demonstration of unique imported items.
- **Furniture store.** Basic interior designs, drapes, and accessories.
- **Clothing store.** Current fashion tips or a fashion show.
- **Hardware.** Household repair tips and gadgets.
- **Ice cream store.** Cake decorating tips or making smoothies.
- **Cleaners.** Spot and stain removal.
- **Banks.** Investment strategies and special accounts.
- **Homebuilder.** Energy conservation and landscaping ideas.
- **Bookstore.** How to publish a book.
- **Liquor store.** How to mix exotic drinks or wine tasting.
- **Beauty salon.** Haircare, styling, and premium products.
- **Computer store.** Web search ideas and new games.
- **Insurance.** What type of insurance you need and how much to get.
- **Photographer.** Quick photography workshop.
- **Music store.** How to keep track of your favorite artists and new releases.
- **Grocery store.** Smart shopping and how to best use your coupons.
- **Manufacturer.** Plant tours and "how it's made" demonstrations.

Another way to get the word out about seminars is to send press releases to all the newspapers, radio stations, and TV stations in your area. Specify that there is no charge for the seminar and everyone is welcome. Because what you're offering is free, many curious people will probably stop by. These people may turn into loyal customers in the future.

Be Customer Friendly

What's going on in your customers' minds? Why did they come to your store, and will they come back? How much will they buy, or will they even buy anything? Do they think your store's atmosphere is customer friendly? How do you find out what's going on in their minds so you can think like them?

You need to understand what customers want in a store like yours and discover a way to provide it. The first thing you can do is be a customer in someone else's store. Shop for things you need and think about what you like or don't like in other stores. Shop your competitors' stores, watch their customers, and listen to the questions they ask. Do the customers stop at the display items or just casually pass by? What do you think these customers want, and are your competitors supplying it?

Ask yourself how you feel shopping at different stores—comfortable or frustrated? Can you eliminate the frustrations at your own store so that your patrons can have a more pleasant shopping experience? They won't always tell you what they want; sometimes you have to step back and observe.

Customer Satisfaction

In retail, shoppers can usually choose from several stores for the same items. But once you have shoppers in your store, they must leave satisfied if you want them to visit you again. Making it difficult and unpleasant to buy from you won't get you very far in generating repeat business and referrals. Here are some ideas to promote customer satisfaction:

- **Have sufficient checkout/payment stations.** The one thing I hate most about retail stores is waiting to pay for a purchase. How do you feel when you're standing in line, there are only two checkout stations open, and several other employees are standing around talking? Probably annoyed. Don't let this happen in your store. Help customers finalize their purchases promptly and pleasantly.

- **Call them back.** For bigger-ticket items, it's a nice gesture to call your customers in one to two days to see how they like using your product or whether they're having trouble figuring out how to use it. A little help and assistance from a goodwill phone call will go a long way. It only takes a minute or two, and it creates future loyalty.

- **Offer free/low-cost assembly.** Don't you hate to buy a bicycle or a bookcase and then have to assemble 82 parts? And, of course, there are only 79 parts when you count them. Usually one screw that holds it all together is missing. Who knows what Flange A on Template M is, anyway? Can you offer quick free or low-cost assembly to your customers?

- **Provide a free carwash.** If you're performing vehicle service, why not return customers' cars cleaner than they gave them to you? Vacuum the inside and have two part-timers do a quick wash with a hose. If you can't do a car wash, why not put a hanging air freshener on their rearview mirror? Customers remember these little extras and may tell others about them.

- **Make sure prices are easy to find.** Price items where customers can easily see the amounts. If the price is not actually on the product, often the small sign gets moved or falls off the shelf, and customers can't figure out how much the item costs. Did you ever consider putting inexpensive barcode scanners around the store so customers can check their own prices? This would be a great convenience that isn't common in smaller stores.

- **Offer free gift-wrap.** Every day is someone's birthday, and busy people have little or no time to wrap presents. Free gift-wrapping is also a great service for forgotten anniversaries, when a customer picks up a last-minute gift on the way home. If you offer free wrapping, you can put out a tip jar, which will help offset the costs. Just don't use cheap materials; make the package look nice.

- **Play soft background music.** Soft music or smooth jazz will help customers relax and will make spending money in your store a pleasant experience. Loud rock music will usually make customers tense and make them want to leave as quickly as possible (unless they're 16 years old).

- **Offer carryout service.** When the bags are heavy or the customer has purchased a large item, such as a television or a bathroom vanity, make a sincere offer to put the item in their car or van for them. Don't wait for the customer to ask; offer first. But use common sense, too. Don't ask a big, burly guy if he wants help with his one bag of groceries—he'll probably take it as an insult. Offer special services only when they are needed most, and remember that every situation is different.

- **Have the manager help.** Have your manager(s) ready and willing to help in all necessary situations. After all, isn't their job to make the store run smoothly and be more profitable? If a shelf is empty and no one's available to restock, have the manager get a few items so there are some for the customers. If there's a logjam at the checkout counter, the manager can open a temporary register to help out until the rush eases. I hate to see a manager standing and watching a problem rather than solving it.

- **Have an in-store directory.** Many of the bigger stores have this, but why can't a small store, too? People who come in and need only one or two things may spend five minutes looking for them. Have several directories placed in high-traffic areas and/or big overhead signs that are visible from all areas. A computer monitor where customers can look up items will also appeal to many people. Naturally, if you put on your directory that an item is located in Aisle 4, make sure Aisle 4 is easy to find from both the front and the back of the store.

- **Entertain customers while they wait.** If customers have to wait for their product or service, such as at a pharmacy or an auto-service store, give them something to do so the time will pass more quickly. A television, magazines, newspapers, games for the kids—all these things help make the wait easier to endure. Coffee, iced tea, and water will help people relax while you provide the excellent service they expect.

- **Have a convenient store layout.** Make it relaxing and pleasant to shop at your store. Put complementary products near each other or build an attractive display for them. Don't block aisles with boxes of unshelved products. Many times, I've gone to a grocery store, only to find that the item I want is behind a stack of boxes and is difficult to reach. Your customers are there to buy, not to work!

- **Place commodity items in front.** Big sellers, everyday items, impulse products, and other things that most people want should be visible and easy to find. Put them in the front of the store or by the checkout area. Some marketers suggest that stores should hide these products so that customers have to walk through the entire store to find them. I'm speaking as a shopper when I suggest that you should use convenient spots for the most purchased items.

- **Demonstrate new products.** When you're trying to sell a new product or concept, show how it's done right in your store. Have an ongoing demonstration or post signs stating when the next one will be. Get customers involved and have them use the product during your presentation. If you can't do a demonstration, consider a mini-infomercial on a television that keeps repeating; place it in the main aisle. People will be reluctant to purchase a new product if they don't know how to use it, so show them how.

- **Offer delivery.** If you're selling larger products, special-order items, or something that's out of stock, offer free or low-cost delivery. In some businesses, such as furniture and appliance stores, delivery is expected—but is it friendly and prompt? The senior-citizen market will usually appreciate delivery on smaller items as well, so find a way to provide this service cheerfully.

- **Refer to other stores when necessary.** If you can't sell or don't stock certain products or you are out of stock on products that a customer needs now and can't seem to find anywhere, create goodwill and send the customer to another store that has the product. This will create a smile and a thank you. And hopefully the next time the customer needs something in your product line, he'll come to you first.

Providing exceptional customer service will make your customers enjoy coming to your store and buying your products. When people really like your store and the way you do business, they tell their friends and relatives, which is how you grow your business.

So You Want to Have a Sale

Shoppers love sales—they're getting something they want and paying less for it. We all like the good feeling we get when we save money. It's the American way—a sale! Some people will even buy things they don't really need now because of a lower sale price.

Be sure there's enough room in your regular price that when you price the items for a sale, you still make a profit.

But you don't want to have a sale going on for the same merchandise all the time, or your regular prices will mean nothing. And you need to have enough margin in your regular price so that when you reduce the price, you can still show some profit.

You want to be sure that your store is as full of products as possible during a sale so that you can promote the sale. An empty store makes the sale look unimportant and will fail to attract passersby.

Here are some other ideas for running a successful sale:

- Choose a name for your sale to generate interest and curiosity in customers. Don't copy a name that a competitor has recently used, though; be original.

- Make sure you have enough products in stock to satisfy your anticipated demand. People will come to leave with the product, not a rain check.

Sales that last more than 10 days are no longer sales. The reduced prices you are offering then become your regular prices in your customers' minds. Why would anyone ever purchase at the regular price again? Have a deadline for all sales and stick to it.

- Have the merchandise fit the type of sale. Don't try to sell your leftover swimsuits at a January ski sale. Sale items should be what your target market wants to buy *now*.

- Your price reduction should be at least 25 percent and as much as 33 to 50 percent if possible. A 10 percent reduction isn't going to entice anyone to make a special trip to your store.

- Items that you put on sale should be regular items carried in the store that sell for regular price before and after the sale. Popular items work best and will draw people in to see the other items that have been reduced.

- Have a time limit. The sale needs to end—don't let it run forever. Consumers will lose interest after a while and ignore all your sales if your items are perpetually discounted.

- Have big displays of commodity items on sale. This makes it look as if you're expecting a big crowd. Ask suppliers to ship extra products on consignment.

- Get the word out. Make sure there are a lot of in-store and window signs about the sale. Hire a sign twirler to attract the attention of passing motorists. An outside banner will also create interest.

- Use newspaper advertising if you can afford it, or use an insert with coupons and a map to the store. Spot radio announcements cost less than 30-second commercials.

- Send a direct-mail piece to all the regular customers on your mailing list about five to seven days prior to the sale.

- Place related items together. If dresses are on sale, have other accessories at regular price nearby. Many people will purchase both.

- Let your customers know of an upcoming sale at the checkout counter. Hand them a flyer announcing the sale and coupons if available.

- If you have a VIP customer list, give those customers a two- or three-hour head start on the sale for the best selection. Do this by invitation only, and they'll feel special.

- Talk to suppliers and see whether they will give you a good discount on the larger quantities you may need to stock for the sale.

- Ask manufacturers of your sale items if they will lend you any display items they have to enhance your store's appearance during the sale.

- Tie a sale in with something like a holiday or an event happening in your town. Making an event out of your sale may even get you news coverage.

- For end-of-the-season sales, see whether your suppliers have any leftover related items you can get at a steal and add to your sale.

Sales are fun and profitable, and they can bring new and repeat customers into your store. If your sale doesn't work, it means that customers didn't value the merchandise at the sale price you set enough to buy it *now*. Learn something from each sale, and the next one will be even better. Also, study your competitors' sales to get ideas for your next one. If a certain type of sale didn't work for your competitors, it probably won't work for you either—unless you are creative and make some changes.

Overstocks, Deals, and Consignments

When buying for your store or distribution company, you'll occasionally be offered special merchandise at special prices. To buy or not to buy—that is the question. Your manufacturer or supplier may have incorrectly estimated the market and overproduced or overstocked certain items. They need to turn their inventory into cash, so they may offer it at cost or below.

You have to make a decision about whether you can move the merchandise to your customers without a long shelf life. The price will be tempting and the sales pitch strong, but don't let that determine your buying decision. It may be a great deal if you can offer it on a special display at a reduced price. If you advertise, can you highlight it in your ad? Will your supplier assist you in the cost of promoting the merchandise?

Above all, you must decide whether your customers and prospects want to own the merchandise. If you can't create interest or there is no perceived need for the product, it doesn't matter how low the price, it won't sell well.

If at all possible, try to get a return clause that allows you to return any unsold product for a refund after 60 or 90 days. This may be hard to get because of the low price, but it never hurts to ask.

Another low-risk option for retailers is selling products on consignment. The retailer receives a supply of products for display or to include in a catalog, without paying for them upfront. There

On overstock deals from suppliers, try to get a return clause that will allow you to return unsold merchandise for a refund. You can also ask for free displays to use during your sale.

193

can be a prearranged time period after which the retailer pays only for the number sold and can return the goods or extend the time for the balance. If the product is a good seller, you can restock or enlarge the display area. If it's a poor seller, return what's left, and you owe nothing for the unsold product.

This is a good method for testing a new or unproven product with little risk. The retailer or cataloger gives up selling space and hopes to get a profitable return. The one risk you take is that if you decide to no longer sell the items, you may get a couple delayed returns. You give the refunds to keep the customers happy, but now you're stuck with a couple of the products back. You already paid for them, so you need to resell them. But if the products were damaged when the customer received them, you should be able to get a refund from the original vendor—put that in your agreement with them.

Always be on the lookout for and open to special offers and deals from which you can make a quick or additional profit. You never know when they will come along, so keep a little reserve available so you can take advantage of them. Sometimes the unexpected or unusual situations can really add to the bottom line. But make a decision based only on the probability of moving the product quickly.

When Goliath Moves into Town

Compete with large competitors by raising your prices and keeping your stock small.

So, your business is growing, you're making a reasonable income, and you have time to enjoy your family. You run your business the way *you* want to, and the customers follow because you know what all your competitors are doing, and you're doing it better. But what happens when a large national chain with low prices and a huge selection decides to open in your selling area? Is it time to board up the windows and move to the retirement home? How do you compete? With higher prices and a smaller selection, of course!

Are you wondering whether I'm crazy? Perhaps, but read on.

First of all, if you're doing your homework and you know what's happening in your area through public notices, you'll have six months or more to prepare, so get busy today. This is a challenge you must face head on so you can turn an adverse situation into a profitable one.

Here are some ideas for how to compete with and prosper over large corporate stores:

- Keep in mind that if your selling area has 10,000 possible customers now, a big store will draw from a larger radius, and your *potential* customer base will double or triple.

- Offer personal service and help customers with their selection of products rather than relying on huge displays.

- Have the ability to order items that are not stocked or that have unusual features.

- Offer free delivery, installation, and removal of any replaced items—or offer a discount if customers can pick the item up at your dock and just have you load it for them.

- Offer larger-quantity price discounts. The big stores seldom offer this, so you'll be a step ahead there—but be sure to provide the same friendly customer service as you always have.

- Make custom gift baskets of similar items for mothers, fathers, girlfriends, mechanics, golfers, teachers, the boss, and so on—you get the idea. Be creative and different.

- Sponsor local youth teams and projects and be there during events to meet and greet people. Keep your business prominent and in constant view on shirts, signs, and handouts. Network with everyone!

- Assign a salesperson to each customer, group of customers, or account and send mailings with offers, coupons, sales info, and new items. Include the salesperson's picture on the opening letter. The personal touch is tough for big competitors to compete against.

- If you're located downtown or in a busy area, offer free valet parking. Many elderly customers will love this and will be very loyal, especially in bad weather.

- Find time to walk around the store (or have the manager do it), greet people, and find out customers' likes and dislikes. Everyone likes to meet the boss and express his or her feelings.

- Have specialty items related to your business that aren't found in other stores. Can you offer goods to target certain ethnic or minority groups so they will regularly shop your store and send their friends?

- Get information on your best customers and give them special advance shopping times for sales and new arrivals. Also try an early-bird discount.

- Open earlier and close later, but be sure to have a knowledge-able staff on hand during the extended hours. Many people work long hours and will shop at later times.

- Create a better store layout for an easier and more pleasant shopping experience. Use visuals and audio enticements to keep people in the store longer.

- Make sure that employees are trained in product uses and benefits. Don't make the customer just pick something off the shelf without knowing how to use it.

- Visit other towns that are your size in your state and in nearby states. Find stores in your industry and talk to the owners to get tips on what they are doing to cope with big competitors. Leave the welcome mat out when they come to your store; exchange ideas.

Big-box stores should not be feared, but should be used as a marketing tool. They rarely offer the personal touch and service that a smaller company can. When was the last time you walked into a big chain store and they greeted you by name? Don't hold your breath.

In your type of business, find out what customers really want most and figure out a profitable way to give it to them. You'll want to offer value-added products and services that are always worth more in the eyes of the consumer.

There's an old saying that a good offense is the best defense, so plan your strategy without fear. You never see a football coach go into a game with no plan and assuming that the team will lose.

Why Offer a Discount?

Discounts are a good marketing tool in special situations. They can be temporary or permanent, but they should be monitored to be sure you're getting the results you intended. Don't have so many temporary discounts or special sales that you give the impression that your regular price is much too expensive. Also, why would people *ever* buy at the regular price if they know that a discounted price or sale is coming in a few days or next week?

Use discounts only for a specific purpose that adds to your bottom line and increases your customer base.

Discounts can be an effective tool when used for a specific purpose that adds to your bottom line either directly or indirectly. Here are some reasons for discounts:

- **Excess or old merchandise.** Perhaps you ordered, stocked, or produced more than you anticipated, and you need to sell the items because they may be obsolete soon.

- **Seasonal sales.** Perhaps the golf or camping season is over, or you have clothes that will be out of style by next year. These items take up valuable selling space.

- **New products.** When something is new and innovative, you need people to try it and talk about it. This is also the perfect time to send press releases.

- **Larger quantities.** This is a common practice in business-to-business sales: buy more and save more. Is there a way to adapt this to consumer sales?

- **Senior citizens and students.** Offering discounts to specific groups can build more sales volume and bring public awareness and goodwill to your business.

- **Perishable items.** Selling at reduced prices is better than disposing of items whose shelf life or expiration date is nearing the end.

- **Supplier discounts.** Perhaps your supplier offers you a big discount that you can pass on to customers. Ask about these regularly and use them.

- **Building volume.** You may want to increase volume and sales so you can receive volume discounts from your suppliers.

- **Increase cash.** When your cash flow needs a quick boost, and you have a lot of product on hand, discounts can be a quick, productive tool.

- **Prompt payment.** Speed up accounts receivable—a discount for payment by a certain date works in many cases. Offering free shipping and handling is another idea.

- **Cash now.** If you're in a business that usually invoices, try a discount for cash in advance or cash on delivery.

- **Competition.** When your aggressive competitors have reduced their prices, you can meet or exceed the discount. Just be careful not to start a price war where everyone loses.

- **Loss leader.** Products can be sold at cost or a little less to encourage buyers to purchase other profitable items.

- **Advertising strategy.** When you're starting a campaign, sales and discounts draw attention to your ad, create interest, and help make your ads successful.

- **Point-of-sale.** When you have a customer who is on the verge of buying but needs a nudge, offer a small discount if the customer buys now.

Discounting should be used—not *abused*—for successful results. It would be great to see a line outside your door, waiting for you to open, because of a special sale. But if you have that sale too often, your sale price will soon become your regular price. The lines will dwindle, and you'll be back to business as usual but at lower margins. Make it known to consumers why they're getting a discount and make a big deal about it.

Use Gift Cards

Gift cards are essentially interest-free loans.

How can you get a customer to say, "Please hold my money until I'm ready to buy something?" With gift cards, of course. Essentially, gift cards are interest-free loans, plus they almost always guarantee a sale. If you're not offering gift certificates or gift cards, consider starting a program right away.

Another advantage to gift cards is that customers don't usually redeem all of the value—or they don't redeem the cards at all. Approximately 10 to 12 percent of card amounts sold goes unused due to lost or misplaced cards or purchases for less than the total value. People move out of town and forget they have the card, or they simply lose it. In such cases, not only do you get an interest-free loan, but you don't have to pay it back!

Businesses of any size now use gift cards. If you accept credit cards, you can process gift cards on the same equipment for a nominal fee.

Gift cards sell well all year round for birthdays, anniversaries, and retirement gifts—and even more so at the end-of-year holiday season.

Now that I've told you how great gift cards and certificates are, let me offer words of caution. If you're just starting or you are a very small business, you need to be protected against someone duplicating your certificates. Never have a paper certificate that's black ink on a white background—they can be copied almost anywhere. If you're using paper, select a colored paper and print in two colors to avoid most copies. Also, include a continuous control number and keep a log of the amount the certificate is issued for.

At our ice cream store, we limited paper certificates to a maximum of $20 so that if there was any forgery, the most we could lose on one was $20. We also wrote the amount in words next to the numeral so the amount couldn't be changed. (For example, $5 can't be changed to $15 if you write "five" next to it.) Each certificate was signed only upon purchase to avoid theft of unsold certificates.

The newest and safest method is to use gift cards, which are available even for smaller business. They are not activated until they're purchased at the register, so if cards are missing, they have no value. In the past, only large companies could afford these, but now there are several companies that cater to the smaller business market. Inexpensive gift card processing software is also now available, and most merchant service (credit card processing) companies also offer it.

Make sure you post signs in your store and on your website so everyone will know you offer gift cards or gift certificates. This is just another profitable way that a small business can compete with the big guys.

Offer a Big Selection

Give your customers a choice of several brands, sizes, and price ranges in product areas in which you want to specialize. (Earlier, when I suggested offering a smaller selection, I meant on items that are not in your basic area of expertise. When you are an expert in one area, people will know that they can come to you for anything in that area.) Everyone won't buy the same-size product at the same price level. You'll have customers whose budget will only allow them to buy the least expensive product. Others will have a larger budget or a desire for the highest-priced products. Don't automatically assume that everyone wants the cheapest product. Some may buy the lowest-priced item and then upgrade on their next purchase, so it's wise to have different price levels available.

> Don't assume that all your customers will want to purchase the cheapest product.

Variety is good. How often would you visit an ice cream store that only had three or four flavors? In your business, you need to have as many "flavors" as you have room for—in the case of an ice cream store, for example, at least 25 or 30. In addition to inexpensive and common items, you should stock more expensive specialty items that some purchasers will be interested in.

You're only going to please a small group of customers with a small selection; the rest will go elsewhere. Give people a bigger choice, and it may also increase your repeat business and referrals.

Senior Sales

The over-60 age group is a rapidly growing demographic, thanks to the baby boomers. Many people in this group have paid off their mortgages, have paid for their children's college education, are empty nesters, and have substantial savings and investments, which means they have money to spend. But remember, they are smarter shoppers and expect good value for their money. Don't ever try to deceive them—word will travel fast.

> The over-60 crowd is a strong demographic for sales. Don't ignore them; they have money to spend.

Can your business offer products and services to this "cash available" crowd? People are healthier and more active now than they were years ago, so the over-60 group can still do things, such as play sports and travel, that previous generations may have given up on at a younger age. Many are retired and have time available when others are working, so use your slow times to sell to them. Make your store senior friendly. Here are just a few ideas you can consider:

- Offer free shopping services or concierge.
- Have an Internet site that is easy to use.
- Don't treat people like senior citizens—just treat them as special customers.
- Offer publications for their age group.
- Offer free home pickup and delivery for services such as cleaning or groceries.
- Feature afternoon/early evening dances and entertainment.
- Share the cost with other businesses and offer a van pickup service for trips to shopping centers and strip malls. Show videos in the van about products and services at the stores or about what's on sale.
- Hire seniors to take other seniors' phone orders during certain hours.
- Manufacture special car accessories for seniors.
- Feature special early-dinner or late-lunch prices and menus.
- Start a friendship-matching service for singles.
- Offer group trips for people with similar interests.
- Offer lower-priced taxi, limo, and bus services for seniors for less busy times.
- Start a local senior activities newsletter sponsored by your store.
- Produce or market health food that is low in cholesterol, fat, sodium, and so on.
- Offer non-high-tech luxury items.
- Feature a special afternoon section in a movie theater that is away from kids and teens.
- Give gift certificates/cards to senior associations and retirement homes.
- Send a van to pick up customers at a retirement home once a week during slow times.

- Offer part-time jobs to seniors and give them a store discount.
- Give a senior citizen discount.

Doing some of these things will surely increase your business from seniors. They're going to spend their money somewhere, so why not at your store? They're also great about referring other seniors if they like your products or services. We're all going to be seniors someday; think about what would entice and interest you.

The Unfriendly Customer

Some people just want to get their business done and that's it. You should be able to pinpoint these customers right away. Always start with a friendly greeting, and if the response is a mumble or nothing, get down to business immediately. You don't know—or *need* to know—what else is going on in the person's life, so complete your sale quickly and professionally.

> Satisfy less-friendly customers by making the transaction all business.

You'll actually make the customer satisfied by not trying to be too friendly and not asking non-business-related questions. Be happy to have their business and money, and say, "Thank you." Never force customers to respond to a "How are you today?" question if they don't want to answer. You should also avoid asking other related questions as soon as you identify the person as this type of customer. If you serve and treat these customers the way they want to be treated, you'll probably have a long-term repeat customer.

The Indecisive Customer

Indecisive customers just can't make a decision on which product to buy or whether to buy at all. They want to see everything and ask all the questions, but when it comes to actually making the purchase, they back off. They say things like, "I have to think it over" or "I'll check with my spouse." They may have made a decision in their mind, but they're afraid to follow through.

> Indecisive customers are sometimes happy to have the decisions made for them.

You might be able to make the decision for them after hearing all their questions. Just pick up the best product for the customer and say, "Shall we go with this one?" Indecisive customers will probably appreciate your help and be relieved to have the decision made for them. Then make the sale quickly and send them on their way. They will likely come back for your help in the future.

Impulse Buyers

Impulse buyers are everywhere—they're you, me, and your customers. How many times have you gone to a grocery store for two items and left with a full bag? We all get that feeling once in a while and act on it. We make or add to a purchase because the opportunity is there, and we don't analyze the decision, check prices, or rationalize like we do with other purchases.

Have useful items within easy reach of your checkout counter or pay station, and you'll benefit from impulse buyers.

This will undoubtedly be the case with your customers sometimes. Be sure you're in a position to take advantage of impulse buying and even create it. Use checkout displays, point-of-purchase racks, colorful packaging, or last-minute offers on phone sales. Use items or offers that are ready to go or don't need much explanation.

Often when waiting to pay in a convenience store, I'll pick up a package of breath mints or get an instant lottery ticket, just because they're there. Have useful and related items within easy reach, and you'll increase sales and profits at no cost to you.

Slow-Day Marketing Ideas

Wouldn't it be nice to have one-sixth of your business *every day* from Monday through Saturday? You'd know how many people to staff at your retail store and how much your bank deposit would be every day. But the reality is that life is tough, and business is even tougher, so you need to make adjustments along the way.

Slow periods could be very normal in your type of business. But just because they're a common occurrence, that doesn't mean you have to enjoy them. Use creative ways to get customers to visit your store when you need them most. Here are some ideas to boost sales on slow days, during slow hours, and in slow months:

- Double coupon values.
- Offer free upgrades.
- Offer free delivery and setup.
- Feature entertainment in the store.
- Offer a free shopper-helper service.
- Feature special sale prices.
- Double points on customer cards.
- Offer 5 percent off everything when it's raining.
- Offer free refreshments and snacks.

- Have senior-citizen discount days.

- Have a drawing or contest.

- Offer a 10 percent discount when your town gets more than two inches of snow.

- Hold a clearance sale that starts on a slow day.

- Hold a product demonstration.

- Have kids eat free with the purchase of two adult meals.

- Offer special coupons for a slow month.

- Hold a short seminar about your products.

When you've decided what will work for your business, you need to make sure everyone knows about it. Put signs everywhere, including on your front door and near cash registers. Send a postcard to your customer mailing list with the news. If you take phone orders, announce these offers on your on-hold recording. Tell everyone you sell to about the new offers, and tell them to send their friends. You might be the only store of your type that's crowded when it's snowing!

Hey, I've Got a Coupon!

Coupons are a great way to get new business and remind old customers to come back soon. Just be careful not to offer coupons on the same types of items or services too often, or your regular price will mean nothing. People will know that if they wait a little longer, they can get a coupon or discount, so why buy now?

Your coupon offer should be easy to understand, have an expiration date, and include your business name, phone number, and location. Make your coupon contingent on a purchase, such as 50 percent off a purchase, $5 off a purchase, or buy one, get one free. And remember that the savings or deal must be of value to customers, or they'll just ignore the coupon.

Always make your coupons contingent on a purchase. Simply offering something for free without a purchase is unlikely to yield much profit for you.

Coupons can be business builders. You can use them to get people who might not otherwise find you to try your products or services. The hope is that they'll like your product enough to come back and buy it again without a coupon.

Tons of coupons are thrown into the marketplace all the time, but the redemption rate is usually less than 10 percent. Some people are fanatics about clipping and using every coupon they see, whereas others would never use one. But regardless of whether your consumer uses your coupon, it still brings attention to your store and products. It's up to you to decide whether and how often coupons can work for your store or on your website.

Get Visitors' Business

If you own a restaurant, a fast-food establishment, or a bar and you're not going after out-of-town visitors, you're missing a chunk of valuable business. What are the chances that out-of-towners will drive by and see your establishment? Probably slim, unless you're on a main thoroughfare. So you need to be a destination for them.

If you're a food-service establishment, visit local hotels and motels so they can recommend you to their guests.

One idea is to advertise on billboards around the city or at the airport, but most small-business owners can't afford the thousands of dollars necessary to do this. So why not make an effort to call and/or visit all of the hotels and motels in your selling area and give them an ample supply of paper menus and/or coupons? You could also offer to give them laminated menus for each guestroom; you can get your menus laminated at most large office-supply companies for a few dollars each. Leave a few extras to replace lost or damaged menus.

Check back every few months to offer new menus and to be sure that the hotel is using them. You might want to offer the hotel manager or concierge a free meal as thanks and to show the quality of your food. This is a great and profitable promotion that can help both your establishment and out-of-town visitors. Don't pass up this business—it only takes a little effort and not too many dollars on your part!

Retail Payment Choices

After you have made the sale, you want to complete the transaction as quickly and conveniently as possible. If you're a retail store, the three common payment options are cash, check, or credit card. If you're not accepting credit cards now, you should contact your bank's business department and find out what processing service that they recommend. There are a few undesirable services out there that have hidden fees and high processing costs.

The total of all the transactions for each day will be processed and usually direct-deposited in your bank account within 24 to 48 hours. You'll lose 1-1/2 to 3 percent of the transaction amount in fees, but it's worth it to keep those customers who pay only this way. Most systems will also accept debit cards, which act like electronic checks. In today's world, you really have to accept most credit and debit cards, or you'll risk losing business.

If you're going to accept checks, use a check-protection company to protect against loss.

When accepting checks, it's a good idea to use a check-protection company to guarantee against losses from insufficient-funds checks. One I have used requires two phone numbers and a driver's license number written on the face of the check to guarantee it. If the check is returned, it goes directly to the check-service company, and they fax us a notice to deduct it from our checkbook. At the end of each month, we receive a payment from them for any returned checks, plus $5 extra per check to cover any bank fees. We get paid regardless of whether they collect on the checks, and we never hear about it again.

There is another system where you feed the check through a small machine connected to a phone line, which approves the check on the spot, but you need to purchase the machine.

Let Their Fingers Do the Walking

If you're the type of retail business that must or should be in the yellow pages or other phone directory, your ad needs to be action-oriented. People don't browse these books; they use them when they are ready to take some action (buying or serious shopping). To create action, your ad should use words such as *free, fast, specialists, fully stocked, big selection, delivery, open late,* and so on.

Make your directory ad action-oriented.

Look at your closest competitors' ads and select a size similar to theirs. These ads can be very expensive, so don't overdo it—but you also need to be large enough to compete. A well-written medium or even small-size ad can draw customers without you going over your budget.

Be sure to select the correct category or categories where your ad will be found easily. Use some type of graphic or illustration to catch people's attention. If you're placing a display ad, there should be a directory rep assigned to your area to help with design. In most cities, the monthly fee is added to your phone bill, so you have to keep payments current.

Your prospects will probably take one quick look at your ad in their search, so make it the best you can. Once people decide on another company or store, they probably won't be looking in the same category for a while.

You can make an offer in your phonebook ad, but if it's a discount, remember that you'll have to use it until the next book comes out, which is usually in a year. Rather than have the customer clip out your ad, use a code number for the offer, and you'll be able to keep track of the response.

The yellow pages are also gaining ground online, and people are using them from their computers and phones. Be sure to have some presence there. Keep track of where new customers are coming from and spend your ad dollars where you're getting the most response. Don't let pushy salespeople for these services talk you into something if it's not working.

Store within a Store

If you have 1,000 to 2,000 square feet or more, here's an idea to enhance a selling area: Create a mini-store in one section of your space and sell different or related products. You might decide to move one group of products you're now selling to one specific area and put temporary walls or partitions around it. This can generate attention for this product group and be a pleasant new experience for your customers to browse. Decorate the area in the theme of the products and make it different than the rest of the store. If you can use part of your front window as one of the walls, you can even attract passersby to stop and look.

Keep It Clean

In any type of establishment where food is served, cleanliness should be a top priority. Don't overlook or ignore it, because your customers surely won't (nor will the Health Department). Your customers may not say anything in words, but their reaction will show in the lack of repeat business. Don't leave dirty or messy tables for any length of time; clean them as soon as you can. A clean store gives customers the feeling that the food is also prepared in a clean and fresh manner.

Many customers will also form an opinion of your business from the condition of your restrooms. Check them regularly and kept them smelling fresh. You can rent an automatic sprayer from a maintenance company for a couple of dollars a week.

Free Displays and Signs

Where can you get free displays, signs, samples, and other items to promote your products? From your suppliers, of course. They want to help you sell as many of their products as possible, so they will help you any way they can. If your supplier is a middleman or a distributor, go right to the manufacturer. They usually have displays where you can feature or demonstrate products. If it's an expensive structure, you can ask to borrow it for a week or a month. Because the manufacturer or supplier has trucks delivering all the time, they can probably drop it off if you give them enough notice.

Your suppliers have a lot of displays, racks, and advertising material that they may not tell you about and that is available for your use. It never hurts to ask; if you get a negative response, you're no worse off than when you started.

Position your display in an area for maximum exposure and the best lighting conditions. Products and other merchandise that are at eye level or just above and below it will usually sell the best. Use floor level for extra stock or accessories that aren't the main attraction.

You'll get more interest if you can add a spotlight or colored lighting at the top of your display that can be seen from other parts of the store. I would discourage any flashing lights or sirens, though, because even if they attract attention, most people won't get too close to them. They can be more annoying than helpful. You also don't want to put special displays in an area where direct sunlight coming through a window will irritate potential customers.

If you're just not very creative and artistic when it comes to making displays, you can hire people who do this for a living. Check the phonebook or the web for local interior designers, or simply ask a neighbor or a nearby store who they've used. Most people will be flattered if you tell them how much you like their displays, so they'll be happy to refer their designer to you. Or a local school or college may have students taking related classes who will be willing to do the work for you.

Displays are a fun and profitable way to entice people to buy items they didn't come to the store for in the first place. Change or move your displays often so that frequent customers won't ignore them on return shopping trips.

Action Plan

✓ Make your store look and feel comfortable for everyone.

✓ Don't fear big-box competitors—welcome them.

✓ Monitor and train front-line employees for excellence.

✓ Plan a sale with a purpose.

✓ Design a program for seniors.

✓ Wear your best smile at all times.

"Don't try to fool a consumer, or the joke will be on you."

—BT

Chapter 12

Business-to-Business Sales

- Finding New Business
- Respond Quickly
- You Score Better in Your Ballpark
- You Must Follow Up
- The Lowest Bidder?
- Be Their Associate Buyer
- Reorder Reminders
- All Your Eggs in One Basket
- Taking the Order and Billing
- Late Deliveries and Problems
- Coupons, Bells, and Whistles
- Host a Seminar
- Letters of Recommendation
- Problem Customers

Can a small company survive in the tough and sometimes cut-throat business sales market? Absolutely—you can survive and thrive if you keep your eyes and ears open. In fact, it's usually the smaller companies that first introduce the new, innovative niche products. Rather than have a large, expensive R&D department trying to develop 50 or 100 new products, small businesses search for one or two great innovations. Or, they try to improve existing products that they know their customers are looking for. They usually have a target market in mind before they even develop the product, and that helps ensure success. Being close to your market and customers will give you ideas that the big companies never see.

Even if you're just staring a new business, you can compete with the big boys by offering new ideas for old products and special services that are not being offered now. Ask customers and prospects what new products or services they would like to see or have improved, and then work on it. Remember, the big boys were once little boys like you, with great new ideas. As they got bigger, bureaucracy took over, and the new ideas and customer service probably suffered. Don't let your business slip into a generic mode; be new, different, and aggressive all the time. Keep doing research, but do it with your customers, not in a lab.

A smaller company can provide other businesses with innovative products sold in innovative ways by people who practice (not just preach) great service. A small business can react to changes much faster if it keeps abreast of its market and industry. And, with corporate layoffs, cutbacks, and downsizing, job security in a large company is not what it was years ago. Employee loyalty has fallen, and it shows in their jobs. Business customers are finding that their sales reps are changing jobs constantly, and the new reps have no idea what their needs are, except what they can glean from past orders. Most buyers want and demand that a business supplier learn and remember what their needs are.

When employees become valuable to a small business, their job security is relatively assured, even in economic downturns. They are usually in a position to help the company survive during the slow times by getting even closer to their customers—and in the end, the customer benefits, too, from this attention and service.

Business customers normally purchase more costly items and larger quantities than consumers, so you need fewer customers to show greater sales volume. The main difference between business and consumer sales is that, in many cases, business sales are done through a personal visit, a phone call, direct mail, or a website. This can create a higher selling expense, but it is offset by a greater order amount.

Business sales are somewhat easier because you usually aren't dealing with erratic consumer behavior and fickle buying habits. A buyer for a business will act differently when he leaves the office and becomes a consumer. People usually act professionally in a business-to-business transaction, no matter how fickle they may be in their personal buying habits.

Convenience, service, quality, and reliability play an even bigger part in business sales than in consumer sales. Chances are slim that you'll keep a business customer who has to call you two or three times when there's a problem. They don't have the time, and there's always another vendor waiting to take your place. They expect any problems to be resolved quickly and professionally.

Finding New Business

Three ways of acquiring new business customers are advertising (refer to Chapter 4), telemarketing (see Chapter 14), and sending direct mail (refer to Chapter 6). My favorite method by far for a small business is direct mail. When you send direct mail on a regular basis to specific target prospects, it brings customers and leads to you at a relatively low cost. Advertising does the same thing, but at a higher cost per response. How many small businesses can afford the high price of a half-page ad in a major industry publication? Not many. And further, can they spend the money it costs to run the ad several times for full effectiveness? How many people are going to look at the ad and respond—enough to make it worthwhile?

Your direct mailing gets in a customer's door when you may not be able to.

By the time the next issue comes out, the magazine and your ad in it are likely gone—tossed aside by the prospect. However, business prospects can and do save direct-mail pieces if they aren't in the market for your product right when the direct mail arrives. I've had many calls from business prospects months after sending out direct mail. Many prospects save direct-mail pieces in a file if they know they may have a need for your product or service in the relatively near future.

Telemarketing to set up face-to-face appointments or to sell your products directly is also a good tool if you can reach the decision maker. However, your direct mail and telemarketing will only be as good as your prospects list.

Another way of getting new business is through referrals from your satisfied customers. Referrals can be leads that you receive and follow up on, or the referral may actually call your company himself. These are the best prospects because the interest is already there, and you should be able to close many of the sales.

Whatever method or combination of methods you use to acquire new business, you need to keep doing it regularly. This will replace any lost customers and grow your business by adding sales and profits. A small business (or any size business, really) will not survive without adding new customers regularly. You need to replace the lost ones and keep finding new ones to grow. Test and retest to find the methods that work best for your business; then make regular investments to acquire a constant stream of new business.

Respond Quickly

When you're in the mail-order business or you sell by advertising nationally, you will get a lot of questions and inquiries for information, literature, quotes, and so on. You must answer these quickly. You can respond by mail, fax, email, or even overnight delivery if appropriate. If you respond by mail, use First Class or Priority Mail only—anything less is unimpressive to the buyer or recipient. Always try to get your response out the same day if possible, so it arrives while the potential customer is still thinking about your business. Their interest will wear off the longer they wait.

Always try to respond to queries the same day or the next day if at all possible.

The bottom line is that if you respond quickly to inquiries, you will give the impression that you'll be just as prompt in filling their order. The old business saying is, "Don't delay—do it today!"

When you're using an envelope to send information and samples, put something on the outside such as, "Requested Information Inside." This will let prospects know it's not unsolicited mail, and it will remind them that they are waiting for it.

It goes without saying that you should keep a record of all of your inquires and build a separate mailing list. Always do one or more follow-up mailings to the names on the list until they buy. Or make a quick phone call to evaluate their level of interest and readiness to buy. Email is another method of following up and making secondary offers. Once these prospects become buyers, move them to your customer mailing list.

When you're sending follow-up mailings, test different products at different price levels. A word of caution, though: Some people don't like to get offers from anyone, so give them a way to opt out of your mailings.

You Score Better in Your Ballpark

If you're selling business-to-business products that need a demo or hands-on presentation, give yourself the best chance to lock up the order. If you send a salesperson out to the prospect's site, you risk a lower percentage of orders than if you invite the customer to your site. Once the salesperson walks out your door, you really can't be sure whether he is going to follow the presentation required by your company. He may not even take the correct model of your product to demonstrate—it's been known to happen. Or maybe there's a chance to upgrade the product to the next higher model, but the salesperson doesn't have it with him or doesn't mention it. Perhaps he could've sold add-ons and accessories—if he'd had them with him to demonstrate.

If the prospect has a question that the salesperson can't answer, the rep will have to get back to the prospect with the answer. This interrupts the flow of the presentation, and frankly, it's not always easy to reach some people after the fact. Also, sales reps may not be able to answer questions about credit terms, payment plans, trade-in values, and so on.

So what does this mean? It means you have a better chance of closing the sale faster (especially on big-ticket items) if you get the buyer in your ballpark. And I mean the *buyer*, not the buyer's assistant. Get a person who can make a decision, not just a messenger.

Here are some ideas for how to get your prospect into your ballpark and what to do when he gets there:

- Make your showroom or demo area the neatest and cleanest room in your building.
- Test your demo product in advance to make sure it works! This is very important.

- Keep your showroom near the front door so prospects don't have to walk down a messy hallway and look in offices with cluttered desks. Believe me, they look.

- Have one or two people in your company responsible for keeping the showroom tidy and ready for unexpected guests at all times.

- Have a water cooler and clean paper cups in your demo room.

- Everyone offers coffee, but not too many offer espresso. You can purchase used espresso machines for a few hundred dollars at a restaurant supply store, and it adds a nice touch.

- Have fresh cake, cookies, and/or fruit available.

- Set an exact time and send a limo to pick up the prospect. You can make a deal with a limo company to have X number of trips per month, and you'll probably get a better price.

- Treat the prospect like a guest, not like a dollar sign.

- Introduce the prospect to other important people in your company.

- Alert your credit department so you'll have someone available to answer questions if necessary.

- Have a technical person standing by to handle any technical questions.

- If you're giving a plant tour, advise the plant manager in advance so all employees will be on their best behavior. And be sure the plant is as neat and clean as possible.

- You, the salesperson, and the company should be available to prospects and visitors during working hours and even after hours.

- Demonstrate upgrade products and accessories that should be nearby.

- Show a video of a third-party or satisfied customer using your products.

- Don't leave your guest/prospect alone in your office or demo room for more than a minute or two.

- Remember that when the prospect is in your ballpark, selling can be a team effort.

- Last but certainly not least, remember that a lot of selling ideas come from listening.

You Must Follow Up

Many companies, especially in the business-to-business market, neglect important follow-up. Someone requests information, brochures, or samples, you send them out, and you never hear from them again. Why? Because you didn't call the prospect back and complete the sale. How do you even know if they received what you sent? It may have been intercepted by someone else in the company—or worse, it might've gotten tossed out as unsolicited advertising. You spent money putting this package together, plus your time and your postage, so why not find out whether it's doing its intended job?

Your potential customer requested the information for a reason. It may have been for an immediate purchase, and if your competitors are doing their jobs and following up on requests for information, you may have lost the sale to them. It's a foolish business owner who doesn't follow up on all requested literature that's sent out.

Following up is one of the most forgotten tasks in business, and it causes missed sales. When prospects request information or samples, they have some interest. It's up to you to cultivate that interest and turn it into a purchase.

Set up a regular procedure where one of your employees makes follow-up calls weekly. The best time is midweek, rather than Monday or Friday—most people are in the office midweek. If you get the prospect's voicemail, leave a brief message with your toll-free phone number. Make at least three attempts to reach the prospect. Often he or she has questions and just hasn't gotten around to calling you back for the answers. You've just saved the prospect the trouble and expedited the order process.

Don't underestimate the value of good follow-up; it generates sales and goodwill.

The Lowest Bidder?

It's not always best to be the lowest bidder. Many times I've seen people be proud that they got the lowest price, only to find they've gotten shoddy quality and late delivery or delayed job completion. What is the vendor with the lowest price sacrificing to be so low? Are they using subpar materials or untrained/unprofessional employees, or are they not providing after-sale service and guarantees?

As a business owner or manager, you have to decide whether you even want to be involved in a bidding war. Decide how you want to position your company, and if bids don't fit the picture, don't do them.

Some vendors have nothing else to offer, so they use the low-price strategy to get business. They usually say that they'll make it up on volume. But if the volume is not there, something else will be sacrificed. The vendor may accept more business than they can handle and scramble to fulfill the orders or complete projects because their profit is so low. Something will and does suffer in the process. The product or service will seldom be as good that provided by someone who is making a fair profit.

Is this what you really want when purchasing products or services? Or do you want a good price for the value you're receiving? You'll feel comfortable knowing that your vendor made a fair profit and you received the quality and service you expected. The same is true when you're the vendor: If your profit is too low, it's difficult to provide great products, services, and after-services, which are necessary to keep loyal customers.

Besides, if you lose an order on price and the winning vendor has difficulty fulfilling the order at their low price, you may just get the next order from the customer when they are dissatisfied. So don't go away angry; let the buyer know you're there if any problems arise.

You also don't want to be the highest price unless you're selling luxury items, but try to provide a good price for the value you're offering. When you buy and sell this way, you'll become a more satisfied customer and vendor.

Be Their Associate Buyer

Don't sell them; help them buy.

You may have heard the adage, "Don't sell them; help them buy," and it is wise advice. Do your customers buy several items in specific categories, but you can only supply some of them? If so, why not take over the entire purchasing function in that category? You can keep records of prices, inventory, and order frequency on your computer and supply monthly reports. Provide a complete order-management service, which you can do easily and inexpensively on your computer. It will be difficult for customers to discontinue your service and find it elsewhere without a painful transition.

You can also help customers search for the best prices, quality, and delivery on the items that you don't supply. Because you know your industry, there may be companies customers don't know of that are better suited to satisfy their needs. And you may be able to set up a referral agreement with another company that benefits both businesses. Just be careful not to recommend one of your tough competitors, who may also go after your part of the purchases.

If you can provide this type of service, you're almost assured to receive all the repeat orders for your products, at least for a specified time period. The purchasing agent or person who buys these products knows that if you're not there, they have to do all the work themselves.

Although this is a great inside position, don't get too confident and start charging ridiculously high prices and think customers won't notice. They will check on you periodically, probably without you knowing it. It's a great job if you can get it, but don't abuse it. You can also ask for letters of recommendation that you can use to acquire other customers.

Reorder Reminders

Do you have repeat customers who don't always order at the expected regular time? By *regular time*, I mean when you think they should order or they have done so in the past. An inexpensive way to keep in touch and remind them is through a reminder postcard. Postage for such a card is about half the cost of a regular envelope, and it is still delivered via First-Class mail.

For customers who don't always reorder on schedule, send reminder postcards or an email.

When printing these reminders, use the largest size you can and still pay the postcard rate. Check out the postcard requirements and costs at www.usps.com in advance, so there are no postal surprises later. Always include a photo or description of any new products or services you have, along with your regular ones. To remind customers about reordering, fill in this information on the reverse side:

Another way to send reorder reminders is by email to the person who last ordered. Just be sure that your subject line says "Reorder Reminder," so the recipient won't think the email is spam.

- What they ordered last
- When they ordered last
- A reorder number (if applicable)
- Who to contact to reorder
- Toll-free number and email address
- Current pricing and delivery

You can design your postcards so you can print them on your laser or inkjet printer and then store the information on your computer. Always send the postcard to the person who ordered last time, because if that person changed positions or left the company, it should be directed to his or her replacement. A follow-up phone call seven to ten days later is a good idea if they have not reordered by then. You can find out approximately how much of a supply they have left and when to send another reorder card. It's also a good time to mention any new products you think may interest them.

If you don't make some type of contact to remind them of who you are and what they buy from you, the reorder may go to someone else. You also need to stay in contact in the event that your buyer has left and the replacement buyer doesn't know where the last order came from. If they can't find the previous order, they may go looking for a new supplier. Reorder reminders will also call attention to any other of your products they may need to order. And they reduce the need for last-minute rush orders, which carry a premium charge in many industries.

All Your Eggs in One Basket

A contract is only unbreakable until it's broken.

If you get more than 25 percent of your business from one customer, what happens when you lose that customer? But you can't lose them; you have a contact, right? Well, remember the old saying that rules are made to be broken. You may have a great retail location with a 99-year lease, but it can be broken if a public highway is going through.

You always need a backup plan, even if it's only in your mind. It's hard to think of a quick solution when you're caught off guard, so be prepared. Here are some more ways you could lose your bread-and-butter client:

- If your customer goes into Chapter 11 bankruptcy, a judge can void any contract he feels can help the company survive and get back on its feet.

- A new buyer may have a friend who supplies the same product or service, and that friend may get the next order while playing golf with the buyer.

- Your customer's company may be bought out or may have merged, and so now the customer uses the other company's supplier. Sorry, you lose.

- The owner of the company could die and leave his children to take over and change everything. You will have to compete for their business all over again, and you may not get it.

- A large corporation may decide to manufacture a similar product and sell it at half your price before you can react.

- Your patent may run out, and then it's open season and competitors can rush in.

- Your plant could temporarily shut down, and during the delivery delay, your customer could find a new supplier.

- A dispute or argument could sour your relationship. This should never happen, but it does.

- Your product could become outdated or obsolete if you didn't update it or make needed changes.

- Perhaps your delivery is late too often, and you ignored the warnings.

- Maybe your customer service is rude, slow, and not helpful.

- Perhaps you can't resolve a quality problem on a previous order.

- Maybe you take your customers for granted and ignore their little requests—and someone else doesn't ignore them.

You can probably think of other reasons why you might lose customers, but the more important issue is, what will you do? Have a plan in mind or head off these situations in advance. Don't assume the solution will take care of itself.

Taking the Order and Billing

When selling to businesses, you need to establish an order policy that you and your customer can easily live with. Unlike consumer sales, where the person buying pays the bill, in business the person who purchases is not usually the one who pays your invoice. It's usually sent to the accounts payable department, which makes sure that someone with authority has approved it. The faster you get the approved invoice to the accounting department, the faster you'll get paid.

At our company, we send the invoice to the person who ordered so that person can approve it and pass it on to the accounting department. We always try to invoice the customer the same day the order ships, and we send invoices totaling more than $1,000 by Priority Mail. But an even faster way is to send them via email. And there is no rule that says you can't send an invoice even before the order is finished and shipped; we do this often when our cash flow is slow.

Send your invoice the same day the customer's order ships—or sooner.

The unwritten policy in business is to allow 30 days for payment, but we put Net 20 as our terms. Some companies will adhere to the terms you put down or even pay sooner. Others will ignore your terms and pay in 30 to 35 days, which is accepted without argument as standard business practice.

When taking an order, we always require a signed quote with specs and prices we have given them, or we require them to submit a signed purchase order with a number on it. You need something on paper with a signature to prove that you received the order should the need arise. Your buyer may leave the company, or the company could be bought out while the order is in process, and you want to be sure you'll be paid.

Also, for all first-time customers, we require a 50 percent deposit, which helps our cash flow and lessens the risk with a company that we don't know well yet. The only exception is for large, well-known corporations that will likely balk at the request for a deposit. The risk that they won't pay your invoice is low anyway, and you can easily check them out on the web.

Larger companies may also ask you for references, a W-9, or more information on your business for their records. They may ask for things such as your federal tax ID number and whether you are a small business or a minority-owned company. When you closely follow their procedures and yours, the order-taking and payment processes should go smoothly. And when the first order is finished, you'll both have a track record you can refer back to for future orders. After a few more orders, both you and your business customer will reach a comfort zone, which makes doing business much easier.

Late Deliveries and Problems

Problems on orders for your customers happen for as many reasons as you can possibly imagine. But it's the solution that can save or lose a customer.

These are the things that keep aspirin manufacturers in business. You followed all the procedures, you checked everything twice, and the order should ship on time. Just as you're counting your anticipated profits, you get the phone call from your supplier or customer that something has changed for the worse. Unfortunately, these things happen—we're all human, and business is not perfect. But it's how you handle the problem that really matters. Let's look at some reasons for unexpected problems and late deliveries:

- Your supplier has an order backup.
- Order entry made an error.

- Order processing got behind.
- The finished product didn't pass quality control.
- There are too many people on vacation to fulfill the order on time.
- The order was produced incorrectly and must be redone.
- There's a strike at the plant.
- The delivery estimate was wrong.
- The raw materials are not available.
- The equipment has broken down or needs service.
- The order was misplaced. (This is a bad one.)
- You didn't receive the customer's signed order.
- You're waiting for the customer's deposit.
- It's the busiest time of the year, so everything is late.
- You can't produce the product for the price you quoted.
- You're having credit problems with the factory.
- Several key people have left your company.
- There has been uncontrollable weather or fire damage to the plant.
- There have been delivery or freight company problems.

Once a problem is identified, it should be brought out in the open as soon as possible; don't conceal it. Be prompt in informing the customer and tell them the truth, don't make up excuses. If it's your fault, admit it and try to find a solution quickly. Can you get a similar product or supply from another source to fill in temporarily? Even if it costs you more or you need to pay in advance, it's worth it to keep the customer satisfied until the original order is filled.

The worst thing you can do is lie or blame someone else for the late delivery or other problems; take responsibility and find a temporary solution. If it's a quality or defect problem, you need to rectify it, offer a discount, or do it over. The long-term value of your customer is worth more than a short-term loss or breaking even.

Ask whether your business customer is satisfied with the solution and make a note in the file or computer record so it doesn't happen again. When the customer is ready to order again, you will remember the previous situation and head it off in the future.

Telling the customer the truth about a problem promptly will save most customers and bolster your integrity. So don't hide in the next room; lay your cards on the table and find a mutually agreeable solution.

Coupons, Bells, and Whistles

When selling to business customers, leave the gimmicks at the office and use a straightforward, professional approach.

Businesses are a different animal than retail customers. All the wild excitement of consumer selling won't apply to most businesses. They want a businesslike approach with professional literature, materials, and people. I discovered years ago that coupons for products and services aren't used much by businesses and have a low return. Most business buyers will want your best price regardless of any coupon or special deal.

When our company was going through a slow period, we got the idea to send many of our existing customers a credit memo for $50 to try to get them to order soon. We made it expire in 40 days if not used. It was a new idea, but it only generated modest quick sales. With corporate budgets tight, most buyers will wait to justify every purchase and probably don't want to admit that they ordered early because of a coupon.

Offering prizes, gimmicks, and awards doesn't work too well either when it comes to enticing buyers to order before they're ready. One thing that has worked more often is offering customers a price break to order a larger quantity. For example, when a customer asks for a quote on 10,000 of your product, include the next two higher price breaks, such as 12,000 and 15,000. If the price is lower per unit on the higher quantities, I've seen buyers increase their intended order.

Host a Seminar

If your customer base is local or within 100 miles, why not share some of your industry knowledge with your customers and prospects by having a seminar? The advantages are threefold:

- It's another person-to-person contact with your company.
- Customers can gain knowledge about what's new in your industry.
- Customers can see your company and staff in action.

When offering a seminar of this type, several factors should make it a success and profitable in the long run. Here are some ideas:

- Make it free to attend.
- Keep the time limited to less than two hours, or people will lose interest or leave early.

- Make it educational, not a sales pitch. Customers can hear the sales presentation in their own office and won't travel to your site for it.

- Try to get speakers or trainers from other companies or outside sources to provide variety.

- Send a formal invitation or at least a personalized letter three weeks in advance so attendees can get it on their calendar.

- Make follow-up calls to those who have not responded within a week of the event.

- Offer to pick up anyone who is coming more than 25 miles. Send a stretch limo or a fancy bus to pick up several attendees at one time.

- Offer some type of refreshment but not an entire meal. If attendees eat too much, they may fall asleep during the presentation.

- Select your attendees carefully. You're better off with fewer, more qualified people than with a lot of less qualified people.

- Give them something when they leave—a sample, a small gift, and, of course, extensive literature on your products or services.

- Try to set up follow-up dates with each attendee—within a week, if possible.

- Have a question-and answer-session at the end of the seminar and encourage participation.

- Ask attendees whether they felt the seminar was useful and informative and whether they would recommend it to others.

- Find out whether they would attend another seminar in 60 to 90 days.

Hosting seminars will bring your business customers and prospects to a closer and more personal relationship. Education is a great selling tool, and your attendees should be satisfied if they receive worthwhile information. And, by speaking at a seminar and conveying new information and knowledge, you establish yourself as an expert in your field. When you're buying business products, would you rather buy from a novice or an expert?

Letters of Recommendation

These are one-page letters sometimes called *testimonials*, and they are an excellent selling tool for small businesses, especially if you're a new company. With a short track record, you need to

If you're a new company, letters of recommendation or testimonials from satisfied customers can help you gain new customers and build your business.

prove to new prospects that you know your industry and have satisfied customers. Shortly after a sale or delivery to a customer, ask for a letter of recommendation that you might show to other prospective customers. Let the customer know that it can be short—two or three sentences will suffice—because the person reading it won't spend much time on each one. In many cases, the new prospect will just glance at the letters and assume they are praising you and your company.

When requesting letters of recommendation from customers, stress that the letters need to be on their company letterhead and signed. The act of writing a letter of recommendation actually tightens your relationship with the customer as well. Chances are if they write the letter, they may feel as if they should give you the next order as well.

Getting testimonials is an ongoing challenge because they are usually dated, and you don't want to use them if they're several years old—they lose some of their value. Also, your prospect may wonder what's been going on since then and why you don't have any current ones.

If you aren't using letters of recommendation now, start asking for them today. You need all the ammunition you can get to make business sales, and proof of satisfied customers is a step in the right direction.

Problem Customers

Get rid of problem customers. In the end, they aren't worth your time.

There's a difference between a picky customer and a problem customer. The picky ones you can live with, and if you keep them happy, they are usually very loyal and send you referrals. They want everything just so, so do it for them. But problem customers are going to hurt your business, so get rid of them! Problem customers are the ones who find something wrong on every order. They always want a discount or demand that you give them another product or do it over. They may hold their payment of your invoice due to insignificant complaints. They take up your time, create waste, ruin your mood, and irritate your employees. You can never make them happy, and they are likely to complain about your business to other people and destroy referrals.

There is no winning or bottom line with this person, only frustration and aggravation. I'm sure you can think of a few problem customers right now who you would like to eliminate—do it! You can use the time you save to concentrate on servicing new customers. These problem customers aren't profitable; they're just a nuisance, and your business is better off without them. Always give a prospect or customer the benefit of the doubt at first, but if you can never satisfy them, you're better off without them. Spend your time with customers you can satisfy and that you know will return to your business.

Action Plan

✓ Never stop looking for new business.

✓ Act professionally at all times.

✓ Follow up, follow up, follow up…

"When selling to business customers, be all business."

—BT

Chapter 13

Tradeshows

- Finding the Right Shows
- Reasons for Exhibiting
- Tradeshow Expenses
- Selecting a Space
- Getting Your Exhibit/Display
- Generate Tradeshow Traffic
- Working Your Booth
- Lead a Seminar
- After the Show
- Getting the Most out of Attending a Tradeshow

When you attend a tradeshow, you look for new products and ideas, meet current suppliers or customers, and renew old friendships. When you exhibit, you're part of the show, and potential customers come to see you. If your business sells to other businesses, you usually need to go to them and make your presentation, but at a tradeshow, they will come to you.

Can a small business really afford to participate in these large events? How much does it cost, and will you actually increase profits from exhibiting? These are questions you will need to answer before you write that big deposit check for your space. Have you attended this show in previous years to see who's exhibiting and who is walking the aisles? Do your regular customers normally attend the show? If you don't know, ask them—they'll surely tell you. Also, ask them what other tradeshows they attend regularly. If a majority of your customers go to most of the tradeshows in your industry, who are they talking to—your competitors? Is there a chance you might lose some business if you're not a stop on the booth floor?

Let's face it; exhibiting at tradeshows is expensive. For a small business, it will likely take a big chunk of your marketing budget to be at one or two shows a year. You have to look at tradeshow exhibiting for a small business from more of a results angle. What realistically will you get out of being there?

To stay on top of your industry, you need to attend at least one tradeshow a year, preferably two. Many new innovations are introduced at tradeshows, and you can have a hands-on experience. It's good business sense to be there or at least to send someone from your staff.

When you know that answer, the next question is, can you afford it and do you have enough people to work the show? If you take most or all of your staff from your office, who will run your everyday business and process those regular customer orders? You can't tell a customer who calls your company that someone will get back to him in three days. You must have an even balance between the show and the office for both to succeed during the show time schedule.

One possible idea is to participate in only local or regional tradeshows where you drive back and forth or travel shorter distances with no overnight stays. Booth and travel expenses should be much less at these shows, and you can rotate your staff more easily. If you're new to exhibiting, there are usually several local business expos or tradeshows where you can test the waters and see whether tradeshows are really for you.

Regardless of whether you exhibit, you should attend most or all of the shows in your industry and related ones to review new products that you may want to purchase. Many tradeshows are also connected with conventions that have meetings, seminars, and awards dinners.

If the tradeshow is at a resort, you may be able to tie in a mini-vacation and bring your golf clubs and spouse. For these types of conventions/tradeshows, there should be a spouse/significant-other program to keep your loved one busy and entertained while you attend meetings and browse the exhibit-show floor.

Prices for attending shows are reasonable when you figure in all the information you'll get in one place. Most shows offer discounts for early registration or multiple attendees from one company. There are also discounts available at nearby hotels that partner with the tradeshow and hold blocks of rooms for attendees. You'll probably have your choice of several types of rooms, from bargain basement to the lap of luxury. Your best choice is likely in the middle, because you'll spend most of your time at seminars, on the exhibit floor, and in hospitality suites and less time in your hotel room.

Finding the Right Shows

You need to select the best shows for attending and exhibiting. The shows you attend may be completely different from the ones where you want to exhibit. But always attend the shows that are within your industry, especially if you're not exhibiting. You need to know what's new, who's there, and what's happening. Other shows and conventions to attend are ones that you have an interest in, can learn from, or may buy from.

Even if you're not exhibiting at an industry show, you should attend to see what's new and who's there.

If you have a limited budget, make a list of all the tradeshows available and then arrange them in your order of importance and interest. Obviously, exhibiting will cost a lot more than just being an attendee. Contact the show management or promoter and request information on attending, exhibiting, or both. They will be happy to send it to you quickly. You may be able to find the basics, including the cost, at their website, but look at the printed material as well.

If you've been in business for a year or more and you've sent reply cards for product information, many tradeshows will find you. Unexpected information will come in the mail three to six months prior to the show dates, and usually follow-up info comes after that.

If there are three shows at which you would like to exhibit, but you can only afford one this year, here's an idea to reach the most attendees. As people enter a tradeshow or convention, they fill out a registration form that usually includes a profile. After the event is over, these are entered into a computer, and the list is available for sale by the show management or the promoter in about a month. You can purchase these lists and do your own mailing to the same attendees you would've seen at the show. Send a personalized letter starting out with, "Sorry we missed you at the widget show…" and offer an after-the-show special or unique sale. Most recipients will think you were there but they didn't have time to stop at your booth.

You need to get this type of mailing out ASAP, while the event is still fresh in their minds. If you get a good response from a show list, you may want to consider exhibiting at that show next time.

If you're just starting out and can't afford to exhibit at any shows this year, buy all the lists, do a mailing to each one, and monitor the response. The results will tell you which show will be best for you the following year or when you can fit it in your budget.

When you attend a show that you're considering for an exhibit, look at the people walking down the aisles and see what booths are the busiest. Are they competitors of yours, and do you see any of your customers there? Talk to people at the food courts and see why they came and what they're looking for. Exchange business cards (which you should have plenty of) and call prospects right after the show.

To find a list of tradeshows and conventions, along with contact information, you can try www.biztradeshows.com or www.tsnn.com, or you can simply search the word "tradeshow" on your Internet search engine and find a site that lists all the coming shows. Then search their site by keyword to find the ones that interest you.

If you're looking for smaller local or state shows, check with your Chamber of Commerce, convention/visitors bureau, or state business association. If you want information on a specific show from an association group, check the *Encyclopedia of Associations* in your library reference department. The convention date and contact information will be listed in the directory.

Selecting the right shows will help you budget your available investment and reap the maximum rewards. So do your homework before you write the deposit check.

Reasons for Exhibiting

There are numerous reasons why you might want to exhibit. Among them are the following:

- **Increase sales and profits.** This is probably obvious and will be your real intention for exhibiting. You can find new customers and increase your business overall by letting more people know who you are and what you can provide.

- **Meet and entertain customers.** If you have customers across the country or internationally, let them know you'll be there and send them free tickets for admission. Take as many of the important ones out to dinner as you have time for, or have a hospitality suite. (Do it up first-class.) This may be your one chance every year to let your customers know that you appreciate their business.

- **Announce new products and services.** The right prospects should be there to see what's new and how it will work for them. If you want to create a little suspense, have a countdown or a clock going backward to the official announcement time. A corporate officer should make the presentation at a predetermined and publicized time. Alert the media, and you may even get coverage.

- **Get sales leads.** You should qualify people you meet in your booth with a few brief questions and then code them A, B, or C for future follow up. I've attended shows where I've felt as if a detective was interrogating me before they gave me any information, so don't overdo it. Make visitors feel welcome with a smile and give them your full attention. Your A leads should be the first ones you call back and then B and C.

- **Pick up new distributors.** Are you looking for new or more people to handle your products on a regional basis? Many of them attend tradeshows to add on more product lines. Give special attention to the ones who really want to help you promote your company and products. Meet with them after the show and qualify them.

- **Have show specials.** Do you have new equipment or machinery that's running way under capacity? This is the time to pick up orders at special show prices to fill in these slow times. These customers may become regular customers later—at regular prices.

- **Build a mailing list.** You'll want to accumulate as many prospects as possible for your future direct mail. Ask people to fill out a form for a drawing or simply drop their business card in a bowl. These are people who can buy your products and services that you can't find elsewhere. Don't overlook the possibility of collecting as many names as you can, and encourage all your visitors to participate.

- **Get media publicity.** Reporters from TV, radio, newspapers, trade journals, and magazines will be there covering the show. What can you do to stand out and get attention even if you have a small booth? A big giveaway or drawing or perhaps an unusual announcement may pique the media's interest.

Exhibiting at a tradeshow is expensive, even if it's a local show. But if you need to be there to build your brand, meet customers, and showcase your products, then you must do it. The expense will pay off if you do it correctly.

- **Check out your competitors.** If your competitors aren't there, you're lucky—but they probably are. Stop at their booths and introduce yourself; look around and compliment their exhibit. Stroll by or near their booth occasionally to see what type of traffic they're getting. They will be checking you out too, so don't be bashful.

- **Hire sales reps.** You will obviously meet sales reps from other companies and from your competitors. If you talk to one or more who stands out, you can discreetly give them your business card and let them know you'd like to talk if they are ever looking to change companies. This is not unethical—it's being done every day, everywhere, and probably with your own people.

- **Conduct seminars and meetings.** If you want to establish yourself as an expert, give a free seminar or hold a roundtable discussion. You'll soon be recognized as a leader in your field or industry. Invite everyone you can and send a press release to the media prior to the event. Also have it put in the show program with your photo.

Tradeshow Expenses

Here's where your checkbook comes in handy; you'll be writing checks to all kinds of people. If you planned ahead, you've been saving for this, and it won't be a shock when you see all the outstretched hands. Some expenses can be paid over time, such as for booth space or your new exhibit, but others are due before or immediately after service is rendered.

It's a good idea to budget about 20 to 25 percent extra for unexpected things that come up—and they will. For example, at tradeshows we've had our display light burn out, an extension cord that wasn't long enough, forgotten items that we had to ship FedEx overnight, and forgotten clothing. When you need something in a hurry at a show, you can forget discount-store prices; they've got you, and it's going to be expensive. Just pay it and forget it so you can have a great show.

> Budget 20 to 25 percent extra for unexpected costs at tradeshows.

Here are some expenses you should plan for in advance:

- **Booth/space.** A small business can usually afford only a 10×10 or 10×20 booth because of the high cost, but you can still make big profits by selecting the correct space on the floor plan. In a national show, a 10×10 space usually will cost somewhere between $2,000 and $4,000—maybe more for a premium location.

- **Exhibit/display.** If you don't already have one, you need a display that will attract attention and present your products and services in a professional manner. Get several quotes and designs before you make a final decision. Ask for staff opinions and suggestions for the design and layout.

- **Shipping/freight.** Seven to ten days before the show starts, you'll want to ship your exhibit and other literature (plus giveaways) to the show holding area. Because of the cost of these items, I suggest getting insurance on the shipment and also sending them UPS or FedEx two-day shipping so they're tracked well. Never use the mail or parcel post, because there's no guarantee the package will ever arrive. The show management should provide shipping instructions; follow them exactly.

- **Staff.** How many people will you bring, including yourself? Do they need to be paid, or is this time part of their salary duties? I've heard many companies that include tradeshow time as part of their job descriptions, but they pay a reasonable bonus or an extra amount for each day worked at the show. You could also give employees one paid day off at the end of the show to rejuvenate.

- **Travel/hotel.** Don't forget lodging—you can't sleep in your booth! If your staff is comfortable with the arrangement, a small suite with individual sleeping rooms may be less expensive than two separate rooms. Take advantage of the show's special hotel rates and discounts, and purchase any plane tickets well in advance to get the lowest rates.

- **Food.** Yes, you have to feed your staff and yourself, but be smart about doing it. Food from the tradeshow floor concessions is the most convenient, but the cost is sky high. How can a hot dog the size of your little finger cost $7.50? (Oh, I forgot—they give you eight potato chips and a pickle!) The best idea is to have a big breakfast right before the show opens and a great dinner after—you'll get much more value for your money. Take along a snack to eat during the show, and that should get you through.

- **Union costs.** Every tradeshow I've ever been to that's in a big hall or convention center is subject to union personnel for setup and takedown. You can't use any tools or perform any other tasks that the unions normally do. The only exception is a smaller display that fits together without requiring tools or special skills. All electrical work, moving, and assembly must be done by union personnel—and, of course, you get the bill. Don't bother fighting it; you'll never win. This is not all bad, though, because the union personnel know the layout and have worked many shows before. Don't worry; they'll get done on time, before the show opens, and they can handle most last-minute emergencies. Set up these services in advance, because they may cost more at the last minute.

- **Hospitality suite.** This expense is optional and it can be a big one. If you're going to do it, go all out and make it memorable; don't just serve soda and crackers. You don't have to serve crab and lobster, but get several party trays with food that will impress your guests and will also be their dinner that night. Remember, some people don't eat meat, so have at least one vegetable tray or vegetarian item. You can serve beer, wine, soft drinks, and water. If you're going to include mixed drinks, you should hire a bartender so people don't over-pour for themselves. The hotel can provide an entertainment suite and offer different food tray selections. This is a once-a-year chance to impress and entertain your customers and prospects, so do it right.

- **Cleaning fees.** These won't break your budget, but cleaning needs to be done—and again, only union personnel can do it. Order nightly vacuuming of your booth carpet, dusting, and emptying of your trash. After a long day in your booth, you wouldn't want to do this even if you could. The next morning, you'll walk into a clean and fresh booth ready to snag that next big prospect.

- **Security.** This should be provided by the show management and included in your booth fee. You should also check with your office insurance agent and possibly add a rider for the show. Services during the show and overnight lockup will keep you more focused on your objectives.

These are the basic expenses you have to consider when deciding whether you can afford to be in a tradeshow and whether you can profit from it. Tradeshows are a big business and cost big bucks, but they can offer huge marketing opportunities that you can't find elsewhere. If these expenses are out of your current budget, consider starting with a local or regional show where booth costs and travel expenses will be much less. Then, as you see results, you can move up to national shows. Don't spend money you can't afford, though, because there are no guaranteed results at a tradeshow, just opportunities.

Selecting a Space

When you inquire about a show and request information, you'll receive a floor plan of exhibit space that's currently available. Being a small business or a first-time exhibitor, you won't get the prime spaces, because they go to larger exhibitors or companies who have been there before. Most of the smaller spaces are not in front or on main aisles, but that's not all bad. One area I like to consider is either the right or the left end aisle, where a lot of the smaller spaces are located. When people attend a show, they usually start at one end aisle or the other as they go up and down the show floor. I think the least desirable area is the back aisle, unless you're exactly in the middle of the end of another aisle. These are usually the last spaces to go, and if they're not sold, they're used for rest areas with chairs.

Choose a space on the right or left end aisle to get a fair amount of traffic by your booth.

You don't want to be close to any of your big competitors or any-one selling the same items you are. Ask the show manager who else is in your aisle and try to put in your contract that no exact duplicates of your products can exhibit in the same aisle as you will be in.

Being next to a large, well-known corporation's booth is a good idea because their booth will attract a lot of visitors, which may spill over into your booth. People standing or waiting in the larger booth may see your sign and display, which they might have missed if you were located somewhere else.

You also don't want to be anywhere in a dead-end aisle. The traffic flow will be less than half of the traffic in the other aisles, and there's only one way in.

A corner space is great, but you may have to pay extra for it. The corner gives you exposure and entrances from two aisles, result-ing in much more traffic. You just have to be sure your display will work in a space with two sides open.

Once you've been in a show, you'll have an earlier chance to pick a space for that show the next year. Usually, the more years you do the same show, the earlier you get to choose your space for the next year's show.

When you select the best space available, you'll be asked to sign a contract and pay a deposit, which may or may not be refundable. The balance needs to be paid in full about 60 days before the show, and you can make payments as the time nears. If you're a novice at this, you don't want to learn by making mistakes, so ask some-one else who's been in a show for his or her help and opinion.

Getting Your Exhibit/Display

If your budget is slim, consider renting a display or buying a used one.

Exhibits and displays can be expensive when they are custom made with all the bells and whistles. If your budget is tight, you can buy a used display or even rent one. When you're only doing one show a year, why pay for a custom display that could cost from $5,000 to $20,000? Many large display/exhibit manufacturers will rent a used one if you buy a personalized sign from them. Also, you can save with the purchase of a used exhibit with new signs and add-ons.

If you're only planning to be in smaller local shows, a tabletop display is much less expensive and can also have a lighted sign. It only takes about five minutes to set up, and you can easily carry it in and out yourself.

When you buy a full-size display, shipping boxes should be included, which are very sturdy and will last a long time.

Some new exhibits and/or displays take four to six weeks to complete, so order early enough to have the display made exactly the way you want it. Investigate and check prices from several different companies before you make your purchase. Find out whether the company will make future repairs if needed and how long any guarantee lasts. A good display should last at least four to six years with limited use.

> If you're just starting out in local shows and expos, consider a tabletop display. They can look very professional and are priced in the $800 to $2,000 range.

Generate Tradeshow Traffic

Exhibiting in a tradeshow is a major decision and a big expense. So once you've committed a significant chunk of your marketing budget, you'll want to be sure to get as many prospects into your booth as possible. This can be quite a task, because a smaller business can't compete with the huge advertising dollars the big companies have to spend. You can use direct mail prior to the show for your customers and inner-circle target market, but what about the rest of the potential prospects?

> Before a tradeshow, use direct mail to your customers and target market to generate traffic at your booth.

Here's an innovative idea I've heard about: Most tradeshows have special room rates for attendees at nearby hotels, and blocks of rooms are set aside just for attendees. Contact the marketing department of each hotel and offer to supply door keys for free for all the rooms that will be occupied by attendees. The hotel will know who these people are because the rooms will be identified in the computer when the guest checks in. On the front of the plastic key, have your company logo and a "Welcome to the *X* Show" message or some sort of colored graphic design. You could also put a phrase stating your booth number and that if attendees bring the key when they visit your booth, they can enter a drawing for a prize. On the back, below the magnetic strip, you can include a line saying, "Thank you for staying with us," and include the name of the hotel and the phone number.

The hotel should love the personalized welcome for their guests that they probably wouldn't buy themselves. And where else can you get the type of advertising that the attendee carries in his or her pocket or purse and looks at five or ten times during the visit? The cost to do this for three or four hotels should be approximately $1,000 to $1,500 for four-color printing. But you can't buy this type of exposure for many times that cost. While the big companies are spending $25,000 or more on advertising, you're paying a small fraction of that. Plus, your way is unique and sure to catch the attendee's attention.

Many people don't turn in their keys when they check out of the hotel, if only because they're afraid they've left something behind and might have to go back and check. So offer a discount after the show if the attendee's order is accompanied by the door key with your logo on it. Make the offer good for only 60 days so the attendee won't forget about you. The hotel won't care if the person takes the key, because it won't be used after the show is over, and the hotel didn't pay for them anyway.

But now that the secret is out, you must be quick. As soon as you pay your deposit on a booth space, contact the hotels immediately, before someone else use this idea. And even if you find that another company has beaten you to the punch, try the secondary hotels for the show and others nearby.

Working Your Booth

All your advance planning, expense, and work are about to pay off, because *it's show time!* You've spent the money to get into this tradeshow; now it's time to reap the rewards. How you work your booth will determine how much you'll get out of it. Here are a few suggestions to get maximum results:

- Keep the walk-in front area of your booth open and clear at all times so visitors can enter easily and not have to maneuver around you or your staff to get in.

- Dress professionally and make trips to the restroom to check your appearance as the long day goes on. Keep breath mints handy and use them often.

- Don't sit behind a table or anywhere else; stand with a friendly smile even if it hurts or you're tired. The next person stopping by could be the big one. If you must sit and rest, go to a rest area for a few minutes.

- Have water in your booth to refresh yourself and staff between visitors; you're going to do a lot of talking. Moist towelettes and hand lotion are also refreshing.

- Don't eat food in your booth; it's bad manners, and the food looks awful sitting on a table while you're talking to someone. If you're hungry, get a quick snack at the concession area.

- Greet visitors with a simple hello and give them a minute or two to look around. Then ask a few questions about where they're from and whether they use your type of products.

- Try to get a business card from each visitor and make notes on the back for future reference. You can also code visitors as to their likelihood as prospects.

- Make sure you have enough staff in your booth to handle any expected number of guests. People won't wait very long if no one is available to talk to them.

- Ask visitors whether they would like to take literature with them or whether you should mail it to them after the show. There is usually too much to carry, and they will appreciate receiving it back at their office.

- Have a demonstration of your product or service and post times when it will start. If you can't demo, consider having a TV with a company video constantly showing its use.

- Have a contest or drawing for prizes and encourage everyone to enter. If you're giving away a BMW, you'll get a lot of entries (just a joke!).

- Don't leave your booth unattended.

- If your regular customers or a great prospect stop by, invite them to your hospitality suite that evening. Don't just tell them where it is; give them a little card or invitation with the room number on it. It's more impressive.

- Try to create a situation or event in your booth that will attract media attention to get some free publicity. You want as much media attention as you can get—it's free.

- Give your booth staffers a 15- or 20-minute break every two hours so they'll return refreshed. Going long hours without a break may make them a little grouchy and less friendly to your visitors.

- Don't turn your back to the booth entrance and aisle. If you're talking to someone, guide that person to the side so others can enter your booth easily and browse.

- Have a last-minute meeting with your staff every day of the show to remind everyone of your goals and what you expect to achieve. Be open to all questions about situations from the previous day and head off any problems that may have occurred the day before.

- Record your exhibit in action so you can review it after the show and make changes and adjustments for the next tradeshow. Show the video to your staff and ask for suggestions. Each tradeshow exhibit should be a little better than the previous one.

Lead a Seminar

Offering to lead a seminar or a breakout session at a tradeshow or expo will make you look like an expert. Regardless of whether you're paid for it, it's worth the effort.

If you want recognition and attention drawn to your booth, be a speaker or have a roundtable discussion with you as the main figure or moderator. Most tradeshows and conventions will have certain times set aside for their educational sessions. Meet with show management well in advance to offer your speaking services in the areas where you're an expert. Ask whether there are any specific subjects they want to present that you know well. You want your subject matter to be of interest to as many people as possible so that most of the seats will be full. If the seminar is not during exhibit times, have your staff fill some of the seats but give them up if more people arrive.

Once you've given a successful seminar, you'll be noted as an expert on your subject.

If you're giving a speech during a tradeshow, ask the show management to include the date and time in their show brochure and program to get the most advance publicity. You can also have a sign or poster in your booth to help increase attendance. At the end, of the seminar, invite everyone to your booth to ask any questions they have about your talk or related subjects.

If there's a large awards dinner or meeting, offer your services as an awards presenter or to introduce a well-known speaker. You'll get a lot of exposure, and people will recognize you later on the tradeshow floor.

Speaking to smaller groups at tradeshows can be good experience for future speaking engagements. Someone in your audience may even invite you to speak at their future event—for a fee, of course. So get involved; don't just sit in the audience.

After the Show

Well, it's over—you've survived three or four days of grueling personal contact with all the prospects that you hope will soon become your customers. Now you can go back to the office or store and just answer the phone with your order pad in hand.

Not quite! If you're ready for the facts, your work has just begun. If you ignore the next steps, you just wasted your time and money being in the show. Follow-up should start right away, or many of the people you talked to will forget you quickly. Get back to your business, handle any immediate situations that came up while you were gone, and then work on your show leads and orders.

Here are a few things you should do when the tradeshow is over:

- Open accounts for any new customers you picked up at the show and quickly process any orders. You want to do this first because it's money that has already been made, and you want to show off your good service.

- Start calling all the people who wanted to set up an appointment and get a date and time before they change their minds and forget you.

- Send literature and product information to all those who requested it, along with a personalized cover letter asking whether you can set up an appointment or conference call.

- Send a letter to let the prospect know that you enjoyed meeting him or her at the show. Enclose some literature to entice future action. Personalize the letter with the prospect's name and business address.

- A couple of weeks later, call those prospects you haven't heard from and attempt to sell to them or visit them. Mention that you met them at the tradeshow.

- Sort through the leads and business cards and decide which you want to add to your permanent mailing list.

- Offer to sell or trade your sales leads with other businesses who want to reach the same target market but aren't competitors.

- Have an after-show debriefing with your staff for new ideas for the future and to discuss what did and didn't work at this show.

- Start planning your next show and what you want to change to make it better and more profitable. Keep a file of ideas and plans that you want to try in the future.

Getting the Most out of Attending a Tradeshow

Don't be wondering what's new in your industry that everyone knows except you. Be at the tradeshow, where you will be one of the first to find out. Find the time and money to attend, because it will always pay off in new knowledge.

You need to attend your industry tradeshows to keep up with current trends and find out what your competitors are doing. At least two a year is a good number to keep you abreast of things. But how can you make this an enjoyable and profitable experience? What if your time is limited, and you'll never get to see everything? Here are some ideas to make the most of the time you have:

- Decide in advance what you really want to get out of the show. Is it finding new products or new suppliers, or is it visiting with current suppliers?

- Study the advance show guide and make a list of must-see booths. Put them in order of importance and list their aisle locations.

- Make a secondary list of booths that you'd like to visit if you have any extra time.

- If you find that there's just too much to see in the time you have available, consider bringing a staff member to split the load.

- Study the floor layout so you know where all your must-see booths are located and how to get to them easily.

- Try to figure out the amount of time that you can allot to each booth and still have time for the others you'll need to visit.

- Sign up early for any seminars and presentations you want to attend to avoid sell-outs.

- Always preregister for the show and receive your badge in the mail before you go. This will keep you from standing in long lines, especially on the first day.

- Wear comfortable shoes. There's a lot of walking and standing at a tradeshow.

- If a booth you want to visit is very crowded, and there's no one available to talk to, consider coming back later. Booths are least crowded at the end of a show day.

- Contact your top two or three exhibitors in advance and let them know that you're coming and what you're looking for.

- If you're getting pressed for time, let exhibitors know you need only basic information now, and you can get more details after the show.

- Take only a minimum of information with you and have exhibitors send additional literature and samples after the show.
- Have a lot of business cards with you and hand them out freely to everyone you have an interest in.
- Have a pen handy to make notes in the show program or on business cards you've picked up.
- When seated at a table in the concession area, network with the other people around you.
- If you stop by a booth and find you have no interest in it, move along quickly.
- Make appointments with those special exhibitors you saw for more information after the show.

There's an old adage that says to prepare a plan and then work your plan, which is what you need to effectively attend a tradeshow. You should always come out of a show with many more money-making ideas than you had before you attended. This is where industry leaders meet for ideas and to share knowledge. Be part of the action; don't just sit on the sidelines.

Action Plan

✓ Plan to attend at least one industry tradeshow per year.

✓ Be on the lookout for new shows with new contacts.

✓ Decide whether exhibiting is worthwhile for your business.

✓ Always follow up on leads quickly after the show is over.

"A tradeshow is like a supermarket with aisles of great products and services."

—BT

Chapter 14

Telemarketing

- Inbound Telemarketing
- Outbound Telemarketing
- Hiring Telemarketing Employees
- Planning and Making the Call
- Telesales Lead Finders
- Cold-Call Fears
- Voicemail Smarts
- Is Telemarketing Paying Off?
- Check the Laws
- Some Final Telemarketing Don'ts

As postage costs, gas prices, and the cost of face-to-face sales calls skyrocket, the telephone remains a cost-effective alternative method of reaching prospects. Over the years, phone rates have actually fallen because of fierce competition in the industry. And how long does it take you to get in your car, drive to see a prospect, and find out he is not in or she can't see you? With telemarketing, you only visit the ones who are expecting you, because you've already made an appointment on your initial call.

But not everyone can call unknown people and make a presentation—some can't handle the rejections that inevitably come. Telemarketing is the quickest form of marketing because you get your answer right away with a sale, an appointment, a "not interested," or a hang-up.

A new idea that telemarketers are using is Internet interaction. While they have the prospect on the phone, they ask the prospect to go to their website and see what they're talking about. It's sort of like a one-on-one webinar.

Telemarketers have gotten a bad name because of the unprofessional methods used by some of them. They are put at the low esteem level of used-car salesmen (sorry, guys). But it's all in how you do it. If performed in a professional non-pushy manner, telemarketing can present valuable offers to the people you call. Let's face it: If it didn't work, would anyone still be doing it?

Businesses selling to other businesses telemarket regularly to set sales appointments, present new products to their customers, and make direct sales. Consumers can be less receptive to telemarketing calls because when they're at home, they don't feel like talking to a salesperson on the phone.

A smaller business should have some type of telesales program in their marketing mix to pick up new customers and prospects. This also provides you with feedback when trying to present new products or services. You'll find out what percentage of people are interested and responsive and how many have no interest at all. You get quicker answers and indications of any real interest in your product or service.

Telesales can be inbound or outbound, and the two are quite different. Let's look at some characteristics of both and what makes them work.

Inbound Telemarketing

When your prospect or customer calls your business to place an order, respond to an ad, request service, or inquire about literature or information, it is considered an *inbound* call. You have your next new customer or order on your phone; what more could you ask for? This is the time to up-sell and offer add-ons, special terms, gifts for advance payment, and so on. Because the customer called *you*, chances are very slim that he will hang up during your presentation. This can be a softer sell than an outbound call only because the customer must've had some interest to call in the first place. These can be your objectives for an inbound call:

- Make a sale.
- Complete a sale.
- Make a free offer.
- Explain an advertisement.
- Create value for your company.
- Gather customer information.
- Add to your mailing list.
- Up-sell products or offer payment discounts.
- Handle complaints and returns.
- Provide a help line for customers.
- Enforce goodwill with customers.
- Up-sell additional services.

Do you have a separate direct line for these calls, or do they go through an operator, a voicemail system, or a receptionist? If the calls are answered or intercepted prior to getting to you, does the person answering the call know how to handle it properly? Are all your inbound-call personnel trained to deal with all of the aforementioned objectives, or do they need to transfer the call for some of them? Your caller will be more relaxed and receptive if the person who answers can help with any and all such situations.

Have you ever called a company for help or to order something and been transferred to someone else who supposedly could help you—only to get the person's voicemail because he or she was busy? This frustrates callers, who were talking to someone but have now gotten someone's voicemail instead. It can be the kiss of death to put an inbound caller on hold or transfer him to someone's voicemail. Some callers won't leave a message—they'll change their mind and just spend their money elsewhere. If you *must* put someone on hold, and they have to wait more than 15 seconds, at least have hold music or something to pass the time. Dead air seems twice as long, and some people might hang up and not call back. You spent money somewhere to get them to call, so take advantage of the fact that they did, and don't lose the customer.

Remember that a first impression is created as you pick up the phone to answer an inbound call. Most people are on guard and don't know what to expect when they call to inquire or order from you. The first 10 seconds is important if you want repeat orders or a positive response to up-sells.

If you're doing an infomercial and you expect a lot of calls, you may need to hire a temporary inbound call service that can take the calls and orders. It doesn't matter where the company is located, because all customers really care about is the toll-free number. You can also use telesales services when you're doing a huge direct mailing at a specific time of the year, and you don't have enough staff to process the calls. When the big rush is over, the service can refer the calls back to your staff.

The only disadvantage to not taking all the calls yourself is that the telesales service has no stake in your business and nothing to gain except their hourly pay. Whether the rep treats your customers well will probably depend on his or her mood that day.

When hiring this type of service, see how they deal with you when you make your first inquiry. If they are courteous and easy to talk to, they may also be affable to your callers. Ask for and check a few references with other companies they have worked with. If you're spending the big bucks it takes to do this promotion, you don't want to lose even one order; you want and need them all.

Before you finalize your agreement, ask to speak to the supervisor who will handle your project and stress that you want their people to be courteous and pleasant to all the people who call. You want their reps to be pleasant to non-buyers as well, because a small percentage may call back. Let the call center management know that if this promotion works, there will be others coming.

Outbound Telemarketing

You only have a few seconds to pique a person's interest on a sales call. Don't waste those precious seconds asking, "How are you?" Just say hello and get on with it for the best results.

Not everyone will want to do this, but most people can with a little practice and confidence. You know it's done every day, because you probably get called regularly with one offer after another. But let's face it: If it didn't work, no one would be doing it. There are different reasons to call customers and prospects, and each one has its own personality. Some good reasons for using outbound telemarketing are:

- To make an immediate sale
- To explain a limited-time offer
- To get a buyer's name
- To qualify a prospect
- To set up a personal appointment

- To follow up on an order or service
- To update a mailing list
- To follow up on direct mail
- To send product literature
- To direct the customer to your website
- To ask customers for referrals
- To up-sell a current order
- To see whether a customer is satisfied

If you're trying to make an immediate sale or offer, you need to stress urgency and call for action now. Offer some incentive to order today, such as free shipping, an upgrade, or a gift of some type. Most of these calls will be to sell smaller or medium-size products, and if you don't sell them on the first call, it's probably over.

If you're calling to set an appointment with a business or an at-home buyer, your main goal is to get the day and time confirmed so there will be no surprises later. Mention the date and time again just before you hang up: "I'll see you Thursday at 3 p.m." If you're calling to follow up on a medium or large purchase, such as a car, a house, a stereo, or furniture, you can suggest add-ons, extended warranties, or service agreements. If the person is happy with his original purchase, add-on sales are much easier. If there's a problem with the customer's purchase, do everything you can to rectify it. After the problem is solved, you can go back to the original purpose of your call.

In our plastic membership-card business, we sell cards to a lot of associations, museums, and credit unions, so we call and ask for the membership department right away. When we reach the membership department, we quickly explain that we supply all types of membership cards and would like to send a free folder with samples and ideas. We tell them we'd like to know the name of the person who makes those decisions so that we can mail the folder directly to his or her attention. We always get it in First Class mail the same day. We follow up about a week later and now know the person to ask for when calling back. Our success rate for getting the correct name for the free information on the first call is more than 70 percent.

If you're planning to do an expensive mailing of catalogs or literature, you can call to verify an address, confirm the decision maker's name, and let him or her know what to expect in the mail shortly. The price of the call will be less than the wasted postage if you have an incorrect name or address. If you're calling after a mailing, ask whether the person needs additional information or more samples or if he has any questions and is interested in placing an order. If the person is planning to order, you can offer to take the order now and mention reasons for not waiting, such as short supply, quick delivery time, or a possible future price increase. If the person is not interested, you can ask a few questions to see whether he is really a prospect or should be taken off your mailing list. Or you can just try again at a future time.

A small business has to watch expenses, so don't mail to someone who is not a bona fide prospect. If it sounds as if a customer is almost ready to order when you talk to him, you can mail information Priority Mail or Next Day Air if the size of the possible order is worth the additional expense.

Hiring Telemarketing Employees

People who are successful at telemarketing are a different breed from other employees. Not everyone is cut out for this job and able to perform it successfully. They need more breaks and shorter hours so they can be refreshed and ready for each new series of calls—telemarketing is hard work.

A positive attitude is the number-one trait to look for in a potential telemarketer.

The number-one thing to look for when hiring a telemarketer is his or her attitude. Being positive regardless of what happens on the call is the only way to be successful on the phone. Telemarketers who can keep a smile on their face will also sound better on the phone. When telemarketers are good, your business will see positive growth results. Put them in the right environment, with the right products and target list, and how can you *not* prosper? If telemarketing is right for your business, the right telemarketer will make you a winner.

Look for these qualities in each potential telemarketer you interview:

- A pleasant phone voice
- Speech that is not too fast or too slow
- Speech that is loud enough but not overly loud
- Proper grammar and correct pronunciation of words
- A positive and optimistic tone
- Good listening skills and knowledge of when to stop talking

- Someone you would enjoy having a conversation with
- The ability to be persistent without being pushy
- A sense of humor without being silly
- An up-to-date knowledge of current events and news
- A friendly attitude
- Enthusiasm
- Confidence and a reassuring tone
- Experience
- A persona that you would buy from

You also may look for other qualities that pertain to your industry. Don't settle for less than you're comfortable with, or you'll just have to do it all over again. Do a trial run through your script or outline and listen to see whether the person is comfortable doing it. Be sure to interview people face to face and over the phone to get a complete picture before hiring them. This may seem like a lot of steps just to interview a telemarketer, but remember: They are representing your company to everyone they call.

To find your telemarketing personnel, you could run a newspaper ad or a Craigslist ad, but those should be your second choices. Before you get to that level, try a few better choices first:

- Referrals from friends and business associates
- Interested people from college public-speaking classes
- Likable telemarketers who call you
- People from drama and acting schools
- People you meet and enjoy talking to
- Service-oriented salespeople in stores
- A local Toastmasters group

Finding, interviewing, training, and motivating telemarketers is a never-ending task because you can never have too many people who bring you sales and growth. It's a good idea to consider both experienced and inexperienced people, because a smart company won't let a great telemarketer get out of their grasp, so good experienced telemarketers can be hard to find. Always be in the market to talk to a great one—you may stumble upon an exceptional telemarketer when you least expect it. Find out who the person is and how to contact him or her again.

Planning and Making the Call

Preparation and execution are the keys to making successful outbound calls. You need to know the reason why you're calling and plan your goal accordingly. When you've reached your goal, the call is over—don't oversell and lose it. Here are some ideas for successful outbound calls:

- Know as much as you can about whom you're calling. This gives you an edge, and you won't be playing catch-up during the call.

- Know your objective and reason for the call and guide all questions in that direction.

- Sell yourself on your company and products or services so you're convinced that your call is what is best for the prospect. If you can't sell yourself first, how can you sell anyone else? Make the call with confidence and resolution.

- Use an outline of what you want to cover so you can stay on track and moving in the right direction. If you need a script, try to memorize it so it doesn't sound canned and boring. Sound natural and try to adapt to the other person's personality.

- Don't say, "Do you have a few minutes?" "How are you today?" or "Do you want to save money?" The person you called will know you're an amateur and will probably say "No" and hang up. You don't really care how they are today; you don't even know them. This is not a personal call; it's business.

- If you don't know the decision maker's name, ask the operator who to talk to and the correct spelling of the person's name. If a recording answers the phone, and you don't want to listen to the whole story, press 0, and you'll usually get a live operator. Be courteous to the operator—he or she knows a lot more than you do, and you want that person in your corner, not across the ring.

- When you're connected to the correct decision maker, introduce yourself by name and company. A simple "Good morning" or "Good afternoon" is enough before you start your presentation. (It's not a pitch—a professional gives a presentation, while a snake-oil salesman gives a pitch.)

- State your reason for calling and proceed to give the reasons why the person should agree with your presentation. Don't talk so fast that it's hard to understand—a short pause now and then gives the person you're calling a feeling of less pressure.

- If the prospect begins to ask questions about your company, products, or services, you should take the lead in the conversation because you're the expert. The person will feel more confident if you control the discussion but don't dominate it. In fact, most people will expect it. If you act wishy-washy or speak quietly, your chances of closing a sale or getting an appointment are significantly diminished.

- Know your product or service well and have additional reference materials near the phone to answer questions you need help with. If you can't find the answer or you don't have the authority to answer the question, give the person a specific time at which you will call them back. When you call at exactly that time, you can tell the operator you have a phone appointment with so-and-so at 3 p.m., and would the operator please put you right through.

- If the prospect wants to talk, stop and listen. The person could be giving you valuable information that you need to close the sale. Or he could be telling you why he won't purchase, which you can use as an objection to overcome.

- When speaking on the phone, imagine that the person is sitting across the table from you. Don't speak too fast or too slow, too loud or soft. You're just having a conversation that you should be in control of.

  Helping people buy always gets better results than selling them.

- If you're trying to set a face-to-face appointment, suggest a few times and ask the person what's the most convenient for him. If he agrees to a day and time, confirm it again just before you hang up so it's fresh in the person's mind and he will be expecting you. Keep your calendar in front of you so you don't set appointments too close together—you don't want to be late.

- Avoid using hard-sell tactics where all you do is create stress and unfriendliness. People hate to be pushed into something and are more receptive to being guided in the right direction. Pressuring and forcing people to make a quick decision will probably result in a negative one.

- If you're making a lot of calls on a regular basis or telemarketing is your life, consider investing in a hands-free headset. Such headsets make it easy to make multiple calls without fumbling with the receiver each time. Always buy the best-quality headset you can afford, because your voice will sound more natural and have less background static.

- Enjoy telemarketing; it's a chance to talk to a lot of different people who have different needs. You may be able to fill their needs and wants and make money, too! If you enjoy your work, it will be apparent in your calls, and your prospect will be more relaxed and responsive.

- One last idea: If you have a list to call that's in alphabetical order, try starting at the end and working backward. Chances are those prospects in the X, Y, and Z categories haven't been called as much and may be easier to work with—they may buy anything! Other telemarketers may have used the same list and given up before they got to the end.

Telesales Lead Finders

If you outsource telemarketing to generate leads for your business, monitor what the telemarketers are doing. Add your phone number and those of other employees to the list you give them to call. You'll find out firsthand what your prospects are hearing. If the call needs adjustment, don't tell the caller who you are—just notify your rep right away.

In a telemarketing sales effort, when the selling price of an item or service is higher, you can use lead finders as the initial call. They are usually paid less than sales closers are, but you should give them some incentive to do the job to the best of their ability. Compensation for lead generation can be a set amount for each qualified lead or a percentage of the sales that are closed. Some of the advantages of lead finders are:

- They can qualify prospects to see whether they are possible customers.

- They can validate your call list and help you delete obsolete businesses and phone numbers.

- They can record changed addresses and phone numbers.

- They can find the correct decision maker by name and extension.

- They can make several calls, if necessary, to reach the decision maker.

- They can create interest in your product or service.

- They can set up the sale for the closer or salesperson.

- They can evaluate the lead and rate it on a scale of one to four.

- They can help you build your mailing list with interested prospects.

If a prospect is ready to buy, a salesperson or closer should be available to accept the call right away. Don't leave the prospect on hold too long, or he may get cold feet and hang up. Develop a system where the closer will be on the phone with the prospect within ten seconds. Once the prospect decides not to buy and hangs up, it's will be difficult to get him back on the phone.

Lead finders are an important part of your telemarketing program, so keep them happy and well compensated. If you are having a lunch or dinner meeting with your face-to-face sales reps, include the lead finders. They are the ones who open the first door, and they should share in the benefits. Everyone should work as a team for the best results, and all levels of your sales staff should know each other.

Cold-Call Fears

Unless you're in a retail-store business, you and your staff will probably have to make cold calls to get new business. Direct mail will set the stage for a cold call, but you have to make the call. By following a few basic rules, you'll get more sales or appointments than your average salesperson.

Cold calls aren't as bad as everyone says if you just relax. Don't think about making the call; just pick up the phone and do it. When someone rejects your proposal, don't take it personally—the person doesn't even know you and just isn't receptive to what you're calling about.

- Believe in yourself and know that you can make the cold call successful.

- Believe in your company and the products and services you're presenting.

- Decide in advance whether you want to close a sale or set an appointment.

- Keep the call short and to the point. Explain why you're calling and how it will benefit the prospect.

- Stop and listen for a response—let the prospect talk.

- Answer any questions promptly. Don't hesitate or hide anything.

- Expect to win, and you will most of the time.

- Don't take rejection personally; just go on to the next call.

Make several cold calls, one after the other. Once you get in the rhythm, the momentum will make each call easier. Stay positive and practice the Golden Rule.

Voicemail Smarts

Often when trying to make a phone presentation or get an appointment, you will reach the decision maker's voicemail. This may be on purpose, because decision makers can't possibly take every sales call they get. The message you leave will determine whether you'll get a call back or if you'll get through the next time you call.

If you get a person's voicemail when making a sales call, be brief, straightforward, and honest, while piquing the person's curiosity.

For every voicemail message, you should keep in mind four things:

- Brevity
- Straightforwardness
- Honesty
- Curiosity

Don't use statements such as, "Mr. Peters, I have something very important to talk to you about." That's a giveaway that you're afraid to say why you're calling, and you'll almost never get a call back. Don't tell your entire story in your message, but pique the person's curiosity with a clue as to why you want to talk to him. Leave some information about why it will benefit the person to return your call. Offer to explain further on the phone or in a personal appointment.

Let the person know the best time to call you back or when you will call him back and then follow through. Being honest and straightforward will catch more prospects than using mystery and deceit. After all, the reason for leaving a voicemail message in the first place is to get a response.

Is Telemarketing Paying Off?

If you're calling prospects to set up appointments or for lead generation, you actually can see what it's costing you to obtain a new customer. First, you need to know the number of leads it takes before you get one customer—two, five, ten, and so on. When you know this, you can find out the cost of generating one lead by adding all your telemarketing costs over a week or month and dividing by the number of leads you were able to get. Multiply your lead cost by the number it takes to get one new customer, and you'll know the telemarketing cost to acquire one customer. Add in the cost of your salesperson, and you'll find the total expense needed to acquire one new customer.

If the amount scares you, it should—you're paying it! Now you can find out whether you made a profit by dividing the sum of all new order amounts by the number of new customers. Figure your percentage of profit and see whether it's higher or lower than the sales cost. If you're near the break-even point, you can consider whether your customers will be repeats and how often to see whether your strategy is paying off.

Even if you're not making a profit on the order, do everything you can to entice the customer to reorder. Reorders will always produce more profit than a first order just because there is a much lower sales cost. Actually, there may be no sales cost at all—you just take the order and process it.

If you train your telemarketing people well, they should become more efficient and reduce the average cost of a lead. Practice and fine-tuning will pay off in the long run, and you'll quickly get to know who your best telemarketing people are.

Check the Laws

Most states have laws governing when and how you can do consumer telemarketing. Normally, you can't call after 9 or 10 p.m., and there's a fine for each offense that's reported. Fines can be steep, so be sure you check with your state offices before you start.

Some areas even have phone upgrades where you can't get through if you're a telemarketer. And you must follow the laws pertaining to the Do Not Call list. Excessive complaints can lead to an investigation of your business and possible cease orders.

However, most of you won't have these problems, especially if you're calling businesses during normal business hours. You may need to check out additional laws pertaining to calling interstate to see whether they apply to you, though.

It's difficult enough to do telemarketing, so don't ignore the laws and spend valuable time defending yourself. Chances are that people who don't want to be called will be hostile and never buy anything, so why bother?

Some Final Telemarketing Don'ts

- Don't be rude or disrespectful to the business's gatekeeper or screening person.
- Don't use high-pressure and hard-sell tactics.
- Don't be discourteous if the person isn't interested.
- Don't forget to reward your best callers and lead generators.
- Don't use slang or off-color words during your presentation.
- Don't let an irate or depressed employee make telemarketing calls.
- Don't forget to leave the door open for future calls.

- Don't forget to ask for referrals.
- Don't forget to introduce yourself by name and company when the prospect answers.
- Don't call a restaurant during lunch or dinner hours.
- Don't forget to thank the person as you end the call.
- Don't give up after a string of nos.
- Don't hang up when someone is talking.

Action Plan

✓ Hire only telemarketing employees who have a positive attitude.
✓ Plan and rehearse your call first.
✓ Check all your state calling laws.
✓ Don't take rejection personally.

"Practice the Golden Rule when telemarketing."

—BT

Chapter 15

Customer Loyalty

- Get Close to Your Customers
- Ways to Create Loyalty
- Ways to Destroy Loyalty
- Your Business Personality
- What's Your Brand?
- Customer Cards and Tracking
- Loyalty Breeds Referrals
- Tell How or Tell Who
- A Doctor's Loyalty

Is there any loyalty left in customers minds? Do they really care, and can you create loyalty? The answer is *yes* to all of these— if you plan and work at it. If you are starting a new business and you have no loyal customers yet, you will need to create some loyalty quickly.

Never underestimate the value of loyal customers or take them for granted— they are too hard to come by.

You're in luck, because many people like the comfort of frequenting the same business for years. Customers may test a new business once, but they'll usually go back to their original place the next time.

Remember, though, that a satisfied customer is not necessarily a loyal one. Loyalty builds up over time and with a series of satisfactory experiences, plus a good feeling during the sale. This doesn't happen overnight; it takes time, and you work on it all the time.

In most cases, loyalty has nothing to do with price. Really loyal customers like what you offer, learn to expect quality, and return to get it. But if you ever lose their loyalty, it is very difficult (if not impossible) to get it back.

When I lived in Chicago, I went to the same barber for 12 years, until I moved. Now I've been with a new barber for seven years. I want to know that I can relax there and know that my haircut will be done exactly the way I want it done, and it takes repeated visits to get that feeling. A lower price or a new salon would not get me to change unless I had a reoccurring problem with the barber I was using.

You can establish that same feeling in any type of business, from a printer to a clothing store to a shoeshine stand. Loyal customers will build your business and guarantee that you'll *stay* in business.

If you think of loyalty as part of a train, with all of your other business functions following it, then loyalty is the engine that pulls all the others. In a small business, customer loyalty and retention are even more important than they are in a corporate giant. Large corporations can always mass-advertise and get a new crop of customers—they do so regularly. But smaller companies don't have that kind of budget for advertising, so they need to keep all their customers once they get them.

In this chapter, we'll look at ways to create and destroy loyalty. A small business can usually get those answers through their sales and profit reports—if you've built customer loyalty, that will be reflected in your sales and profits.

Sustaining loyalty is an ongoing course of action.

You should be aware of when a regular customer hasn't come into your store or called to place an order for a while. If you're used to getting their business once a month, but now three months have passed, it's time to find out why. Just because a customer is loyal after a year, that doesn't necessarily mean the same customer will be loyal after two years or five years. Creating loyalty isn't a one-time process; it's an ongoing course of action. After you create loyalty, you must sustain it. Consistently high quality and personal service will go a long way toward sustaining long-term loyalty. But only one recent exception can destroy many past good experiences.

And what about loyalty in franchises? When you travel and want a quick fast-food meal, you may look for a familiar logo because you know that the quality will be more or less the same as it is back home. That works to the advantage of franchise owners when it comes to out-of-towners, but for them to keep their local customers, they need to add friendliness and cleanliness to their store's personality. You can develop your own store personality that customers will remember, and if they like it, they'll keep coming back.

The same is true for business customers. If they see a specific personality that you've established and they feel comfortable, they'll continue purchasing from your company.

Regardless of whether you're selling to businesses, opening a retail store, running a franchise location, or doing consumer sales, this chapter will help you learn how to create and sustain customer loyalty.

Get Close to Your Customers

Remember when you first started your business—how difficult it was to get those first customers to take a chance and buy from you? If you're starting your business now, you'll quickly learn first-hand that it's a challenge to build your customer base. If you don't want to do that all over again, all the time, you need to keep those customers coming back regularly. You can do so by getting close to them and staying close. A number of customers will help you build your business because they:

- Order often
- Place large orders
- Pay their bills quickly
- Send referrals and friends
- Are easy to work with
- Give you new product ideas

- Tell you their likes and dislikes
- Are patient when problems arise

These great customers belong on your A list to receive your best prices and service all the time. Your employees should know who these customers are and go that extra mile when dealing with them. These are the people with whom you want to continually discuss what new products and services they want and how you can provide them. Keep these customers informed about what's happening in your business. Give them advance notice of any price increases so they can stock up at the old prices. When you're considering adding a new product or service, ask what they think and value their opinion—use it in making your decision. Most such customers will feel honored to be asked and will likely give you their true opinion.

When any problem occurs with an order for your A-list customers, solve it promptly and to their satisfaction. Have your employees alert you personally so you can follow up and make sure the problem is taken care of. A quick call from the top (you) shows customers that you really care about them.

Solving a problem is the number-one key to loyalty. Every business has problems, and people are not shocked when they happen. How quickly and fairly they are rectified makes all the difference to a loyal customer.

You might also consider giving your A-list customers your home phone number or your personal cell number. If you'd rather not give your home or cell phone, give them your home email address so they can reach you in the evening or on a weekend if some emergency arises. Getting back to your customers in off hours, even if you can't help until the next business day, will go a long way in showing your concern and willingness to help.

Your next group of customers will be the majority group consisting of regular buyers who you can reasonably count on for business. This is your B list, and your staff should treat them with respect, concern, and helpfulness. This group of customers is reasonably loyal, but they may occasionally flirt with other businesses to see what's going on and whether they can get a better deal somewhere else. Many customers can be enticed into experimenting with a newly opened business just to see how it's different from yours. They may be given little perks and once-a-year gifts or rewards. They probably won't change for small differences, but they may be swayed by big offers.

Often, if these customers try another source and it doesn't work out, they will come right back to your business. You need your B-list customers, who you can count on about 75 percent of the time, to help grow your company and provide a stable customer base. Some will move up to your A list after time, especially if they have tried other sources and come back to you. Don't neglect this group; handle their requests and problems promptly.

Your casual customers will fall into your C list and will provide sales and profits, but you can't always count on them. They will change sources on a whim, and you won't see or hear from them again. But you may pick up C-list customers from your competitors in the same way. C-listers don't have loyalty to any business and are sort of "here today, gone tomorrow" customers. These are the ones who probably won't tell you when there's a problem; you just won't see them again. If they really like your products or services and your way of doing business, they may eventually become B-list customers, but they'll never be on the A list. Their personality and character won't allow them to make a serious commitment to any one business over the long term. But regardless of their lack of loyalty, you need their business, and you and your staff should treat them professionally.

Then you come to your lowest-level customers—your D list. You'll never get any loyalty from them—but do you even want it? They will buy from you only when it's convenient for them, and they're always looking for a better deal. They don't care whether you make a profit or you go out of business tomorrow. D-listers are often unpleasant to do business with and may come up with unreasonable demands and silly complaints.

When selling to your D list, be sure they check and okay everything along the way. They often like nothing better than to find a little problem and demand a discount. Exercise caution when selling to your D list, and when the aggravation outweighs the gain, stop doing business with them. You can suggest that they buy from one of your competitors and let the competitor try to handle their annoying ways.

Few, if any, of these types of customers will ever move up to your C list—it's not in their nature. Have a set policy when dealing with these customers, and let your employees know how to handle them.

Ways to Create Loyalty

We all want customer loyalty, but are we willing to create it, and do we even know how? You must establish an overall environment or atmosphere for your business that sets you apart from your competitors. Here are some ideas for how to create customer loyalty:

- Provide exceptional customer service.
- Offer convenient business hours.
- Create a perception of high value.
- Make the customer feel important—when possible, learn and use the customer's name.
- Ensure regular owner/manager contact.
- Provide personal service and attention to customers.
- Greet everyone with a smile.
- Have a friendly refund and exchange policy.
- Show a sincere desire to help.
- Follow up with the customer after a sale.
- Offer faster checkout and payment.
- Offer faster order processing and shipping.
- Establish customer-friendly policies.
- Have an outstanding guarantee.
- Provide service to special-interest groups.
- Have a welcome sign on your door.
- Offer a selection of specialty products.
- Solve problems immediately.
- Have a rewards or payback program.
- Stay open late to accommodate a customer.
- Ask customers for new product input.
- Alert customers of new product arrivals.
- Feature perks for frequent customers.
- Send convenient reorder reminders.
- Keep your business reputation clean.
- Keep your store neat and clean.
- Tell customers often that you value their business.
- Have an open-door policy for questions.

- Give a little extra with each order.
- Have an attitude that the sale is never final until the customer is satisfied.

Make your own list of ways to create loyalty and post it everywhere. Make it visible in the general office, in the break room, by the copier, and even on the bathroom wall. Don't let your employees (or yourself) ever forget what needs to be done. Print the list on colored paper so no one will miss it.

You'll notice there was no mention of price in this section. That's because price doesn't create loyalty. Customers who buy based on price alone are loyal for one purchase only and then are off to whoever has the best price the next time. Forget price and develop the other magnetisms that really create customer loyalty. Provide the little extras, and customers will notice that they like doing business with you.

Ways to Destroy Loyalty

Just as you can create loyalty, you can overturn it easily if you're not careful and you don't pay attention. Don't make buying from you difficult, time consuming, or an overall unpleasant experience. You'll drive your customers into the waiting arms of your competitors. Here are some ways to destroy loyalty:

It takes a year or more to create customer loyalty but only five seconds to destroy it. Human nature makes us remember the unpleasant things that happen to us longer than the good things.

- Provide poor customer service.
- Feature out-of-stock items or unstocked shelves.
- Ignore customers or treat them indifferently.
- Do not reinforce good customer service.
- Have poorly displayed merchandise.
- Forget about customers on hold.
- Don't return phone calls or emails.
- Have a sarcastic or grouchy attitude.
- Make customers wait in long lines to pay.
- Offer shoddy or poor-quality products.
- Open late or close early.
- Have voicemail answer the phone 24/7.
- Have a no-refunds policy.
- Have business hours that suit yourself.
- Leave a customer's question unanswered.

- Have a long delivery time.
- Have employees who ignore customers when they're in the store.
- Drag out the process of solving a problem.
- Have a "no exceptions" policy.
- Show up late for appointments.
- Under-staff your store or phone lines.
- Reduce your guarantee to 24 hours or make all sales final.
- Have a dirty or messy store or office.
- Have poorly dressed or poorly groomed employees.
- Feature high price and low quality.
- Run out of popular items.
- Don't keep customers informed on their order progress.
- Have payment terms of cash or C.O.D. only.
- Don't thank customers for their order.
- Don't acknowledge a frequent customer.
- Don't train your employees effectively.

Some of these may sound amusing, but they happen every day in some businesses. If you could go back and look at some businesses that have closed, you'd probably find a lot of these situations. During tight economic times, customer loyalty plays a big part in your survival and growth.

Your Business Personality

The dictionary defines *personality* as "distinctive individual qualities, considered collectively." Just as every person has a personality, so does your business. After a year or so in business, certain traits, manners, and characteristics will emerge and be picked up by your regular customers. Your customers will be able to see whether you're only out for the almighty dollar or you really care about serving and helping people.

Even a franchisee develops its own personality and individual qualities. The products and the system are the same as at other franchise locations, but the character and attitude are different because of different owners for each location.

Your attitude as an owner will work its way into your business and be known by your employees and customers. We develop our personality and character early in life, and so will your business. A tough, egotistical, and unfriendly business demeanor won't go very far in creating loyalty from your customers (and your employees). You want to portray helpful, pleasant, and reliable feelings to everyone who enters your little empire. Yes, you're the owner, the king of your castle, the emperor of your domain, but you won't have any subjects in your kingdom if you don't create the correct environment. You need customers to feel as if they can refer anyone to you and that if you can't help them directly, you'll point them in the right direction. If you create this environment and personality for your business, your customers will start to feel more comfortable buying from you, and it will take a big misstep to get them to change to someone else.

I prefer to fly on one particular airline because of the miles and because I've achieved a certain status level. So if this airline flies where I'm going, I'm on it. It sometimes costs a little more than the low-price carriers, but I have a good chance of being upgraded to first class because of my status level. And I'm so used to this airline that I feel comfortable and secure in my seat. I know what to expect and how I'll be treated. If I use another airline from time to time, I get a little anxious at first because it's so different. I'm sure this is exactly how my favorite airline wants me to feel.

You can create a similar feeling about your company if customers know you'll take good care of them. They will become fond of your business personality and visit you often.

What's Your Brand?

Your brand is how your customers and prospects distinguish you from other businesses in your industry. The brand can be your logo, your name, a specific type style, or even a slogan that's easy to remember. If you're a doctor, an attorney, or an accountant, your brand is your name, so use it often and everywhere. Take every available opportunity to promote your brand. Display it on all ads, literature, signs, and business cards so it becomes familiar to your target market.

Promote your brand at every possible opportunity.

You want everyone, including your customers and prospects, to know your brand and rely on it. Once your brand is established in your target market, people will begin to feel that:

- Your brand is their best choice.
- They're comfortable with the quality.
- They're comfortable with the price.
- Your brand is worth a premium.
- Your brand has value added.
- Your brand has a reliable level of performance.
- Your brand offers consistently good service.
- It's guaranteed.

Brand recognition can build long-term business rather than one-time orders. Work to keep your brand in front of your customers so that another choice won't be an option. You don't have to be a Fortune 500 company to establish your brand in your target market—you can use publicity, word-of-mouth, and advertising to do so.

Customer Cards and Tracking

Using frequent-customer cards is a give-and-take situation. You give customers rewards for buying, and they give you their personal information, which you can use for marketing purposes. Small companies can use frequent-customer cards with a computer program that keeps track of purchase activity by a customer number. Or, cards can be as basic as a punch card that offers "Buy 12 and get 1 free." If you opt for the latter method, use a specially shaped punch as a security feature, so people can't use a standard hole-punch to falsify their cards.

What, when, how, and why your customers do certain things is the foundation of successful marketing. If you can get them to use loyalty or rewards cards, you will have all their purchasing information, and you can use this to send them targeted coupons or rewards based on their purchasing habits or history.

The signup form for your cards gives you the customer information you can use for other promotions and mailings. If you ask for customers' birthdays (without the year), you can send a card a few days in advance. If you have a retail store, you can include a "Happy Birthday" coupon that entitles them to a free item or 30 to 50 percent off a purchase during the week of their birthday.

The casino industry uses customer-tracking cards to the highest level. They know when their guests are playing, for how long, how much they are betting, and how often they come to the casino.

They get all this information and give you a free buffet dinner. Is it worth it? You bet! (Sorry—couldn't resist the pun.) Casinos also know what states and cities most of their customers come from, and they use that information to target their advertising, direct mail, and email. Instead of spending millions of dollars going after the wrong market, they concentrate on the areas where they get most of their regular customers. Repeat advertising and mailing in these areas gives them maximum results.

Customers show loyalty and use the cards because they want the free dinners, free shows, and occasional free room. They also feel comfortable gambling where they know all the rules and some of the casino personnel. Everybody is happy, but it's the business that makes the money. Casinos have this method so fine-tuned that they can predict what their betting volume and win will be by who's staying in their hotel.

Small businesses can use these concepts on a smaller scale and at less expense. Your customers just want to know that you appreciate their business and that if they are loyal to you, they may get something back eventually. You don't have the financial resources that a casino has, so how do you get started in this area? Here are a few ideas you can consider:

- Use customer punch cards—with or without signup forms.

- Have a birthday club—send a card and a coupon.

- Issue customer cards and write or buy a computer program to keep records by customer number.

- Have your cash register programmed to accept a customer number and tie it to purchases.

- Offer a frequent-dining card if you're a food-service establishment.

- Issue cards for advance admission to special sales or new product showings if you're a furniture or other big-ticket-item store.

- Find another small business and have a cross-promotion card that is good at both stores.

- Let a school sell your discount card as a fundraiser—that way, you get the customers.

Loyalty Breeds Referrals

We all know that customer loyalty means repeat business, which we all need to stay in business. We also need to grow our business, which means adding new customers. In addition to all the advertising, direct mail, signs, and so on, are we overlooking the least expensive source? Satisfied and loyal customers can increase your business by referring new customers to you.

Referrals can help your business grow exponentially.

Referred customers are usually less apprehensive than other new customers are when first purchasing from you because they have friends, relatives, or acquaintances who are already pleased with your products or services. And when referred customers become satisfied customers, they too will send referrals, and your business can grow exponentially!

Provide some incentive for those who send you referrals that then become your customers. It can be a small discount, a free gift, or more points on their loyalty card. Some people may be very loyal to your business but won't refer other people unless you ask them, so ask them. If they don't want to be involved, ask for the referral name and call or mail that person and mention your customer's name. This type of free word-of-mouth advertising is one of your best marketing tools. The power of a referral is stronger than most advertising.

Tell How or Tell Who

Occasionally, a potential customer will visit your store or call your office in search of a product or service that you don't provide. It's easy to say, "Sorry, we can't help you," and move on to something else. Chances are such potential customers won't return unless they're absolutely sure you have what they want—or they may never return. Why should they? You gave them no help at all.

Help people find what they need even if you can't provide it, and you can't lose.

Why not build a little loyalty even if you can't make a sale? Tell the customer where or who can fill his needs, and you'll make a friend in the process. The next time the customer needs your product or service, you're sure to be at the top of his list. You want customers to come to you first, even if you can't make the sale. Not only will you get their regular business, but also many will refer others to you. You just can't lose by making a business friend by helping people find what they need.

If you keep getting similar requests for things you can't provide, try to create a cross-referral deal with another company who can. You can both come out ahead and have happy customers. They will send you people who need your products or services, and vice versa. It's a win-win situation.

A Doctor's Loyalty

Wouldn't every small-business owner like to have a doctor's following? Your clients and customers wouldn't look around before using your products and services, and they wouldn't compare prices or even look at competitors' advertising. They'd be willing to wait 20, 30, even 45 minutes to be served, and although they wouldn't like it, they also wouldn't walk out.

Did you ever hear of someone saying they were going to get three quotes before an operation? Maybe three opinions, but not price quotes. Price is not usually a factor when physical health is the concern. Loyalty and comfort are the issues, not price. So how can *you* create this type of loyalty in your business?

You need to instill a desire and comfort level in customers' minds that your business is the only one where they will purchase your type of products or services. It's almost like a mini-brainwashing, where they ignore all your competitors because they know you are the best source for them. You'll probably never achieve a doctor's level of loyalty, but even half as much will go a long way in growing your business. Remember, price only makes a difference when everything else is equal. Find a way to create and sustain that strong loyalty, and you won't have to worry about your customers comparing prices.

Action Plan

✓ Always be looking for ways to create customer loyalty.

✓ Get to know your clients and customers.

✓ Promote your brand whenever possible.

✓ Reward those who send referrals.

"If you want loyalty without any effort, get a dog."

—BT

Chapter 16

Customer Service

- Keep Your Customers
- Wear Your Customers' Shoes
- The Customer Is Angry
- Customer Service Don'ts
- Look Down to See the Profits
- Rally the Troops
- Reward Great Service
- Employee of the Month
- Don't Lock 'Em Out
- Pay Attention
- One-Hundred Percent Satisfaction
- Transaction Time
- The Good, the Bad, and the Real

With so many franchises, discount stores, and fast-food restaurants everywhere, we've seen the quality of service and friendliness in retail business become all but extinct. And industrial, business, and manufacturing personnel seem to be inflexible and even less helpful. You get greeted by voicemail rather than by a businesslike human voice. Exceptional service and empathy for the customer are difficult to find, especially in many larger companies that feel you have to buy from them because they have numerous stores and massive advertising budgets. They flood the media and think that a majority of buyers will heed their call.

This is where a small business can make the most headway against competitors and grow a business—with customer service. These two words alone tell the story:

Customer. A person who buys from you and pays you money for your product or service.

Service. To help people with any question, problem, procedure, or decision in a professional and friendly manner.

How can you possibly have a successful business without both parts? Some business owners have tried, but most have failed. When quality and prices are similar, who are you going to buy from? Probably the company that treats you the best and is the most helpful.

You want repeat business from about 95 percent of your customers, and the only way you're going to get it is if they were happy and satisfied with their most recent purchase. When you consider the lifetime value of a customer, the money and time you spend on perfecting your service looks very cheap. These lifetime customers are the people who will support you during business slowdowns and poor economic times. They are also the people who will refer their friends, relatives, and business associates.

Great customer service means more than just doing the ordinary; it's over and above what is expected—that little extra. It doesn't just happen; you must make it happen by constantly training, reviewing, and reminding your employees. Without customers, their job (and yours) is non-existent. No money flows into the business to pay them if there aren't satisfied customers who purchase regularly from the business. This sounds very simple, and you'd think everyone would know it, but people can forget it if they're not reminded.

When you visit a fast-food restaurant or a large corporate store, you sort of expect to be treated with indifference and a cool attitude. Or you get that fake smile and artificial, "How are you today?" Most of these establishments (though not all) concentrate on training their employees in how to do the job correctly rather than in how to treat the customer. They rely on their expensive advertising to bring back customers for special offers instead of creating an atmosphere that makes customers want to come back of their own accord. Perhaps people are just getting used to this treatment and keep buying because they think there's no other choice. A small business can offer another choice and take away some of these customers. Smart business owners know this and use it to their advantage.

As a small business, you probably don't have a massive advertising budget, so you should take the easier, cheaper, and better way: outstanding customer service. If I'm at a fast-food restaurant and someone is extremely helpful, pleasant, and attentive (believe me, they stick out), I'll give the person my business card and let him know that if he's ever looking for a job, he should give me a call. These outstanding employees are rare, and when you find one, you should always leave the door open for future contact should the situation arise. If the person's employer is treating him right, he probably won't leave, but if the employee is *not* being treated well in his current situation, you've created an opportunity.

> Customer service is an area where a small business can excel over a large corporation—but only if you train, retrain, and monitor your customer contact employees. Be the type of company that your customers enjoy doing business with, and they'll be back.

If you're lucky enough to have one of these outstanding employees on your staff, handle him with care and let new hires observe him in action.

Keep in mind that when your employees aren't happy, it will spill over to your customers. Are they seeing people who enjoy their jobs or grumpy, sarcastic clock-watchers? When your customer contact is on the phone and not in person, the same feelings are transmitted by tone of voice or attitude. If you're smiling on your end of the phone, customers will know it on the other end. The same is true if you're in a bad mood—customers will be able to tell, even over the phone.

As a small business, you can provide excellent customer service at very little cost, and this can be your catalyst in outsmarting your bigger competitors. The care and friendliness you provide is just as important as your products and services and should not be overlooked. Customers will remember this, and you will profit from it.

Keep Your Customers

As a small-business owner, you know better than anyone that repeat business is essential—even critical—to keep your doors open and foster growth. Your customers' continued business is the foundation on which any prosperous enterprise is built. Think about the amount you spend on advertising, direct mail, and publicity to get a new customer—and then remember that it costs nothing but effort to keep them coming back.

If you can't afford a big-bucks ad campaign, your other option is to keep customers coming back by providing outstanding customer service.

Large companies rely on repetitive advertising and expensive promotions to get customers because they can't always control their customer service and personal attention. When you think about going back to a fast-food restaurant, do you remember their last big advertising campaign on TV or the person who served you? My guess is that you remember the advertising, which costs big bucks that a small business can't afford. So why not take the easier and more economical way of attracting customers? Repeat satisfied customers will build your business faster than anything else.

According to the White House Office of Consumer Affairs, 56 to 70 percent of customers who complain to you will do business with you again if you resolve their problem. If they feel you acted quickly and to their satisfaction, up to 96 percent will do business with you again, and they will probably refer other people to you.

Here are numerous ideas you can adapt to your business to keep your customers coming back:

- **Use the customer's name often.** How important do you feel when you walk into a business and hear, "Hi Bob, how are you today?" Find a way to remember names and associate them with faces. You'll convey a good feeling right from the first contact.

- **Give more than you promise.** Deliver more quickly, add a little extra to the order, charge a little less than your estimate, upgrade at no charge, and so on. We all like pleasant surprises; they happen so seldom.

- **Hire friendly people.** A smile on your employees' faces and in their voices will help customers feel comfortable doing business with you. The words *friendly* and *smile* should appear in all your help-wanted ads.

- **Say thank you.** We all want to know that our patronage is appreciated; after all, we're spending our hard-earned money. These two simple words should be in everyone's vocabulary at all times—they never get old.

- **Ask for customer input.** What new products or services do they want, and will they purchase them? What don't they like—selection, prices, business hours, long lines? Then change what you can.

- **Change with the times.** Products, services, benefits, and technology change quickly and constantly, so don't remain stagnant. What was popular yesterday may be obsolete today and gone tomorrow. Stay on top of the trends in your industry.

- **Calculate the long-term value of a customer.** How often does he buy from you, and what will he buy over 10 or 20 years? The numbers will surprise you, but the only way to receive that business is to keep the customer satisfied with great service and value.

- **Match—or, better yet, exceed—what your competitors are offering.** This doesn't mean launching a price war, but you can find ways of doing the same thing better or faster. Be an innovator, not a copycat. Create word-of-mouth advertising by incorporating your new ideas.

- **Show customers the benefits rather than the features.** They want to know what it can do for them, not technical jargon or shoptalk. How will your products make their job or life easier? That's what sells!

- **Reward customer loyalty.** Use frequent-buyer programs, coupons, scratch-offs, special gifts, and so on. Implement early notification of sales, early-bird offers, preferred customer lines, and special attention for frequent customers. Everyone likes that little something extra that makes him feel important.

- **Treat employees well.** Their enthusiasm and pride for your business will come through when assisting your clients and customers. Encourage suggestions and create a feeling of trust and respect. Well-trained and compensated employees will stay longer, require less supervision, and cost you less in the long run.

- **Do constant research.** You can make sure you're satisfying customers by using surveys and comment cards. Have an employee-of-the-month program and let customers vote and add their comments or special requests to their vote.

- **Stay in contact.** You need to be in your customers' minds every time they need to buy something in your industry. Develop and use mailing lists from orders, contests, or business-card drawings. Send to people who are already customers more often than you do to random prospects. Give them a new offer or a reason to purchase again.

- **Handle problems and complaints promptly.** Not every order or purchase will go smoothly—it's just part of being in business. It's how you resolve the problem that really matters. Listen to the customer's view and satisfy him as quickly as you can. Don't sidestep complaints and make the client ask twice.

- **Provide customer education.** An informed and knowledgeable customer is a better consumer of your products and services. Offer verbal instructions and ideas along with easy-to-understand brochures. Have on-site classes at no charge for anyone who wants to know more about your industry.

- **Cross-train your employees.** When someone is off or on vacation, there should always be someone who can step in and handle a customer's questions. A factory can't have one part of its assembly line idle, or the entire operation stops. Don't let there be any gaps in your service or operation.

- **Give VIP treatment.** Giving special attention, offering special hours, letting them meet the owner/president, and providing other perks can make customers feel like you really appreciate and need their business—which is true. The airlines do this at little expense by providing preferred check-in lines and upgraded seating. Find something you can offer to make your customers feel highly valued and special.

- **Get testimonials.** Letters and comment cards from satisfied and enthusiastic customers are great selling tools for use with new prospects. No one wants to be a guinea pig, and past performance can create a comfort level for new buyers. You probably won't get letters from satisfied customers unless you ask, though, so always request them.

- **Assess your customers' needs.** Always be thinking of ways to improve your products and services to fulfill your customers' needs and wants. Often little changes can add big value and increase sales, referrals, and repeat business.

- **Use your employees' ideas.** They have everyday contact with your customers and often will have suggestions you didn't think of. Always reward ideas that you use. Stress the importance of sharing ideas on the very first day and remind employees of this at periodic meetings.

- **Use your customers' ideas.** They know what they want to buy, so how can you get any better input? Sell what they want to buy, not what you want to sell. Get out in your store or on the phone and ask them.

The bottom line is that you work hard and spend money to get customers, so don't let them escape when you have them. Do anything and everything necessary to satisfy them and keep in contact. Keep them coming back over and over again, and your business will prosper and grow. If you let them make their next purchase elsewhere, you'll have to start all over again. Remember the old real estate phrase, "Location, location, location?" Well, in small business, it's, "Repeat, repeat, repeat."

Wear Your Customers' Shoes

Are you really treating your customers the way you would want to be treated? Yes, it's the old Golden Rule, and it never gets stale! You must show empathy and understand what the person on the other side is thinking and feeling. Have you ever gone into a store or called a company and said later, "I'm never doing business with them again?" It happens every day somewhere—is it happening at your business? Do you actually know? Remember, these people tell other people, who may not try you even once because of what they've heard.

If you're not visiting most of your competitors' stores, offices, or websites, you're missing vital marketing information. How can you be better than your rivals if you don't know what they're doing?

Here are some ideas and suggestions to help you live and work by the Golden Rule:

- Be a customer at your competitors' businesses. See what they're doing and then do it better. What can you offer that they're not? Or how can you provide better service? Look at their customers' faces—are they happy?

- Review your refund, replacement, and return policies. Are they done with courtesy, and are they easy for your customers? Do you back up your guarantee 100 percent? Do your employees treat customers who return items in a friendly and cordial manner?

- Listen in on or record customer service call-ins or walk-ins and see what's happening to your customers. Are they being treated like you would want your parent or spouse to be treated? Be sure to let your employees know that you're doing this.

- Look at your hours of operation. Do they accommodate all your customers, early and late? Or do you stay open only when you feel like working?

- If you're selling nationally, do you open your phones a little early and stay a little later to service all time zones? Do you promptly return all voicemail messages and email queries?

- Set your business up to accept credit cards. Everyone can—all retail outfits, distributors, manufacturers, lawyers, doctors, accountants, and so on. It's important, even if you only take Visa and MasterCard. Ask your bank about merchant services.

- Survey customers to ask what new products they would like to buy from you.

- Walk around your store with customers to see how they shop. Are most items easy to find? Is there someone available to help customers if they need it?

- Watch your customers' faces or listen to their tone of voice on the phone. Doing so will help you know whether they enjoy doing business with you.

- Offer gift cards so your customers can give them to friends and relatives. Most merchant service providers have a program you can use.

- Always put your friendliest and most informed people on the front lines.

- Treat complaints as an opportunity, not as a nuisance. Resolve them quickly and fairly.

- Periodically work the front lines yourself to observe your customer contact firsthand.

- Have literature, business cards, and samples of your product or service free and readily available.

- Offer a free trial offer to build confidence in your company.

- Smile! It doesn't hurt, and it exercises your facial muscles.

- Observe customers from outside of your business. Are they leaving in a good mood and do they look satisfied? If they're shaking their heads, you need to make some quick adjustments. Find out what their dismay is about.

- Never cheat a customer even if you can. It will always come back to haunt you, and you will usually lose more than you gained.

- Consider what products, services, or benefits you want to offer your customers and prospects a year from now. Are you working today on ways of providing them? Don't wait until the last minute and let a competitor initiate a great idea before you do.

The Customer Is Angry

No matter how hard you try to please your customers, you'll have to deal with an angry one at some point. You could hang up on the person or tell him to leave, but you'll surely lose his business forever. Why not take the other approach and save the customer's business? The customer is going to buy again from someone, and it might as well be you.

Here are some ideas on how to handle angry customers:

- Let them vent and get it all out so you know what you're dealing with. Don't offer any solutions until you know the entire situation. Don't interrupt them; just listen.

- Apologize for the problem but don't accept any fault at this point, especially if you weren't there when the problem occurred.

- Ask questions to help you understand what the problem is. Go over the problem from beginning to end and learn all the facts.

- Empathize—show them that you know how they feel and can see their point. Let them know you will try to offer a resolution as quickly as you can—and then do it.

- Don't argue with them. It will get you nowhere at this point. Regardless of who you think is right or wrong, you want to save them as customers.

- Thank them for bringing the matter to your attention. Assure them that you're working on the resolution. If you can't offer an immediate resolution, make sure you have their contact information.

- Offer a solution and see whether it's satisfactory for them. Or, you might offer two or three choices from which they can select. You want customers to be comfortable with any solution.

- Do what you promise and follow up to make sure the customer is satisfied with the final situation. If you delegate the solution, stress that it's to be handled cheerfully and then check to make sure it was. You don't want the solution to become another problem.

- Let customers know that they can contact you directly at any time and that you appreciate their business.

These steps won't work in every instance, but they should resolve many situations and save those customers. When you consider the long-term value of a customer, a little setback now seems insignificant. After a problem is resolved, discuss it with your employees so they will know how to handle a similar situation if it arises again. You don't want the same problem to happen again if you can avoid it.

Customer Service Don'ts

This section covers things that you don't want to happen in your business if you want to prosper, especially in tough economic times. Many small-business owners are not aware that these things are even occurring, because they fail to check on their customer service people regularly. You need to be on top of your customer service at all times because your customers experience it every time they buy.

Copy this list of customer service don'ts and review it at least once a month. If you wait too long to think about these things, the damage will be done and can't be reversed. When customers are lost because of poor service or indifference, it's very hard to get them back. These things are simple to correct if you know they're going on.

- Don't argue with a customer. You can lose in two ways—the argument and/or the customer.

- Don't forget to say thank you after each sale or order.

- Don't ignore anyone who enters your store or business; acknowledge the customer's presence.

- Don't ever cheat a customer, even if you can get away with it.

- Don't leave anyone on hold for more than a minute without checking back with the person.

- Don't treat all customers the same. Decide whether a person needs more or less attention and then help and act accordingly. Some will want to buy quickly and leave, while others will want to spend some time making a decision.

- Don't promise things you can't or won't deliver; always be honest.

- Don't tell a client that you will call them back at a certain time and then not do it.

- Don't let poorly trained employees serve customers.

- Don't have business hours only to suit yourself. The customer will go elsewhere if you're not available.

- Don't screen customer service calls; take them all promptly and professionally.

- Don't underestimate the value of repeat orders—they're like gold!

- Don't underrate the lifetime value of a customer.

- Don't be too busy to talk to your customers.

- Don't let voicemail answer all your calls; be available during business hours.

- Don't allow front-line people to be rude or discourteous. If they're having a bad day, send them home.

- Don't let your phone ring more than four times before you answer it.

- Don't make prospects wait more than 24 hours for a price quote or an estimate.

- Don't close your office, store, or factory so you can go on vacation.

- Don't forget to reward regular customers—they deserve it.

- Don't make customers wait any longer than absolutely necessary to pay for their purchases.

- Don't substitute products on an order without first getting the customer's approval.

- Don't wait to solve a problem or make a refund—do it now!

- Don't think a regular customer won't leave you. They get offers from your competitors all the time.

- Don't forget to contact customers you have not heard from for awhile.

- Don't ignore customer suggestions; welcome them and use them if possible.

- Don't provide poor quality and charge for top quality.

- Don't neglect to answer email questions promptly.

- Don't promise a delivery time that's impossible to keep.

- Don't run out of a hot sales item and not give a rain check.

- Don't treat a customer like a subordinate; customers are really your bosses.

- Don't try to fool your customer, or the joke will be on you.

Can you add more don'ts of your own to this list? Some of these may sound a bit ridiculous, but they happen in businesses every day. Decide which don'ts are the most important for your business and let all your employees know what they are. Remind them that without satisfied and repeat customers, no one has a guaranteed job. By following most of these don'ts, you can have the best offense against your bigger competitors.

Look Down to See the Profits

After visiting a fast-food establishment for coffee and a breakfast sandwich, I left shaking my head and wondering who made the decisions there. I was second in line at the only open register and had to wait almost five minutes to get waited on (and there were about four more people behind me). The person taking the orders was a little confused, couldn't find a coffee lid, and had to repeat the order of the person ahead of me several times. More than 10 other people behind her were standing around and talking or handling the drive-through window. Why didn't someone else jump in and open another register? This was not the first time I'd had a similar experience at this store or others like it. I'm sure most of you have experienced similar situations, and it's very frustrating.

At large franchises such as this one, the corporate office makes the policies and major decisions, instead of the stores. Executives sit around trying to figure out their profits but forget where they really come from. They need to get their heads out of the clouds and look down to where the money is really being made. There are real people down here, not just numbers, and they're your customers. They're standing in line, waiting to give you money, so help them out! Spend less on advertising (we all know who you are) and more on supervision and training. It's time to rewrite the training manual and serve your customers better.

Alas, these large corporations won't listen to me, and that's good for all you small-business people. Take away their customers by giving them better service.

Big companies can't out-service your customers if you don't let them. The caring attitude you can provide just isn't there in a huge company.

This is where you can attack the national companies and fast-food franchises. You can and should pay attention to how your customers are treated. You need these customers to come back and purchase over and over again. Beat big companies at their own game and take away their customers. It's not very hard to do if you think about it. If your products are excellent, there should be no reason for customers not to line up at your door. But don't let the line move slowly, or they may leave.

Even if you have five or ten stores, you can still be in charge of your customer care. Visit your stores often; don't just assume that everyone is doing what you expect. Hire a mystery shopper to give you a firsthand account of what's really going on. If you own a restaurant or a fast-food place, give friends or relatives money for dinner and find out how they were treated. Then praise your employees or make any adjustments where needed. You can have all the sales and profits that the big guys are passing up.

Rally the Troops

When was the last time you had a general meeting with all your employees? You should do it regularly so everyone is on the same page in his or her job. Monthly meetings are the best for stores, offices, or manufacturing businesses. Always schedule for an off time and not when customers need to be served or attended to. There's little more annoying to a customer than calling and being told that everyone is in a meeting. A Saturday morning or a weekday morning before you're open for business is best for most small businesses. By having your meetings in the morning rather than in the evening, your employees can get fired up for the day and can implement many of the ideas you discuss right away.

Meetings should be mandatory events, and anyone missing two or three in a year should seriously consider moving on. This sets a bad example for everyone else.

Keep meetings to two hours or less and pay employees for this time. After two hours, your personnel—especially the non-office ones—will get bored and lose interest. Paying them for the time they spend in the meeting should easily come back to you in better customer service, repeat business, and more satisfied customers.

Always pay employees for their time when you have a meeting, and you will get not only better attendance, but also better results after the meeting.

Always make an agenda and plan to divide the time you have among things you want to discuss. Some topics to bring up during your meetings might be:

- New products and services
- Special sales or offers coming
- Suggestions from employees
- Suggestions from customers

- Contests and bonuses
- New customer service ideas
- Procedures (new and old)
- New policies or changes
- Problem and mishap corrections
- Customer complaints
- Grievances
- New-hire introductions
- Retirement goodbyes
- New babies, weddings, and so on
- Birthdays during the month
- Employee anniversaries with the company
- Employee rewards and awards
- Ask for new employee referrals
- Employee questions
- An in-house supplier presentation

If you have multiple stores, offices, or locations, bring everyone together at a central location. It doesn't have to be the main office, just a location that is easy for everyone to get to. If someone has to come more than 20 miles to the meeting, they should be given a small stipend for gas.

Always end the meeting on an upbeat note—something positive employees can take back to their job.

Reward Great Service

Some employees will naturally be great customer service providers, and others will need to work at it. It doesn't matter how great customer service happens, as long as it *does* happen. When you observe your employees over a period of time, giving your customers and prospects the friendly, helpful, and professional assistance you expect, then reward them.

Small, unexpected rewards can go a long way toward keeping your good employees satisfied with their jobs.

This doesn't necessarily mean that you need to give the employee an immediate or large raise, although it could. Little things add up and are appreciated, especially if they aren't expected. A few extra dollars in the tip jar, a longer lunch, a gift card, or a paid afternoon off shows that you are aware of the job the employee is doing and you recognize his or her efforts. There doesn't have to be a constant or weekly reward or bonus, but it should happen often enough to be fresh in employees' memories.

The smart thing to do is make everyone else in your business conscious of these little perks, which are available to everyone. When you give rewards, post it on the bulletin board or break-room wall. Let employees know that great customer service is not a one-day incident but an overall attitude. Keeping your employees happy, content, and motivated makes them better at their jobs and handling your customers. Better, satisfied, and compensated employees make fewer mistakes and need less supervision. So, you can give a little and get a lot in return.

Employee of the Month

If you have five or more employees, that's enough to start an employee-of-the-month program. This reinforces employee loyalty and results in improved customer service. In many cases it will also reduce turnover because there's always a goal to strive for. Employees know that if they do a good job and provide extra effort, they can receive a little more in their paycheck. And if they aren't selected one month, there's always next month, which is not very far away. Employees can get a paycheck anywhere, but are their efforts recognized in a special way?

It may not seem like much, but recognition for a job well done makes employees feel great. This can motivate other employees to step up their service as well.

The monthly decision can be made as a joint effort so everyone will be involved. The boss or supervisors can account for 50 percent of the vote, while co-worker votes can make up the other 50 percent. Or, you can figure out a way to let your customers vote. Voting can be anonymous so that friendships and popularity contests won't come into play as much.

If you have more than 50 employees, you might want to reward the first- and second-place winners so employees will know there's a decent chance to be rewarded.

Let your employees decide what rewards or prizes they want within a preset price limit. By allowing employees to decide, you know that the prize is something they really want and will work to win.

If you have room in your budget, consider a bigger prize once a year for the best of the best. You can make the selection from the 12 previous monthly winners and make a big deal about it. Take a picture and send a press release to your local and neighborhood newspapers. Most people love to see their picture in the paper as a winner of anything.

Your employee-of-the-month program will make working for your business more than just a job to most employees. It's now a place where employees are appreciated and rewarded for the extra effort that really helps a business grow. Employees should always think of their job as a place where their efforts are appreciated. Any money spent here should come back to you tenfold.

Don't Lock 'Em Out

If a customer wanted to enter your store and make a purchase, would you say no and lock your door? Well, it happens every day at franchises, big company stores, and small businesses. If your sign says you close at 9 p.m., and a customer is walking in to make a quick purchase, should you refuse him? If you make a habit of this, you're likely losing hundreds or thousands of dollars every year, plus revenue from all the irritated people who won't come back or send referrals. It's more like anti-customer service, and it definitely won't create goodwill.

The smart idea would be to let the customer know you're closing and ask whether you can help him find something. If you're a fast-food restaurant or a convenience store, how long can it take for one more purchase? It's foolish to refuse any sale just to save five minutes. The long-term loss is much greater than you think. You not only don't get paid for that sale, you won't get all the profits from repeat business if the customer doesn't return. Stay and serve your customers; make it part of your employee training so your employees will do it when you're not there, too.

Pay Attention

When you or your staff is serving retail customers, give them your complete attention until the transaction is finished. Don't talk to co-workers or friends, be on the phone, or show indifference to the customer. This should be part of any training program for new employees and reinforced regularly. You can hang a sign in the back room or employee areas to stress how important this is.

Customers get frustrated when they want to ask a question or discuss the transaction and they can't get the attention of the person who is supposed to be serving them. I've even had a young salesperson with headphones on bouncing up and down while the music was blasting into her ears. She couldn't hear anything I was asking. If an employee has to lift up an earphone to hear you, it feels as if you're bothering her. This sort of employee behavior should never be allowed in your store.

Another customer annoyance is when an employee is on the phone discussing something personal while people are waiting for service. You should have a policy of no personal calls (unless there's a real emergency), and cell phones should be off for anyone working in a customer service area.

Also, your employees' friends should not be allowed to come into the store and talk to your employees for more than two minutes during working time. And if friends are there to be customers, they should be waited on at the same speed as any other patron— the employee should promptly move to the next person when the transaction is finished.

If you don't have set policies in force, some employees (especially younger ones) may try to see how far they can test the limits, which weakens your customer service. So explain the rules and policies and observe your employees to verify that they are following them. Repeated violation of these customer-attention policies means that this employee is not right for your business and should be replaced.

Also, be sure to call or drop-in unexpectedly to see what's happening when you're not there. If you can't trust an employee, how can you keep him? You need people who believe in and follow your customer service procedures. It's the only way you can leave your business and know everything is being done correctly. Customers should receive the same excellent attention regardless of whether you are present.

Sam Walton said, "There is only one boss: the customer. And he can fire everybody in the company from the chairman on down, simply by spending his money somewhere else." Indeed.

One-Hundred Percent Satisfaction

The best, the ultimate, the front of the line… Can this be achieved by anyone, with any product or service, at any time? It's very hard to be 100 percent satisfied with anything, because you can almost always find some little thing you would change or improve. Think about it: Are you 100 percent satisfied with your car, your job, or even your marriage? Probably not, but if you're even close, and there's nothing better available or it's too much trouble to change, you grin and bear it.

According to John Woods, "The purpose of a business is to create a mutually beneficial relationship between itself and those that it serves. When it does that well, it will be around tomorrow to do it some more."

Every small business should strive to get as close to 100 percent satisfaction as possible. If your customers and clients are more than 90 percent satisfied, you'll likely keep most of them without much difficulty. It's easy for people to repurchase or reorder from their regular source, which can usually be done quickly. It's more trouble to change where you purchase, because there is always the unknown factor.

The only way to know how pleased customers are with your products or services is to ask them and listen to their comments. What you consider a minor issue may be very important to them—don't ignore it, or you'll create ill will. If another business comes along and solves that issue, and everything else in your two businesses is equal, you may lose that customer and others like him. And by the time you find out the customer is gone, it's too late to do much of anything about it, because by then he has become comfortable with his new source. You'd have to find another issue or problem to solve to get him back as a customer.

Putting in the effort into attain close to 100 percent satisfaction from existing customers is so much easier than trying to win them back later. Have brainstorming meetings with your employees to come up with ideas to get closer to 100 percent satisfaction. Consider everything from store layout to attractive displays, faster service response, the way you answer your phone, and so on. Little things can make a difference and get you closer to your goal. When you add all the little things together, they really add up.

Your goals in these brainstorming sessions can really be twofold:

- Find ways to get closer to 100 percent customer satisfaction.
- Find ways to provide the things your competitors are not doing so their customers will become yours.

With either goal, you come out ahead.

Transaction Time

How long do customers have to wait to pay you? Why do they have to wait? Do you have enough registers open for the number of customers currently in your store? Do you have enough customer service reps to handle people waiting on hold? Even one hang-up or walkout is probably a lost sale. You've spent valuable time and money to get customers into the store, so once they've made a decision, take their money! Don't make them stand in line like school kids—it gives them time to second-guess their purchases.

Technically, a person is not a customer until the transaction is over. Don't let potential customers get buyer's remorse while standing in line. If you're the owner or manager of the store, why not open a register yourself until the line lessens? These people came into your store to make a purchase, so let them pay—quickly and cheerfully, of course. If you don't, someone will get fed up and walk out. And then you've not only lost a purchase, you've also lost that person's repeat business and possibly referrals.

When you're standing in line, time seems to go more slowly. Make an effort to provide quick, pleasant checkout service. And on phone orders, don't leave people on hold too long—a manager should be able to pitch in as needed. Remember, you're not the electric company, where customers have to wait—your customers *do* have other choices for where they can spend their money.

If it's the holiday season or you're just overwhelmed with customers that you didn't expect, have some type of backup plan to process them quickly. Even hiring a call center for off hours can help during very busy times. You'll have happier customers who want to come back, and that always builds your business.

> People have more things to do than time to do them. Once customers make a decision on the product or service they need, they want to pay and get on with their lives. Don't make them wait any longer than necessary to pay.

The Good, the Bad, and the Real

Following are customer service situations that have actually happened to me or my family or friends. Some are positive, and some are negative—you be the judge.

- The sign on the building said One-Hour Cleaners, and I needed a pair of wrinkled slacks cleaned to wear to a dinner that evening. It was 1 p.m., and I asked whether I could pick up the pants at about 4 p.m. I was told not until tomorrow. I mentioned the one-hour sign and was told that it was only the store name, not how they do things. I went somewhere else and got the pants cleaned in time for dinner.

- I bought a pair of slacks at Nordstrom that had to be altered and went to pick them up about five days later. When I tried them on, they were a little long, but I couldn't wait there until they were fixed. My salesperson said they would deliver the pants to my office soon, so I gave them my business card and left. I expected them in three or four hours, but they arrived in 45 minutes, much to my surprise.

- I took my car to a well-known auto-service place for an oil change and a tire rotation. I was told it would take 30 minutes, and I went to the waiting room. After about 40 minutes, I inquired as to the status and was told it would be another 20 minutes (or one hour total). I told them they had said 30 minutes, and the man replied, "I meant 30 minutes after we finished our lunch."

- I went to a family restaurant, ordered a sandwich, and asked whether I could have chips or coleslaw instead of potato salad. The waitress said there were no substitutions allowed. When the meal came, it had fruit on the side; they had run out of potato salad and had to substitute.

- When we owned an ice cream store, we ran out of vanilla on a hot Sunday afternoon. Because vanilla was our biggest seller, it put us in a real bind. All the suppliers were closed, so we called our local rep on his cell phone. He went to the storage freezer and brought us some vanilla within an hour.

- A new employee at our ice cream store was serving an older couple. The man asked for one dip of rocky road. The server said she didn't know what a "dip" was and unless he said "scoop," she would not give it to him. I jumped in and took over. Needless to say, she didn't last long.

- I thought the cleaners closed at 6 p.m. on Saturday, but it was really 5 p.m. I needed a suit back to wear to a musical that evening, so I called at about 5 p.m. to make sure the suit was ready. The employee said the store was closing—but they were nice enough to wait 20 minutes until I arrived. They have gotten a lot more business from me since then.

- A major gas station had a sign that said it closed at 11 p.m.
  I got there at about 10:45 p.m., and the pumps were turned off
  or not working. I went inside, and the teenager on duty said he
  was closing early. He had to meet some friends at 11 p.m., and
  he told me to come back the next morning. I just found out that
  they closed down recently. I wonder why….

- A fast-food walk-in restaurant that gets very busy at lunchtime
  came up with a smart idea. Everyone is in a hurry at lunchtime,
  so they have a person with a clipboard taking orders from
  people standing in line. When you get to the register, you hand
  the order sheet to the cashier, and everything moves more
  quickly. Why doesn't everyone do that?

- Several years ago, I bought a new Mustang. Before I drove
  away, I asked whether the dealer had checked everything. Later
  that evening, I noticed that one headlight was out, and I was
  irritated. I called the salesman the next day, and he told me,
  "I don't make the cars; I just sell them." I never bought another
  car from them.

- At a fast-food hamburger franchise, I had to wait in line for an
  unusually long time because of a couple of big orders ahead
  of me and a reduced staff at the establishment. I was getting a
  little impatient after five minutes, and so were the people
  behind me. The alert owner or manager noticed this and
  offered all of us a free upgrade to a meal at the price of a single
  hamburger. He also jumped in and helped fill the orders.

- I purchased a new second home about 900 miles from my
  native Chicago. Six weeks before closing, I went to a store that
  sold a variety of home products; I thought I would get good
  prices and service if I purchased most things there. I ordered
  carpet upgrades, special tile for the bathroom floors, a big-
  screen TV, and all the window coverings. The saleswoman who
  helped me pick out the window coverings assured me that it
  would only take three to four weeks for a custom order, and we
  had six weeks. I wanted to set an exact date and fly out to be
  there for the installation, and she told me that would be no
  problem—that they would hold everything at the store. I gave
  a 50 percent deposit (several thousand dollars) and was assured
  that everything was set because I had ordered well in advance.
  I checked in a couple of times over the next few weeks and was
  told everything was on schedule. So I bought my plane ticket
  and arrived at my new house a week after closing for my 10 a.m.
  appointment with the installers. When no one had arrived by

10:30 a.m., I called the store and was told my salesperson was off sick. After 10 minutes, I found out that I wasn't even scheduled for installation that day because she had forgotten to order two items. I had to fly back the next week and was never able to reach the salesperson again. I eventually talked to the owner and was given a few extras, but not enough to make up for two plane fares.

- My regular barber knows that I hate to wait and I'm always in a hurry. She normally opens her shop at 10 a.m., but she comes in at 9:15 whenever I need a haircut, so no one is ahead of me. I've been going there for every haircut for the past three years, and I plan to continue doing so indefinitely.

- I slipped on the ice while getting into my car. I banged my head on the edge of the window and cut myself just above my eye. The cut wouldn't stop bleeding, so after a half hour, I went to the local walk-in medical office. They fixed everything and sent me on my way. The next day I received a call from the physician's assistant, asking me how I was and whether I had any questions. I was pleasantly surprised because I've never received a call like this from a medical office before.

- We needed 300 copies on blue paper made quickly, so we went to a well-known copy store. We asked for 100 folded and 200 flat, and the person wrote that on the order form. When we picked up the copies an hour later, they were all folded. When we complained, the employee said that just because it was on the order form, that didn't mean the person who ran the copies would read it.

- I recently had little time for lunch on a busy day, so I stopped at a well-known national coffeehouse for a gourmet brew and a low-sugar scone to eat. The scones were on display near the cash register; however, I was told that they stop selling breakfast items at 11 a.m., so they couldn't sell me one.

- During a visit to a large national office-supply store some years back, I was trying to find a ribbon for our typewriter. I hadn't purchased this item before, so I wasn't sure where to find it, and I asked someone stocking a shelf in the copy-paper section. The employee said he didn't work in that section but would call someone. The loudspeaker announced my situation, and I was told to stand in the center aisle and wait. After a couple minutes—which seems like a long time when you're just standing there—I decided I would just go back to my office, order it from the catalog, and wait the extra day. As I was leaving, I noticed about five people in line to check out and only one cashier. There were about 20 people working or talking in that store but only one checkout open. I guess they had already made enough money that day.

Action Plan

✓ Show empathy for customers.

✓ Have convenient business hours.

✓ Train and retrain front-line employees.

✓ Don't make customers wait to pay you.

✓ Be available for customer comments and complaints.

"When you're serving a customer, you're also serving your business."

—BT

Chapter 17

Financial Crisis

- Financial Crisis Planning
- Know What You Need
- Unemployment Numbers and You
- Banks and Small Business
- Hold Your Prices
- Defer Debt
- Reduce Fixed Expenses
- Sell Off Anything
- Keep Marketing
- Network, Network, Network
- Contingency Plans

Every six to nine years, the world economy experiences a slow-down or a flat growth period. Some of these adjustment times last longer than others, and some are more severe than others. Most, though, are mild and let businesses and the stock market adapt to changing times. These are not new happenings; the cycle has been going on for as long as business records have been kept—and maybe longer. It's just a normal part of being in business, and nothing about it should create any extreme fear. You need to deal with these slowdowns when they occur and put business as usual on the back burner.

Not every economic slowdown is called a recession, but they should be treated as if one could be on the horizon. If the economy falls into a strong recession as it did in the early 1980s and circa 2008, you must be ready to cope with it if you want to have an ongoing business. Things can happen quickly, and news reporters always add fuel to the fire and make it sound worse than it really is. As a result, the public believes the news and cuts way back on spending, which makes the situation worsen. Then the snowball effect sets in, and the slowdown is seen everywhere. In more severe recessions, there can be an overall negative growth period that lasts from six months to as long as two years. Many jobs and businesses will be lost during this cycle.

I'm not an economist, but I've been through five or six of these economic slowdowns in my business career. I can tell you firsthand that none of them has been fun, and a couple presented serious challenges. What you have to realize is that these slowdowns are going to happen, and they will affect how you do your business. If you don't adjust and pay attention to what's going on in the economy and in your business, you could end up in a financial crisis. How do I know this? Because it happened to me early in my small-business career. I learned many lessons that I never forgot and will never ignore during any slowdown.

This chapter is about things you can and should do if you are in (or even close to) a financial crisis. The more you know in advance, the better your business will be able to survive and sometimes even grow during these turbulent times.

Financial Crisis Planning

Of course, if you plan ahead for any possible financial crisis, you will be in much better shape if it happens to you. But how many of us really take the time to have a plan or two waiting and the reserve capital to back it up? If your business is doing great now, it's human nature to think it may always be like that. So you over-spend, over-hire, and over-expand as if the cash flow will never end. Then, without any warning, sales and orders start to slow down. You may even ignore it in the beginning. You let down your guard and operate as if you have blinders on. But as your slow-down gets worse, you scramble to repair the damage and make adjustments that you hope are not too late.

This reminds me of a poker game I played in years ago. I was having a good night and winning a lot of hands. I took risks that I normally would not take, but most of them paid off. It was near midnight, when I was planning to leave, but the cards were coming great, and the other players were easy to read. I had a sales appointment the next morning at 9 a.m....but what could another hour hurt? After all, I was winning! So I stayed until 1 a.m., then 2 a.m., and then finally left at about 3:30 a.m., when I was well into a losing streak. I finally got to bed after 4 a.m. and caught a few hours of sleep, which was not enough to make me well rested for my appointment later in the morning. As a result, I was half-awake and late for the meeting, I forgot to bring some of the product literature, and I hesitated in answering some of the prospect's questions. We didn't get the order, and I had no one to blame but myself; I wasn't prepared and didn't treat the appoint-ment as a priority. I thought we would get the business anyway, but we didn't. I vowed to never let that happen again.

Many businesses don't plan for an economic crisis or a severe business slowdown and are shocked when it happens. The question is not whether it will happen, but when—will you have a basic plan to get through it and save your business?

Planning for a possible financial crisis will put you in a better place to handle one if it ever happens in your business or in life in general. I don't know anyone who has lived a long life who can say he never had a crisis or two along the way. These things can and will happen; don't overlook or dismiss the signs and think the problem will go away. You wouldn't do that with serious illness, so why do it for your business? A little preparation and the courage to use it when necessary can keep your business stable or even save it in some cases. Make a file called Financial Crisis and keep adding to it as you come up with new ideas. When you need them, these ideas and framework for survival and a quick recovery will be there waiting for you to use them.

Know What You Need

The main point you need to address in any financial recovery plan is the minimum amount of cash flow you will need to sustain your business during slow periods. Sit down in a quiet place where you can concentrate and list all of your fixed expenses first and then your variable expenses. Add about 15 to 20 percent for miscellaneous things that could come up, because they always do. Add up everything to see what your monthly total is. If you don't have enough money coming in to cover the amount, turn the list face down and list your expenses again—but this time try to list even lower amounts for each item. This may sound a little low-tech, but it often helps to see the numbers on paper in front of you. Do this every week or so to see whether anything has changed or can be adjusted.

It never hurts to ask whether fixed expenses can be adjusted in any way during tough economic times.

When you know what you will need to keep your business going, you can use that information to plan how to get the cash flow you need. Most fixed expenses are not negotiable—or are they? Many times I have contacted our office landlord and asked to pay 20 or 30 percent lower rent during tough times and add it to the end of the lease. Or you might offer to extend your lease by a year if the landlord gives you a month free now. If you've been paying on time for several years, there's a good chance the landlord will work with you.

If you have a vehicle loan or a credit line to pay, you can sometimes miss one payment a year with no penalty—just call and ask. The interest accrues, but this respite may provide the short-term relief you need. Many credit card companies will also work with you on lower monthly payments and may reduce the interest rate for six months to a year—ask them. No one wants to put you out of business; they just want to be paid, so tell them how you can do it. Make the first move—don't wait until they call you about a past-due account.

Unemployment Numbers and You

News reporters like to tell us that unemployment is rising and consumer spending will suffer from it. But even if there's 10 percent unemployment, it means 90 percent of eligible workers are employed and spending money. They may be more cautious and want more value for each dollar, though, so find a way to offer that, and they will do business with you. Make people feel that your products or services are worth what they're paying for them and add extras services or perks at no cost to the customer.

Even the 10 percent who are not working are spending money for essentials. They are living off furlough pay, savings, or government money to get them through the unemployed period. They just have to be more selective in their purchases.

Another opportunity that is available to you during periods of high unemployment is hiring good people who are not working because of layoffs or closed companies. This is an unfortunate situation for the unemployed, but it's there, so take advantage of it if you can. These potential employees might not be available to your small business during normal times (you may not have the budget to hire these people under normal circumstances), but they are now. Interview in depth to see who has ideas and experience that can help your company right away. They may love the new challenge and be willing to accept a lower salary and/or lesser benefits than they were getting at their previous job. Even if they only stay a year or so, you can learn from them, and what you learn is yours forever.

> If people are unemployed or worried about being unemployed, they will spend their money more prudently. The smart businessperson will show customers a better value, better service, or that little extra that will comfort customers when spending on purchases.

Economic slowdown is also a time to look seriously at any employees currently on your staff who are not performing up to the level you expect from them. If you've had meetings and talks with them in the past, and you aren't seeing any results, maybe it's time to replace them. Some people value their job more than others do, and in tough financial times you want to retain the employees who *do* value their employment. Don't threaten the lesser employees, because that's only a temporary solution—just let them go. There are probably many people in the job market who will eagerly strive to meet your expectations. If handled correctly, this situation can benefit your business and may even open new doors for the person you let go. Some people are in the wrong job and need that nudge to move on. Explain your current situation to them, but be firm.

Banks and Small Business

During economic slowdowns and recessions, banks (especially the larger ones) first tighten credit for small businesses. They seem to forget that small businesses generate more than half of the gross domestic product (GDP) and create more than half of all new jobs. Banks don't always understand how a small business works; they just look at numbers on financial reports to make their decisions. So they shy away from what they don't understand and concentrate on big business, which could actually cost them more in losses.

Some small businesses with great credit status have a difficult time getting financing, and that's a shame. And when credit *is* available, most big banks charge increased costs and higher interest rates. So small companies must cut back on hiring, expansion, and growth, which also fuels the slowdown. Sound like a vicious circle? It is, and the people who see it usually aren't in a position to change it.

Building a relationship with a bank begins long before an economic downturn or recession arises. When the financial markets get tight, your bank may stand by you and provide the capital you need if you have a solid, longstanding relationship with them.

Banks are in the business of lending money and collecting interest from creditworthy customers. But they often forget who their real customers are and that they would struggle without them. Some banks make small-business owners feel apprehensive or inferior when they ask for financing, instead of welcoming them with open arms. Banks put up an invisible fence around themselves and try to protect money that's not even technically theirs. They fail to realize that if no one is borrowing money and paying interest, their business is in danger, too. The banking profession is a noble one, but hey guys—help us out down here!

When you use a bank for your checking account and debit or credit cards, you should keep track of what's going on daily. Almost every bank has online banking available, and it's wise to check your accounts every morning before you start work. This will help you ensure that previous deposits have been recorded and tell you what checks have cleared. It gives you information on how quickly suppliers are receiving and depositing your payments. When you're in the middle of financial problems, every penny counts every day. Online banking will also let you transfer money between accounts if you have more than one. And you can pay your credit card bills online and wait until the last day before a late charge is added.

Local banks that are not part of large conglomerates provide some hope for small businesses. They understand small business better and often personally know the business owners. Although financial reports are important, small banks can look between the lines and see what's really going on with a business and its short-term and long-term potential. They can even visit the business premises (which I think every bank should do) and watch the company in action. They can talk to the employees and even some of the target customers to assess future growth. Is the business they are lending to on the cutting edge of ideas and technology or just trying to pay last month's bills?

Small local banks can and should take this lucrative market away from bigger banks, and some have been doing it. When loan amounts get larger than a small bank can handle, they will partner with other local or regional banks to spread and share any risk. Get to know your local bankers and invite them to a coffee shop where you can talk on neutral ground about your needs now and in the future. A relationship needs time to develop, and you want to be connected if an unexpected crisis hits your business.

Hold Your Prices

During any financial crisis, you may have a tendency to try to cut your prices to the bone. This could have a very short-term effect on cash flow, but it may hurt you in the future. When you reduce prices so much that people feel you're desperate, the purchasers who buy your products or services will never look at you the same again. They will expect you to either go out of business or just hang on by a thread. They will worry about after-sale assistance and returns, and they may not purchase gift cards. This strategy could cause them to shy away from any products that need future service or replacement parts because they're afraid you won't be there to help them. They might never even consider your regular price again and always expect or wait for the deep discount. And they might be hit-and-run customers who have no loyalty to your company and will go elsewhere to spend the rest of their money.

When your competitors drastically reduce prices to increase cash flow, don't get caught in the fever. The lower prices sacrifice profits, which you need to pay expenses and employees.

It's okay to have some special sales and reduced prices as part of your marketing strategy, but always have a deadline when the sale will end. Or use the powerful phrase "While Supplies Last" so customers know that when the product is gone, the sale is over. Keep sales brief and customers guessing when the next one (if any) will be held. Then they will buy at your regular price, which has more profit in it.

Large companies have what they call *loss leaders*, which are commodity products sold at or below their actual cost, but a small business shouldn't do this unless they plan to discontinue the item. You need some profit to pay your expenses, and you can't always make it up on other items. The old idea of making it up on volume won't work very well for smaller businesses, either. Transportation, storage, and sales costs will eat up any profits you make. If you're in any type of financial crisis, you must have some profit in your cash flow to pay urgent bills.

Never get into a discount war with any business, large or small. There are no winners in a discount war, and any publicity you get will take time to turn into future profits. If you're up against a big-box store, they won't let you win, and they can even take losses on the products. Your business will be seen as a loser in customers' minds. If you don't participate and you sell the same item at your regular price, you'll still get some business from loyal customers. But if you try to deep-discount and risk losses, you'll have to sell 20 times as much to achieve the same total profit—and you still won't beat out the big-box store.

You might consider adding a special free service rather than trying to deep-discount to fight a low-price competitor. Free delivery, free assembly, gift-wrapping, or 800 hotline availability can go a long way for some buyers. Create the feeling that your regular price has a higher value tied to it, and some buyers will see it.

Defer Debt

If you can't make your payments on time, there are ways to defer some of them to keep your business operating. As I mentioned earlier in this chapter, you can request to skip a payment or add it to the end of the payment terms. This may be possible for bank loans, vehicle loans, credit lines, or equipment loans. Call your bank, credit union, or finance company and explain that you're having cash-flow problems and would like to skip a payment now and make it up later or add it to the end of the contract. I wouldn't use the term "financial crisis," though, because it may alarm them and cause other problems. Act and speak in a professional, optimistic manner, and they should be able to offer you some option for relief now. If you're at least halfway through any loans or payment terms, you may be able to refinance for a longer term, reduce the interest rate, and have smaller payments.

With business credit cards, I have found that they will offer a repayment plan at lower interest if you get behind two or more monthly payments. However, it's a shame that you have to wait that long and they won't help you when you're current. Always ask credit card companies for three things:

- Lower interest on balances
- Lower monthly payment amounts
- Refunds for recent late and over-limit charges

Ask for all three of these things. The company may refuse your request, but you are no worse off than before you asked, and they may agree to one, two, or even all three. Credit card companies don't really know you, and they are unsecured creditors, so telling them you won't be able to continue paying on time is a bad thing. Instead, say that you intend to pay everything owed on time if they will give you some help with your three requests. After you get their help, try your best to keep up with payments, because they probably won't help you a second time.

This is also a good time to limit the number of credit cards that you have as open accounts. Request that all but two of the accounts be closed so you're not tempted to start using the cards again.

Reduce Fixed Expenses

Fixed expenses are supposed to be set and not negotiable, but anything is negotiable if you persist and explain the situation. Our office landlord let us pay 50 to 70 percent of our normal rent during a serious slowdown in our sales for about four months. For five years, we had always paid on time, so the landlord didn't want us to move because of a short-term problem. When we were able to pay the full rent again, we added a little extra each month, which was applied to the previous shortfall balance. In another instance, about two-thirds into our lease, we renegotiated a new longer lease and asked for two or three free months at the beginning of the new lease.

Basic utilities are usually impossible to negotiate with, and that's what I found with the electric and gas companies. But our phone-company rep actually knew a little about our company, and because we had a couple of other options for phone service, he was willing to help us. We had about eight lines, including phone, Internet, fax, and merchant services. Because we were getting more emails and fewer phone calls than before, we wanted to

You can negotiate any expense during tough times if you approach it correctly. Many business owners are afraid to even ask, but a negative answer is no worse than what you started with.

cancel one of our regular lines to save money. It was under contract, but the rep waived the cancellation fee, and we had the line disconnected. Then, about a month later, he called and said he could reduce our basic monthly charges by 50 percent for the following three months. That saved us about $130 a month, which was much appreciated. I never thought the phone company would consider helping us, but it's proof that all you have to do is ask. The worst that can happen is you'll get a no, and that's where you started anyway, so what's the harm?

Many business owners think that payroll is a fixed expense, but there is room to adjust. Although you can't change the tax part, you can change the total payroll amount. During a severe financial crisis, you can ask your employees to accept a temporary base-pay adjustment and/or reduced working hours. Explain that you are offering this before you have to make cuts and layoffs. You may find that some people welcome fewer hours and if they can still keep their jobs. Others will grin and bear it as long as it's not a long-term situation.

If your employees refuse to concede anything, you have no choice but to make layoffs where you feel necessary. Unfortunately, the business's overall survival is more important than the bad feeling you get from making layoffs. This is the tough part of owning a business, but sometimes it must be done. And for sales surges during your slowdown, you can use temporary personnel to fill the gaps.

Another way to cut payroll expense is to find areas that you can outsource. This will allow you to reduce salary, benefits, and employer taxes. Just be sure that the company to which you are giving the work will perform up to your standards. Before you outsource, check a few references from some of their current clients to make sure that they are satisfied and the work is done on time. After you've turned work over to the company, it will be difficult and time consuming to change again.

If the company to which you outsource can't do 100 percent of the work, give the rest to a current employee to handle in-house. You might even consider a current employee who can do work at home on off hours with the help of his or her family.

Sell Off Anything

If you're in or close to a financial crisis in your business, you obviously need money to keep operating. So what products or equipment can you sell quickly at fire-sale prices? You must have a tight inventory and get rid of any obsolete or soon-to-be obsolete items in a short time. Keep inventory at a bare minimum and use just-in-time ordering. Schedule your product delivery so it arrives when you are just about to be sold out. That way, you won't have an open invoice to pay for products you don't need right now. If a customer gives you a big order, see whether it can be shipped directly to him from your supplier so you don't have to handle it at all—just bill it and collect the money.

If you're going to be doing any new outsourcing, will there be any equipment or even office furniture that you won't be using anymore? Why not turn it into cash to help your current situation? List unneeded items at a fair price on eBay or Craigslist and move them out quickly. Many businesses will buy used furniture and equipment if it's in reasonable shape and the price is right. Don't keep looking at things in your business that you won't use again—turn them into much-needed cash. Vanity about an office full of furniture is not a concern right now. Make a list of all items of value in your business and then decide what you can do without. Artwork and collectables should be at the top of the sell list.

> Don't keep furniture or accessories that you won't use. Sell them to bring in much-needed cash.

If you have delivery trucks or vehicles, decide whether it's less expensive to outsource that service. If you can find a company to deliver your products and treat your customers like you and your staff do, you can sell your delivery vehicles. If you do this, for the first few weeks after the outsourcing, call many of your customers and ask about timely deliveries and how efficiently they were handled. If there are more than a couple of complaints, change companies immediately. If you have to sign a contract to get a low delivery rate, make sure there's a clause in it that says the contract can be voided because of customer complaints—and then don't hesitate to do it. They are supposed to be servicing your customers, and they must do it according to the requirements that you set up. Don't accept any exceptions or excuses; find another service quickly.

Keep Marketing

When things look their worst, rely on marketing to bring the business back to life. Smart marketing brings in new business, retains old business, and increases your cash flow.

One thing you should do during any financial crisis is keep marketing to get new business and customers—especially if sales are slow and you feel that you are losing market share. If your current customer base is not producing the sales and profits you need to survive and grow, you must broaden your scope to draw in more.

This is easy to say, but how do you actually do it? Start by testing new markets that may be able to use your products and services. Be willing to make adjustments to what you are currently selling to appeal to those markets. Look for new products and services that will complement your current ones, attract new sub-markets, and interest your present customer base. New products are out there; you just need to find them. Do Internet searches and attend industry tradeshows where new ideas are often introduced. Don't stand like a deer in headlights and wait for creditors to run over you—go on the offensive and bust out of your financial crisis.

I have a speech called "Five Cheap Marketing Ideas" that includes ideas you can use in any economy—but even more so in a financial crisis. These consume few or none of your marketing dollars, which you have a shortage of anyway. Here's a brief description of the five ideas, which you may be able to use now.

- **Use cross-promotion.** Partner with one or more non-competitive businesses that are marketing to the same target customers. Refer buyers to each other using word of mouth, discounts, and incentives.

- **Create positive publicity.** Make your business and yourself known in your target market. Be an expert, tell the media, and create word-of-mouth publicity.

- **Treat customers like dogs.** Many of us treat our pets better than we do other people—they are pampered and loved members of our family. Treat your customers as well as you treat your beloved pet to make repeat customers so loyal that they don't even consider your competitors' sales.

- **Use direct mail.** Direct mail can help you reach your best prospects at a reasonable cost. Always test new lists before you use them and make a good purchase offer with a deadline in your direct-mail piece.

■ **Find a better way.** If you have been coasting on past sales and growth, you may have ignored new ideas and changes. Add new value to your products and services before competitors take away your customers.

Another way to keep marketing and create cash flow now is to pre-sell products and services with a discount or a reduced price. For example, you might offer $45 haircuts for $35 each if customers prepay for 10 haircuts. You can even make the haircuts transferable to other people, because those people may be new customers. Or you could use a loyalty card that offers something free if the customer reaches X number of points in a certain time period. The loyalty card can be high-tech, with a magnetic stripe or barcode, or it can be as simple as a plastic punch card. Regardless of how you do it, people will tend to remember your business and keep coming back—and refer other prospects.

During any tough financial period, it's important to keep sales coming in, and continual marketing will do that. Buy business cards by the thousands for you and all your staff. Give them out freely and leave them in any stores and offices that will allow you to. People will pick them up and save them for purchases now and in the future.

Write a one-, two-, or four-page newsletter with articles of interest to your target customers. Leave them in banks, cleaners, restaurants, or wherever you're allowed. This will also make prospects feel that you are an expert in that industry, and they'll contact you with questions. Your should always be thinking, "How can I promote my business when finances are low?" The ideas will come, but it's up to you to use them and create results.

Network, Network, Network

Many years ago, when I was starting out in business, I thought networking was just a waste of time. Boy, did I find out otherwise—and I probably lost a number of potential customers before I woke up. Networking, which is similar to word-of-mouth publicity, is a powerful marketing tool. It's also marketing that you can do in a financial crisis, because the cost is minimal or free. You'll meet many business professionals at Chamber of Commerce meetings, Toastmasters clubs, and events for the BBB or other organizations, and it's usually free to attend the first couple meetings.

Networking is free or inexpensive, so don't overlook it as a marketing tool, especially in times of financial crisis.

People go to these events to network and exchange new and old ideas about their business. Always dress and act professionally when attending and limit alcoholic drinks to one or none. When you're there, you *are* your business.

People you meet won't know you're having financial problems unless you tell them. And if you do tell them or they have heard it elsewhere, explain that you're looking for ideas to turn your business around. Most people will respect your tenacity and really try to help. Listen carefully, because that's why you're there. Make short notes on the backs of business cards from new people you meet. Ask questions and then keep quiet and learn from their responses.

When you find organizations that you feel are beneficial to you and your business, take the next step. Join and participate in their meetings and activities. Run for an officer position or volunteer at a fundraising function. You will also realize that there are things you know or have experienced in business from which other members and guests could profit.

Meeting people who can directly or indirectly benefit your business is essential to any financial recovery. Get involved with organizations in your industry and use social media to connect regularly and exchange information.

The best way to share those ideas and look like an expert is to offer to speak at one of the meetings. Usually, each meeting will have about 20 to 25 minutes for informative speakers. Get on the schedule for a future month and start writing an outline of your main points. Never read a speech word for word, but use your outline to remind you of the main points you want to cover. Practice your speech two or three times before the meeting and be sure it fits in the allotted time.

When you're not offering to speak to peers and other interested people, why not write about your knowledge? It costs you nothing but your time, and it could make your name known in your industry. Offer your articles for free to trade publications in your field and let them know you are available for any paid assignments. Find related trade magazines, newspapers, websites, and newsletters in directories in your local library's reference department. Always save copies of your published articles and show them to prospective customers and clients. You can even show them to banks when you are applying for credit lines or loans. They also come in handy when you're looking for a publisher for a book you've written. It might be the little extra edge that gets you new business or the finances you need. Customers and clients trust people who they feel are experts, and published articles help create that trust.

You can network anywhere and everywhere, 24/7/365, so be ready and available. I've met possible customers in line at a supermarket, at a play, at a sporting event, or while waiting to make a deposit at our bank. Just smile, make a general comment about something current, and see whether they want to have a short conversation. Your smile usually will put people at ease for the few minutes you have available. Always offer a business card and ask for theirs if it's relevant. You may be surprised by what can happen from this short encounter. You may find your next new customer who is looking for a new place to buy from. And by the way, did I mention that all this networking is *free*, which is exactly what you need if you're trying to survive a financial crisis?

Contingency Plans

We have all heard the saying, "Things will get worse before they get better," and sometimes it's true. But don't think that because you're going through tough times in your business, it can only get better. I can tell you from experience that there is always another problem lurking around the corner. This doesn't mean you should be ready to give up, but it does mean you need to be prepared. I've had two or three major things go wrong during a short time period, and I've dealt with each one separately. But if you have some type of contingency plan already in place, you can more easily weather the storm.

A general wouldn't go into a battle without a backup plan in case something went wrong. The same is true for your business—be ready for anything.

Take the time now to jot down a few notes in case any of the following situations arise. File them away and add to them whenever you can. If one of these situations arises, you'll be glad you had ideas ready.

- Your business building burns down
- A key employee leaves or dies
- Sales drop 50 percent or more
- All of your computers crash
- A main supplier goes out of business without notice
- A big competitor cut prices by 50 percent
- You get sick and cannot work
- All your employees walk out
- You have a family emergency and have to be away from work for a month

- The bank calls your loan or cancels your credit line
- New technology destroys your market
- Suppliers force you into bankruptcy

The list of possible crises could go on and on, and it doesn't matter whether there is a recession, a financial crisis, or anything else happening—any of these things could happen. But having a few plans ready and waiting can take some of the sting out of it and make recovery quicker. When a tragedy or disaster strikes, your mind is not always clear and able to come up with solutions. Even rough notes or an outline will give you a head start in the right direction.

When a financial crisis hits your business, use all the mental and physical tools you have to get through it. When creditors see your dedication to solving your problems, most will stand by you. And if another crisis happens in the future, you'll be well equipped and ready for it.

Action Plan

✓ Plan ahead for what could happen.

✓ Know what you will need to stay in business.

✓ Renegotiate any debt possible.

✓ Find and use inexpensive marketing.

"The biggest enemy of failure is success."

—BT

Chapter 18

In the End

- Know Your Competitors
- Cultivate Your Ideas
- Risk Taking
- Small Business Networking
- Cornucopia of Information
- Buy Your Umbrella When the Sun Is Shining
- Why Businesses Fail
- Strength in Numbers
- A Final Thought

We all want to be a success and achieve wealth, fame, and self-esteem. Some of us are willing to work harder and longer than others, but that shouldn't always determine the outcome. It's your drive, desire, and perseverance that will help you win in the long run. Success rarely comes on its own; you must pursue it relentlessly. Don't be satisfied with the status quo; keep searching for a better way, because you know it's out there.

As soon as you get ahead of the pack and slow down, the pack will be gaining on you. It's hard to get to the top, but it's even harder to stay there. Once things start going downhill, they go faster and faster, like a big snowball, if you don't stop it. Don't ignore your competitors and adversaries; they all want to be a success too.

Know Your Competitors

Whether you're a mature, growing, or new business, you will have competitors. Other businesses out there want to outsell you and take your customers. The secret to survival and growth is to know as much or more about them as they know about you. And don't think that because you haven't heard anything from them lately, they're not keeping an eye on you—they are. Competitors know what you're doing all the time and are trying to come up with their own ideas to counter yours.

Don't ignore competitors; instead, learn as much about them as you can. The person who believes he has no competitors will be caught off guard and will surely fall.

If you're a retail business, you should be aware of every other business within a two- to three-mile radius of your store, regardless of whether they are competitors. Every time you see a building going up or a building permit on a window, stop and see who's moving in. If you sell to other businesses, know your five biggest rivals in the market you serve—local, state, national, or international. Check the Internet often to see who is new in your industry or target market. Be sure to subscribe to all the trade magazines in your industry—many of them will be free. And a local business journal may list new businesses, as will your state's Secretary of State website. Don't be too busy to know who your competitors are and what they're doing.

By knowing the answers to the following questions, you just might keep a step or two ahead of your competition:

- **Exactly who are your competitors?** In retail, you can simply check the phonebook and drive around your main selling area. If you're in business-to-business sales, you can search your industry on the web or check directories at the library. The reference department will have books like the *Million Dollar Directory* and Dun & Bradstreet directories. Another idea is to search ReferenceUSA by SIC code and the state or area you serve.

- **Are your competitors big companies, franchises, or small businesses?** If your competitors are big public companies, you can easily find financial information from any of the stock-service companies. If they're franchises, you can check the franchiser's website and find out information such as how long they've been in business, what their franchise fees and royalty fees are, and so on. If they're small businesses, finding financial or other information will be more difficult, but in some cases your banker may be able to help.

- **What are your competitors' strong points?** What do your competitors stress or emphasize in their promotions, advertisements, or yellow-pages listings? What are people saying about them, and why would anyone buy their products or services? Which of their products or services might be better than yours? Can you do it better or at least the same—and are you trying?

- **Do your competitors have niche products?** What are your competitors offering to customers and prospects that is unique in your industry? How are they promoting these products or services—or are they? Are they always offering something new or relying on the same old line? Are any of these niche products patented, or can you quickly develop and offer a similar product? Do you have any niche products that they can't match?

- **Are the owners active in the business?** If the owner is an absentee, it will take him longer to find out about any changes you make. In a retail business, you'll want to find out whether the owners actually work regularly in the business or just visit occasionally. When you have sales or promotions or you offer new products, an onsite owner can respond more quickly. Use this to your advantage whenever possible.

- **What is their pricing strategy?** How do your competitors price their products or services—expensive, rock bottom, or middle-priced? Are they looking for the low-price customer or giving the impression of the high-priced luxury? Maybe they're in the middle and able to go up or down based on market demands. How does their pricing compare to yours? Who adds more value and service?

- **Are your competitors opening new locations/offices?** Is your competition expanding? How will this help or hurt them and you in the marketplace? Do you need to expand or add locations to keep up? You may be able to find out about their expansion plans if you know any commercial realtors or brokers. You can also check city public records for any new building permits.

- **How many employees do your competitors have?** You may be able to find this out by visiting their store or office and asking people who work there or their customers. Are they hiring, laying off, or downsizing by attrition? Do they have more or fewer employees than you for a comparable amount of business?

- **How do your competitors pay their employees?** Are they paying above, below, or about average for your industry? Have you talked to any of their employees—are they satisfied with their wages? Usually the quality of work performed will be in proportion to the level of pay they receive. Are your competitors providing any benefits to their employees?

- **How are customers treated?** One way to find out is to be a customer or hire a friend to browse their store or call their business. Are they courteous, helpful, and informative? Are you left standing at the checkout or on hold for a long time? Do they cheerfully accept exchanges and refunds? Do they explain product benefits and features? Is buying from them a pleasant experience?

- **What are your competitors' weaknesses?** Your competitors will have some areas you can attack by doing them better. Do they offer poor quality, rude service, a small selection, or late delivery? Are they always out of stock on popular or sale items? Do their store or delivery vehicles need a good cleaning? Are they understaffed, which makes their service slow? What can you offer that will lure away their customers and keep yours from buying from them?

- **Where are your competitors?** Are they near or far from you? If they're a retail store, are they easily accessible? Does it matter where they are as long as you both have toll-free numbers and/or websites? Are your competitors near your customer base?

- **How do your competitors market?** Do your competitors use a lot of print advertising in newspapers and/or magazines? Are they on the radio or television regularly? Do they have large, attractive signs at their location and elsewhere? Do they do direct mail, and are you on their mailing list? Do they offer coupons and frequent-customer cards? Are they selling on the web, and how is this promoted? Do they sponsor nonprofit events or are they highly visible for national causes? Are they doing more or less than you are? Can you afford to compete with them in the advertising and promotion marketplace? Do they do more marketing at certain times of the year?

- **How do your competitors react to you?** When you make changes, have special sales, offer new products, or have promotions, do they counter with similar offers? Do they do nothing or seem to pay no attention to you? If they do respond, how quickly? Do they try to outdo you or just match what you have advertised? Do they let you do your promotion and then have one of their own at a later date?

- **Are you afraid of your competitors?** Does thinking about your competitors keep you awake at night? Will they come out with products or services that will make yours obsolete and put you out of business? Do you run your business more on the defensive rather than the offensive? How can you turn some of the negatives into positives?

These are questions you want to keep asking yourself and answering every six months or so. Don't think that the situation today will be the same a year from now. Even if you're not making changes, you can be assured that your competitors are. And don't ignore your competitors, because they aren't ignoring you. Find out as much information about them as you can and use it to your advantage whenever possible.

Cultivate Your Ideas

How do you get new ideas? This is a question I've often been asked, but there's no one simple answer. Flowers and plants grow when the soil is fertile, not when it's hard like clay. So will your ideas grow from your mind when it's open and full of knowledge.

Some great new ideas are never seen because people don't use them. People are afraid that they will fail, but short-term failures are only part of the learning process.

I don't mean only knowledge from school, but also knowledge from life and observation. Be aware of what's going on around you and in other businesses. Be a sponge for information and have a big appetite for knowledge wherever you can find it. Learn from others—question why they are doing something different and think of how you can apply this to your business.

You'll get many ideas daily or weekly, and you need to sort them out to determine which ones to put into practice. The first step is to write down any ideas so you don't forget them. Often another idea will come into your mind, take over, and bump out the previous one. You need to assess all your ideas, so keep track of them. When you're ready to qualify ideas for a new product or service, ask these questions:

- Is it an original idea?
- Is there a specific need for it?
- Will it be affordable to buy?
- Will it be affordable to implement?
- Can it be perfected in a reasonable time?
- How long will it take to be profitable?
- How long before it will become obsolete?
- Who or what is the target market?
- How quickly can the competition react?
- How much will it cost to promote?
- How should it be marketed?

Don't think that you never get any ideas, because you do. Recognizing them and using them is what really matters in your business. Keep abreast of what's going on in the business world by reading or scanning business publications and journals. If you don't want to subscribe to them, most are available at the library. Your industry trade publications and newsletters will show you changing market trends and give you ideas using those changes.

And believe it or not, watching TV commercials will give you insight into what the bigger companies are doing and give you ideas for how you can jump on the trend or counter it.

Make three files for your ideas—one for now ideas, another for later ideas, and a third for questionable ideas. When you have time to try an idea, go to the appropriate file.

Risk Taking

If risk taking sounds risky, well, it is. Rarely does a small business grow or even survive without some element of risk in its marketing mix. This doesn't mean you should spend all your money on every wild idea that comes to mind. But if a new idea, procedure, or product gives you a good feeling that it may be successful, you need to take the risk and put it to the test.

You certainly don't want to put your entire business on the line for one new idea, no matter how good it sounds. But take a calculated risk to see whether your idea can be profitable and unique to your business. If you see that your chances of success are more than 50 percent, it's time to move forward.

One of the best-known risk takers was Sam Walton. He wasn't happy unless he had some new idea or better concept in the works at all times. I've listened to his audio book, *Made in America*, many times, and I always come away with something new to try. Most of us will never achieve his level of huge success (nor do we even want to), but how he got there is the real story.

Opening your own small business was probably the biggest risk you've ever taken. Risks are part of being in business, so analyze them and act according to your best judgment. Taking calculated risks can open many doors to your future growth.

> Don't be afraid to make an investment in your ideas; you never know whether it might be the one the world has been waiting for. Just don't over-risk and bet everything on one venture until it has proven itself.

Small-Business Networking

Networking is important for anyone, but it's even more important for the small-business owner because we can't afford the massive advertising that big companies can. It's a chance to let potential customers know who you are and that your business exists. When you're at a meeting or a business event, you *are* your business. You never know when you'll meet the golden goose or the great new client you've been waiting for. Always be ready and willing to network.

Networking can be done anytime, anywhere.

Try to attend as many local meetings or Chamber of Commerce events as you have time for. You probably won't be able to afford to join all the different organizations that have meetings, so go as a guest of a member. Most organizations will let you attend one or more meetings before insisting that you join. If you're really pressed for time or want to attend more than one meeting at the same time, just arrive early for the cocktail or mixer hour and discreetly leave before the formal meeting starts. That way, you can rush to the next meeting and network at the end of it.

You can join any of the many organized networking groups that favor local businesses. Before you pay your member dues, just be sure you will benefit from the meetings and any leads you will receive. Be a guest at a couple of meetings before you join.

You can network anywhere or anytime. Whether it's on the golf course, in a supermarket, or waiting in line at a restaurant, be ready and willing to network. But meetings will offer the most opportunities for getting to know a wide variety of people. Here are some ideas to make the most of your networking time at a meeting:

- Arrive early enough to use the entire networking time. Other people who arrive early are there for the same reason, so take advantage of it and try to meet everyone new.

- Stop in the restroom when you first get to the meeting and check your appearance and your teeth.

- Dress professionally so that you look successful. People like to talk to those who look like winners, not losers.

- Walk around the area with a smile and assess who is there. Then you can plan the time to spend with each new person and still meet the rest.

- Eat conservatively; it's hard to talk with your mouth full. Have a light snack before you go so you're not starving.

- Keep drinks to a minimum. You're there to network and meet new people, not to party. You don't want to fall asleep during a boring meeting and embarrass yourself, and you certainly don't want to be known as the drunken guy at the meeting.

- Briefly say hello to anyone you already know. Then go on and meet the ones you don't know.

- Have a short introduction ready to introduce yourself. Ten to twelve seconds is long enough.

- Have a confident attitude but don't be cocky; you want people to like you.

- Exchange business cards with people who can benefit you directly or indirectly.

- Have a pen (and a spare) ready so you can jot notes on the back of business cards for future reference.

- It's best not to conduct business while networking. Set a future time, such as a lunch or an appointment.

- Keep an open ear and open mind for things you may be interested in. You are someone else's networking target too.

- Talk to as many people as you can without cutting anyone short. You can always go back to an interesting person if there's time left at the end.

- Don't leave immediately when the function is over. Wait and meet the speakers and other VIPs.

- If you really like the group or organization, offer to speak at a future meeting.

- The next day, send a "nice to meet you" note to everyone from whom you have a business card. Enclose two of your own cards with the note and hand-address the envelope.

- Follow up as promised with all the people you said you would call. Do it within a week or at least send an email.

After you leave the meeting or function, you need to decide whether this is the type of function you want to attend regularly. You want to invest the time you have available where it will do you the most good. There are many choices of meetings available, so you can always try another if the first one isn't a good fit.

Most newspapers publish a list in the Sunday or Monday edition with times and contact information. Another source of meetings is your local or nearby city business journal. Don't be afraid to travel to another city within 100 miles to attend a new meeting; it may be well worth it. Try to budget as much of your time as you can for attending meetings, and you should see results over time.

Don't forget about networking outside of meetings, too. A few years back, I was sitting in the waiting room of a quick oil-change place, talking to a lady with kids about our mailing lists. Her husband was in the computer business and eventually purchased one of our computer user lists. It sounds like an unlikely place to meet a business contact, but you never know who you'll meet and when.

You can also make contacts that you can refer to friends or associates if your business can't use them. Don't underestimate the power of referring contacts to someone else who can help them. You will probably get a two- or three-fold return over time. Of course, you must be sure the company you're referring to is reputable and will do a good job for them.

Networking should be automatic, wherever you are and whatever you're doing. A good networker will always seek out new people and introduce himself. You'll notice at Chamber of Commerce or other business meetings that most people stand around or sit with people they know or are friends with. This doesn't get them very far in the new-contacts game. The good networker will venture up to someone standing alone and start a conversation. The objective is to meet and get to know all the new people at any meeting before it's over. If there's lunch or dinner, good networkers will find a table where they know few (if any) people. By the end of the meal, they want to at least be familiar with everyone seated near them. Good networkers create an opportunity out of every encounter.

Don't forget to network when you're out of town and learn what's happening elsewhere in your industry. Whether you're on a vacation or a business trip, an hour or two of time investment can pay off in big rewards. Find some time to open the yellow pages and find other businesses like yours. Call or just go visit them, ask for the owner or manager, tell him who you are, and exchange ideas. Because you're a non-competitor from another city, you can both open up to each other. You're bound to find something you didn't think of and can use as soon as you get back. Give your host some ideas that you're using effectively in your business. Of course, invite him to stop in if he ever comes to your city. Always keep an open-door policy for anyone coming to your business from out of town. Be a visitor and a good host—it's a valuable learning experience.

Cornucopia of Information

Your best free source of information, open seven days a week, is your local library. Even though your taxes pay for its operation, it's available at no cost whenever you use it. If you haven't been there lately, I suggest you find time soon. There's so much information there that you can spend an hour just figuring out what to use and look at. Make the library a destination at least once every 60 days.

You will find directories with hundreds of pages of new possible customers with contact names. The reference department will have information on all the media companies you can use for publicity. If you can't find what you're looking for, a reference librarian will cheerfully guide you in the right direction (no tipping necessary!). Most of the books in the reference department are not available for checkout, so bring a pen and paper to jot down any details you want to take back to the office with you. If you're checking out books on marketing, sales, or any subject, don't take just one; take three or four so you have different ideas from different authors.

Many libraries have copy machines so you can copy full pages of information from reference books that you can't take with you. Bring change or dollar bills so you're prepared if you need them. You never know when you're going to find a list of potential customers or ideas in a reference book and want to start using the information right away.

> The public library is a great source of information for businesses. Much of the information available in the reference department is not available online, so you need to visit personally.

Many libraries in medium and large cities have websites where you can go directly to other sites with information for which the library has a subscription. If there are publications or websites you would be interested in but that aren't available, make a request to a librarian or write a letter to the library's executive director. If they get enough requests for the same thing, you just might get it. You could always cheat a little and ask your friends and relatives to help you out and make similar requests.

A small-business owner who's serious about growing his or her company should visit the library weekly or at least twice monthly. Using every resource available is what the winners do, so use your library regularly. When you're out of town and have extra time on your hands, stop at a library there and pick up some new ideas. They may have directories or publications you don't have in your city. It's certainly better than sitting in a bar—and a lot less expensive, too.

Buy Your Umbrella When the Sun Is Shining

Isn't it great when your business is doing well? You can't wait to get to work and see how much money you're going to make every day. If you worked hard and long for many years, you don't ever want to go back to those tough beginnings. You want to keep making money at a fast pace and increase growth every year. That's the way it's going to be, so let's go on a cruise and have fun for two weeks! Slow down—there's more to it than that.

Small-business owners put in many hours at a low income to build a profitable business. If you stick to it and persevere, you finally reach the light at the end of the tunnel. But you don't really want to go back and travel that tunnel again, do you? So how do you keep from sliding back into those tough times when just staying in business was a real challenge? You have to plan for the difficult times ahead, regardless of whether you think they are coming. And I can tell you from 30 years of experience in small business that tough times can and will sneak up on you.

Plan and prepare when times are good and when the money is available, because if and when things change, the money may not be available. Business goes in cycles, and slow periods will come, so you need to be ready. Here are a few ideas you can use to be prepared for any downturn:

- Pay down any credit lines you have so they are available when you need to use them again. You'll save all the interest with a lower balance, and financial institutions like to see these paid down and may even increase your limit.

- Reduce balances or pay off any company credit cards you have. This will release more available credit and save that high interest you're paying.

- Apply for new company credit cards when your credit is very good and you can get them at a low interest rate. Transfer other higher-interest balances to these new accounts.

- Put money away in a company mutual fund, especially if the market has been down lately. It may even appreciate before you need it. A money-market fund is the next best choice, or if you're really conservative, a CD is the most secure.

- Prepay insurance premiums so they won't become a burden later. You may even get a small discount for paying in advance. Call your agent or insurance company service department and make your best deal.

- Stock up on stamps or fill your postage meter when excess funds are available. This is a necessary expense that won't creep up when funds are short if you've stocked up when times are good. Stamps and postage are good anytime and can be listed as an asset under prepaid postage. If you're planning for a future big mailing, you can make a postage deposit at a reputable mail-fulfillment house.

- If you are paying your suppliers very well or early, you may be able to negotiate better terms or discounts. If you speed up their cash flow, you are going to move up on their favorite-customers list.

- Take advantage of larger-order quantity discounts. Stock up on your bestselling products before costs rise if you have enough storage or warehouse space available.

- Do things for your employees that you can't do when times are slow—pizza parties, small gifts, bonuses, and so on. They will remember these things and help you through the tough times.

- Buy things you know you'll need now, when they're on sale. This is the time to take advantage of all those bargains for which you get offers. Have someone scan all the sales literature you get to find products you order regularly.

- Do any needed equipment maintenance now, while it's easy to pay for. This means manufacturing as well as office equipment. Breakdowns during tough times can be a real disaster. Review all warranties and get preventive service done when it's easy to pay for.

- Stock up on office supplies, such as copier and printer toner, Post-its, pens, copy paper, and so on. Buying other supplies and forms in larger quantities can also offer a savings.

- Do any research or product testing when you can easily afford to pay for it. The secret to reversing a downturn later may be a new product or service. Be ready to move ahead quickly if and when the need arises.

- Start your customer-appreciation program when you can easily pay for promotional items, loyalty cards, scratch-off cards, and other little bonus items. Have a contest and give away a nice prize.

- Test new mailings or direct-mail pieces when you can easily pay for the extra postage. That way, you'll be ready if market conditions change and you need a quick influx of new customers. Testing during good times will save you money on future mailings.

A small business is a lot like the weather—the sun can be shining one minute, and shortly thereafter a storm will start. So don't wait until it starts raining to buy your umbrella; have several of them ready in the closet. And remember, it even rains in the desert once in a while, so don't think it won't happen to you and your company. This is why the big companies get into a slump and their stock drops 50 percent—they didn't plan for it. But if you're smart and prepared, you can dodge those puddles and survive until the sun comes out again.

Why Businesses Fail

Thousands (if not millions) of new businesses start up every year. Especially with home-based businesses so easy to get off the ground, there's bound to be even more in the future. Many full-time employees even have off-hours small businesses that don't compete with their employer. That seems to be the fad of the 2000s—to have some type of business entity to call your own. A lot of the after-hours ones are borderline hobby businesses, but the goal is still to make additional income. It's so easy to start your business, just like getting married. Get a state license, a name, a phone number, and a mailing address, and you're in business. But like a marriage, a small business is not always easy to get out of (and it can be expensive). I can tell you about both firsthand!

Keeping your business in business is an ongoing effort and just part of your many duties and obligations. Don't have the attitude that everything will work out on its own, because often it won't. Start making adjustments early when you see declines in any part of your business.

Everyone wants to open small, get lots of orders, make lots of money, and eventually sell out for millions. But sometimes—more often than not—there are many bumps along the road to success. How you maneuver around those bumps determines your outcome. If you want a successful business that stays in business, you must pay attention to what's going on and make necessary adjustments along the way.

Usually, when a business fails, it's a combination of several things that build up over a period of time. Rarely does one problem result in the doors closing in 30 days. You'll see in the following list that tough competition is *not* among the major reasons. Every business has competitors; that's the American way. So don't think you can blame your problems on them—it's a copout that won't work. In fact, competitors actually make you a *better* business. But here are some real factors that cause business failures; if you see ones that you can change in your business, I suggest you do it today:

- **Poor customer care.** Also known as poor customer service, this is probably the biggest fault that unsuccessful small businesses have. Customer care is no longer a benefit; it's expected! And if it's not demonstrated in a pleasant and professional manner, customers will spend their money where they're treated better. Give customers a smile and a little more than they expect—it will keep them coming back.

- **Insufficient marketing.** Just opening your store or office, hanging your sign, and saying "The line forms on the right" is not enough. You must advertise, promote, and sell your business to your potential customers. You may have the best product or service, but how can you make money if no one knows about it? You must do some type of marketing on a continual basis.

- **Owner attitude.** Occasionally, you'll find business owners who think they are the king/queen and everyone (including employees and customers) must do their bidding and follow orders. The word about this attitude or business personality will spread quickly and will ruin a business.

- **Poor employee training.** Undertrained service and customer contact people can frustrate your customers and make them wish they went elsewhere. Constantly putting people on hold or saying, "I'll be right back" makes your company less desirable to do business with.

- **Excessive spending.** You don't need the latest model of everything when used equipment will do the job just as well. Lavish accommodations and first-class hotels are not for a growing business; save them for your vacation.

- **Owner neglect.** Opening your small business and not being present regularly is asking for problems. Even putting a competent manager in charge won't work unless you monitor the manager's progress in person. The numbers alone won't tell you about customer care and training.

- **Lack of business knowledge.** If you're not running a franchise, you're on your own, and you need to know business basics. Read books, take courses, or get professional help, because operating a business is more than just sales. Visit the library often to build up your industry and business knowledge.

- **Excessive salaries.** Don't overcompensate your employees or yourself while trying to grow a business. Pay fair-market competitive amounts to new employees and save raises and bonuses for outstanding performance. People should be compensated for reasons other than longevity.

- **Obsolete products or services.** If you're relying on the same products that you had when you started the business, think again. How many people are still playing *Pong*, using 8-track tapes, or wearing men's leisure suits? Get with the times and find or develop new products or services in your industry, or you'll be left behind.

- **Ownership change.** The business is sold or passed down to relatives, and the new owner(s) think there's a better way to make more money. Cutting services and selling lower-quality products is not the answer. Customers become accustomed to a certain level of quality, and if it's reduced, why should they continue to purchase?

- **No cash reserve.** When things are going great, it's time to store some resources for the slow times. Invest unnecessary capital in a money-market or mutual fund. It will be there for your needs when cash flow can't pay the bills, and it's available in a couple of days rather than the month you'd wait for a new loan.

- **Inadequate product mix.** Are your products what the customer is looking for in a business like yours? Do they complement each other and wow customers? Do you offer items not easily found or displayed, or is it time to upgrade your merchandising techniques?

- **Out-of-line pricing.** Are you trying to make your fortune on a few unsuspecting patrons by charging outrageous prices? Customers will soon wise up and disappear. This doesn't apply to being paid for value-added services where you can justify a higher markup, though. Make your prices competitive but still profitable.

- **Loss of a big account.** A small business can't afford to put all its eggs in one basket, because if it loses the basket, the entire organization will be in jeopardy. It's exciting to acquire a large account, but don't change your entire business over it and don't surrender to extreme price pressures. Build your company around small to medium customers, and if a big order comes along, consider it a bonus.

- **Tax problems.** Whether you like it or not, you're going to pay taxes. So you might as well follow the rules and pay them on time. Getting behind on payroll and sales taxes can result in government pressure, penalties, and late fees. Over time, it can grow to an overwhelming amount that the business can no longer handle.

- **Loss of vision.** Why did you go into business in the first place? Getting way off track from the path to your goals can destroy any business quickly. Go find your mission statement and review it or change it for current goals and conditions.

Some business owners lose interest in the day-to-day vision of their business, and that can cause it to fail. If that focus on success seems to be leaving you, either sell or turn over the day-to-day duties to someone you can trust.

You'll notice that competition and economic conditions are not listed. This is because those are normal business situations that every business faces, and they can be controlled. Seldom does a business close because a big competitor moves in, unless the small business gives up without trying to find their niche and get close to their customers. Competitors can make your business even better by calling your attention to increased customer care.

Economic ups and downs have been and will always be here, and you need to have a plan to cope with them. Most business failures occur because of internal problems, not external ones. Maybe it's time to look inside your business and see whether there are any of these monsters lurking around.

Strength in Numbers

Meeting others in small businesses can offer you many ideas to grow your business and survive in tough times. You can become a member of associations and organizations to receive a wealth of small-business information. You'll want to request information to see what the purpose and goals of each are before you join. Many can offer discounts on group insurance and keep you informed of pending laws that affect small businesses. A few such organizations are:

National Association for the Self-Employed
P.O. Box 612067
Dallas, TX 75261
800-232-NASE
nase.org

National Business Association
P.O. Box 700728
Dallas, TX 75370
800-456-0440
nationalbusiness.org

National Small Business Association
1156 15th St NW #1100
Washington, DC 20005
800-345-6728
nsba.biz

American Association for Consumer Benefits
P.O. Box 100279
Fort Worth, TX 76185
800-872-8896

National Federation of Independent Business
53 Century Blvd #300
Nashville, TN 37214
800-634-2669
nfib.com

Score Association
409 3rd St SW 6th Floor
Washington, DC 20024
800-634-0245
score.org

There are also thousands of other associations that apply to specific industries and trades. You can find these listed in the *Encyclopedia of Associations* by the Gale Group in your local library's reference section. Check the index book first to locate your industry and where to find the associations in the other volumes. Most will send you free information and literature to review before you have to sign up and pay dues. If they have an annual convention, you can learn about (and contribute to) the latest things happening in your type of business or industry.

Keeping in touch with your industry means you won't be left behind when changes occur. Business owners who join these associations seem to have a six-month to one-year jump on those who aren't members. Plus, you will have qualified people with whom to exchange ideas.

A Final Thought

We live in a country where opportunity is available to anyone. It doesn't matter what your background is—rich or poor, educated or not, the opportunity door is ajar for everyone. Your desire and drive can get you to walk through that door on your own. People from all over the world are eager to come to America because they know they are free to become successful using their ideas, drive, and perseverance. Most of you are already here, some born with the silver spoon in your mouth—don't let it tarnish. If you have the desire and can handle the risk, do it now! Be the best you can be; it's in your hands now. The quarterback has just thrown you the ball, and the goal line is straight ahead.

"After you've scored a touchdown, start planning for the next one."

—BT

Appendix A

Myths of Small Business

Marketing has always been the engine that pulls the business train. But unfortunately, some people think that if they have a great product or service, the buying public will beat down their door. And they believe that a product or service that is a big hit today will stay popular next year and five years from now. Unfortunately, that simply is not the case.

There are several common myths of small business that you should dispel if you want to stay in business and grow profitably. When you own a small business, you can't just sit back, relax, and watch the money roll in. You must be on your guard at all times, ready to change directions, inject new ideas, and put out all the fires. Be on the lookout for all of these common myths and don't accept them as truth.

- **The lowest price gets the order.** Don't kid yourself; many other factors go into a buyer's decision. The amount people are willing to pay is related to the value they see in a product or service. Price is usually just a scapegoat for another issue; find it, solve it, and receive the sale.

- **Your best employees will never leave.** People who are good at their job usually know it, and you must keep them focused and challenged. There's always someone waiting to steal good employees away from you for their own business, so be vigilant and listen to your best employees' ideas and goals. Include these employees in some decision-making.

- **You have no competition.** Even if you have a unique product, there are other companies trying to develop similar products that are cheaper, faster, and better. Don't fool yourself; you'll have competitors today and tomorrow. Don't ignore your competitors, because they aren't ignoring you.

- **Advertising is a waste of time.** Many people think you can put out an ad, sit back, and wait for all the responses. Unless you're giving away money, it takes time for people to respond, and many will need to see your ad multiple times before they respond or buy. In advertising, persistence and consistent messaging pay off in the end. Use your advertising dollars wisely and monitor all responses.

- **Nobody reads direct mail.** You might be surprised by how many people look at your direct mail and at least scan it to see whether there's something of interest to them in it. I've been sending business-to-business direct mail for 30 years, and I'm amazed by how many people will call back three, four, or six months after I sent a direct-mail piece. Mail to the best prospects regularly with enticing offers.

- **Unhappy customers will always voice their complaints.** Just the opposite is true—most people will not say anything to you if they're unhappy, but they'll never buy from you again. You need to follow up to see whether people are happy with your product or service and solve any problems quickly. Disgruntled customers may not tell you, but they almost always tell their friends.

- **Satisfied customers always send referrals.** Some will, but many won't bother unless you offer an incentive. Give them a reward or a reason to recommend your store or business. A brief phone call or note thanking them for the referral will help you get more referrals and likely a repeat order.

- **Your suppliers need your business.** If you stop buying from a supplier, chances are they won't close down. They need your business if you are easy to work with and pay your bills on time. Make suppliers partners and meet with them regularly to exchange ideas for increasing sales and profits.

- **You'll always get the reorder.** Most companies will check what's new in the marketplace and get price quotes before they reorder—especially on a higher-priced product or order. Get to know what keeps customers happy, provide it, and enjoy long-term business.

- **You can make your business hours fit your own schedule.** Not true! You must be open for business when your customers are available to buy from you—period. If that means evenings and weekends, you must do it or get out of that type of business. Remember, if you're not open, someone else is.

- **Everyone will order through your website.** Not always—some members of the buying public are still a little leery of using their credit card on the Internet. Your website should direct people to visit your store or call your office if they don't wish to purchase online. Check your competitors' sites often and update your site with new offers regularly.

- **You should treat all customers the same.** It's best to respond to each customer the way he or she wants to be treated. Some customers are impatient and don't want to chitchat. Some are very detail-oriented and want you to explain everything. Some are browsers who want to see everything before making a decision. Some are confused and unsure of what they want. Some are price buyers and want your best deal. Adapt to each different customer type, and you'll have more success than if you treat them all the same.

Don't accept any of these common myths of small business as your way of doing business. Markets change, economies change, products change, and technology changes, so you have to change, too. Keep your approach to your small business fresh and exciting and stay ahead of all those competitors who want to take away your customers.

Appendix B

Additional Resources

In my 30-plus years in many different small businesses, I learned a lot from other people. I've built quite a library of business books, tapes, and CDs, which I purchased so they were always available for quick reference. I try to get as many as I can in audio-book format because I'm in the car a lot, and they hold my attention better. You can always check them out from the library or rent them from audio companies, but once you read or hear them, they're soon forgotten. You need to listen to tapes, CDs, or podcasts or read books several times to fully absorb the information.

Following are some good sources for audio books that I have used:

- Audio Editions: www.audioeditions.com
- Books on Tape: www.booksontape.com
- Amazon.com: www.amazon.com/audiobooks
- Blackstone Audio, Inc.: www.blackstoneaudio.com
- Recorded Books, LLC: www.recordedbooks.com
- Audiobooks: www.audiobooks.com
- Audiobooks Online: www.audiobooksonline.com
- Nightingale Conant: www.nightingale.com

Check back at least monthly to see what's new and what's on sale. However, many good business books never make it to the audio stage, so for those you'll need to read the physical book. Most bookstores have periodic sales, or you can buy them online and usually get a discount that way. Many books now are offered in electronic format or for Kindle or other portable electronic reading devices if you prefer to travel light.

Staying informed and reading other success stories will give you an extra edge over the competitor who's only listening to music or reading books for pleasure. Find a business subject with which you need help and purchase several different books or audio books so you can get each writer's ideas. After you've absorbed different opinions, you can decide what will work best for your business. You'll find that once you start reading and listening, you can't wait for new ones to be published.

For a *free* sample issue of our monthly small-business Idea-Letter publication, email idealetter@aol.com or call toll free 877-700-1322.

Index

Numbers

80-20 rule, 177

A

access rights (franchises), 50
action plans
  advertising, 74
  business-to-business, 225
  customer loyalty, 271
  customer service, 295
  direct mail, 102
  financial crisis, 312
  franchises, 53
  prices, 153
  promotions, 122
  publicity, 86
  retail stores, 208
  salespeople, 178
  starting businesses, 13, 39
  telemarketing, 258
  tradeshows, 243
  websites, 137
adding value (prices), 142–143
advertising
  action plan, 74
  agencies, 63–64
  benches, 68
  billboards, 66–68
  budgets, 56–57
  business cards, 64–65
  competitors, 63
  co-ops, 73
  copy
    headlines, 59–60
    hot words, 60–61
    overview, 58–59
  costs, reducing, 72–73
  customers, 57–58
  marketing, 334
  non-ads, 62

  overview, 56
  placement, 61–62
  prospects, 57–58
  publicity comparison, 76–77
  selling, 168–169
  signs, 65–66
  strategies/tips, 74
  telephone
    directory, 205–206
    on-hold messages, 71–72
  television
    direct response, 69–70
    infomercials, 70–71
  testing, 74
  tradeshows, 237–238
  vehicles, 66, 68–69
  walls, 68
  websites, 129–132
advertising agencies, 63–64
advisors (selling), 162–163
agreements (franchises), 48–50
angry customers, 281–282
anniversary promotions, 118–119
articles (publicity), 84
assets, selling, 307
associate buyers, 216–217
associations, 10–11, 329–330
attire. *See* clothing
attitude (customer loyalty), 266–267
attracting customers. *See also*
    marketing
  retail stores, 186–187, 202–203
  websites, 129–132
audio books, 338
automobiles. *See* vehicles
availability (selling), 168–169

B

banks (financial crisis), 301–305
benches (advertising), 68

billboards, 66–68
billing
  business-to-business orders, 219–220
  invoice numbers, 35–36
blogs, 135–136
books, 338
booths. *See* **exhibits**
branding
  customer loyalty, 267–268
  prices, 149–150
brick-and-mortar stores. *See* **retail**
  stores
budgets. *See* **costs**
building relationships
  customer service
    action plan, 295
    angry customers, 281–282
    customer satisfaction, 276–290
    employee meetings, 285–286
    employee of the month, 287–288
    employee professionalism, 288–289
    employee rewards, 286–288
    listening, 288–289
    overview, 274–275
    real-world stories, 291–295
    reviewing current practices, 284–285
    store hours, 288
    strategies, 279–280, 282–284
    transaction times, 291
  customers, 166–167, 175
  loyalty
    action plan, 271
    attitude, 266–267
    branding, 267–268
    cards, 268–269
    creating, 264–265
    destroying, 265–266
    doctors, 271
    levels, 261–263
    overview, 260–261
    personality, 266–267
    professionalism, 266–267
    referrals, 270–271
    tracking, 268–269
  retail stores, 187–191
  suppliers, 36–37
  websites, 130

business cards
  advertising, 64–65
  selling, 169–170
businesses
  associations, 10–11, 329–330
  business-to-business. *See* business-to-business
  direct mail customers, 96–98
  franchises
    access rights, 50
    action plans, 53
    agreements, 48–50
    buying, 45–48
    choosing, 43–44
    entrepreneurs, 42
    finding, 44–45
    franchisor relationships, 52
    initial fees, 49
    manuals, 51
    minimum purchases, 49
    non-compete agreements, 50
    overview, 42–43
    product restrictions, 50
    protected territories, 50
    questions, 45–48
    renewal fees, 49
    retail stores, 21
    risks, 53
    royalties, 42, 49
    strategies/tips, 45–48
    training, 51–52
    websites, 44–45
  home businesses, 17–18
  mission statements, 23–24
  mistakes, 12–13
  naming, 26–27
  reasons for failure, 326–329
  retail stores. *See* retail stores
  small office, 18–20
  starting
    action plan, 13, 39
    creative ideas, 3–5
    marketing, 29–34
    overview, 2, 16
    skills, 6–7
    timing, 5–6
  strategies, 12–13

business-to-business
action plan, 225
associate buyers, 216–217
coupons, 222
customers
diversity, 218–219
finding, 211–212
problem customers, 224–225
deliveries, 220–221
demonstrations, 213–214
following up, 215, 217–218
letters of recommendation, 223–224
locations, 213–214
mailings, 212–213
orders
invoices, 219–220
policies, 219–220
reminders, 217–218
overview, 210–211
presentations, 213–214
prices, 215–216, 222
problems, 220–221
quality, 215–216
response time, 212–213
salespeople, 213–214
selling, 216–217
seminars, 222–223
buyers (selling), 172–173
buying
associate buyers, 216–217
business-to-business, 216–217
franchises, 45–48
tradeshow exhibits, 236–237

C

CAM (common area maintenance) fees, 22–23
cards (customer loyalty), 268–269
cars. *See* **vehicles**
charities, 133
checks (retail stores), 204–205
choices (prices), 149
choosing franchises, 43–44
cleanliness
retail stores, 206–207
selling, 172
clients. *See* **customers**

closing
selling, 163–164, 174–175
store hours, 288
clothing (selling), 172
cold calls (telemarketing), 255
commandments of marketing, 8–10
commissions (salespeople), 176–177
common area maintenance (CAM) fees, 22–23
competitors
advertising, 63
marketing, 334
prices, 140–142
questions, 314–317
retail stores, 194–196
selling, 166
strategies, 314–317
considerations (prices), 140–142
consignments (retail stores), 193–194
consumers. *See* **customers**
contests (promotions), 115–117
convenience (prices), 142
conventions. *See* **tradeshows**
co-ops
costs
advertising, 73
direct mail, 101–102
promotions, 107–108
copy (advertising)
headlines, 59–60
hot words, 60–61
overview, 58–59
cost per response (CPR), direct mail, 99–100
cost plus, 147
costs
advertising
budgets, 56–57
co-ops, 73
reducing, 72–73
cost plus, 147
direct mail CPR, 99–100
fees
CAM fees, 22–23
initial fees, 49
renewal fees, 49
triple net fees, 22–23

reducing
    advertising, 72–73
    co-ops, 101–102
    direct mail, 101–102
    financial crisis, 300, 305–306
    telemarketing, 256–257
    tradeshows, 232–237
coupons
    business-to-business, 222
    promotions, 104–105
    retail stores, 203–204
CPR (cost per response), direct mail, 99–100
creating customer loyalty, 264–265
creative ideas (starting businesses), 3–5
credit cards
    financial crisis, 304–305
    merchant services, 27–28
    retail stores, 27–28, 204–205
    suppliers, 36–37
cross-promotions, 114–115
cultivating ideas, 318–319
current practices (customer service), 284–285
customer satisfaction, 276–279, 289–290
customer service. *See also* **loyalty**
    action plan, 295
    angry customers, 281–282
    customer satisfaction, 276–279, 289–290
    employee meetings, 285–286
    employee of the month, 287–288
    employee professionalism, 288–289
    employee rewards, 286–288
    listening, 288–289
    overview, 274–275
    real-world stories, 291–295
    reviewing current practices, 284–285
    store hours, 288
    strategies, 279–280, 282–284
    transaction times, 291
customers
    advertising, 57–58
    attracting. *See also* marketing
        retail stores, 186–187, 202–203
        websites, 129–132

building relationships, 166–167, 175
business-to-business
    diversity, 218–219
    finding, 211–212
    problem customers, 224–225
customer service. *See also* loyalty
    action plan, 295
    angry customers, 281–282
    customer satisfaction, 276–279, 289–290
    employee meetings, 285–286
    employee of the month, 287–288
    employee professionalism, 288–289
    employee rewards, 286–288
    listening, 288–289
    overview, 274–275
    real-world stories, 291–295
    reviewing current practices, 284–285
    store hours, 288
    strategies, 279–280, 282–284
    transaction times, 291
direct mail
    businesses, 96–98
    consumers, 94–96
    email, 136–137
    targeting, 90, 93–94
employees. *See* employees
financial crisis, 300–301
finding, 38–39
loyalty. *See also* customer service
    action plan, 271
    attitude, 266–267
    branding, 267–268
    cards, 268–269
    creating, 264–265
    destroying, 265–266
    doctors, 271
    levels, 261–263
    overview, 260–261
    personality, 266–267
    professionalism, 266–267
    referrals, 270–271
    tracking, 268–269
marketing, 8–10, 335–336
orders
price quotes, 151–152

retail stores
    attracting, 186–187, 202–203
    building relationships, 187–191
    impulse buyers, 202–203
    indecisive, 201
    promotions, 186–187, 202–203
    seminars, 186–187
    seniors, 199–201
    travelers, 204
    unfriendly, 201
salespeople. *See* salespeople
selling. *See* selling
websites
    attracting, 129–132
    building relationships, 130
    charities, 133
    orders, 131

D

debt, deferring, 304–305
decision makers (selling), 159–160
deferring debt (financial crisis),
    304–305
deliveries
    business-to-business, 220–221
    promotions, 110–111
demonstrations (business-to-business),
    213–214
design
    direct mail, 98–99
    websites, 126–127
destroying customer loyalty, 265–266
direct mail. *See also* mailings
    action plan, 102
    co-ops, 101–102
    costs, 101–102
    CPR (cost per response), 99–100
    customers
        businesses, 96–98
        consumers, 94–96
        email, 136–137
        targeting, 90, 93–94
    design, 98–99
    employees, 92
    layout, 98–99
    mailing lists, 89–90, 92–93
    marketing, 335
    offers, 90–91
    overview, 88

payments, 91
persistence, 91
prospects, 89–90, 92–93
quality, 90
response methods, 91
time
    frequency, 89
    timing, 100–101
urgency, 91
direct response television advertising,
    69–70
discounts
    prices, 196–198
    promotions, 109–110
display (retail stores), 207
diversity (business-to-business),
    218–219
Do Not Call lists, 257
doctors (customer loyalty), 271
downturn. *See* financial crisis

E

economic slowdown. *See* financial crisis
employee of the month, 287–288
employees. *See also* salespeople
    customer service
        employee of the month, 287–288
        meetings, 285–286
        professionalism, 288–289
        rewards, 286–288
    direct mail, 92
    financial crisis, 301, 306
    marketing, 334
    retail stores
        finding, 183–184
        hiring, 184–186
        part-time, 184–186
    telemarketing, 250–251
entrepeneurs (franchises), 42
events
    promotions, 107–110
    tradeshows. *See* tradeshows
exhibits (tradeshows)
    buying, 236–237
    finding, 236–237
    locations, 235–236
    renting, 236–237
    seminars, 240
    strategies, 238–240

F

Facebook, 134
failure, reasons, 326–329
fees. *See also* **costs**
    CAM fees, 22–23
    initial fees, 49
    renewal fees, 49
    triple net fees, 22–23
financial crisis
    action plan, 312
    banks, 301–305
    credit cards, 304–305
    customers, 300–301
    deferring debt, 304–305
    employees, 301, 306
    fixed expenses, 305–306
    inventory, 307
    marketing, 308–309
    networking, 309–311
    outsourcing, 306–307
    overview, 298
    planning, 298–299, 311–312, 324–326
    prices, 303–304
    reducing costs, 300, 305–306
    rent, 305–306
    selling assets, 307
    utilities, 305–306
finding
    customers, 38–39, 211–212
    employees, 183–184
    franchises, 44–45
    suppliers, 37–38
    telemarketing leads, 254–255
    tradeshow exhibits, 236–237
    tradeshows, 229–231
firing salespeople, 177
**fixed expenses (financial crisis),
    305–306**
following up
    business-to-business, 215, 217–218
    selling, 166, 175
    tradeshows, 241
franchises
    access rights, 50
    action plans, 53
    agreements, 48–50
    buying, 45–48
    choosing, 43–44
    entrepreneurs, 42
    finding, 44–45
    franchisor relationships, 52
    initial fees, 49
    manuals, 51
    minimum purchases, 49
    non-compete agreements, 50
    overview, 42–43
    product restrictions, 50
    protected territories, 50
    questions, 45–48
    renewal fees, 49
    retail stores, 21
    risks, 53
    royalties, 42, 49
    strategies/tips, 45–48
    training, 51–52
    websites, 44–45
franchisors, 52
frequency (direct mail), 89

G

gift cards/certificates
    retail stores, 198–199
    selling, 171
goals
    marketing, 7–8
    wish lists, 34–35
grooming (selling), 172

H

hardware (retail stores), 207
headlines (advertising copy), 59–60
high prices, 149–150
high prices, offsetting, 142–143
**hiring employees (retail stores),
    184–186**
home businesses, 17–18
home sales calls, 170–171
hot words (advertising copy), 60–61
hours
    customer service, 288
    marketing, 335

I

ideas. *See* **strategies/tips**
impulse buyers, 202
inbound telemarketing, 246–248
indecisive customers, 201

infomercials, 70–71
information, researching, 322–323
initial fees (franchises), 49
international sales (websites), 136
Internet. *See* websites
inventory (financial crisis), 307
invoice numbers, 35–36
invoices
    business-to-business orders, 219–220
    invoice numbers, 35–36

L

laws (telemarketing), 257
layout
    direct mail, 98–99
    websites, 126–127
leads (telemarketing), 254–255
letters of recommendation (business-to-business), 223–224
levels
    customer loyalty, 261–263
    prices, 149
libraries, 322–323
LinkedIn, 135
listening
    customer service, 288–289
    selling, 160–161
lists
    direct mail, 89–90, 92–93
    email, 136–137
locations
    business-to-business, 213–214
    retail stores, 20–23
        CAM fees, 22–23
        franchises, 21
        realtors, 21
        shopping centers, 21–22
        triple net fees, 22–23
    tradeshow exhibits, 235–236
logos (promotions), 105–107
loss leaders, 150–151
lowering prices, 145–147
loyalty. *See also* customer service
    action plan, 271
    attitude, 266–267
    branding, 267–268
    cards, 268–269
    creating, 264–265

    destroying, 265–266
    doctors, 271
    levels, 261–263
    overview, 260–261
    personality, 266–267
    professionalism, 266–267
    referrals, 270–271
    tracking, 268–269
lunches (selling), 164–166

M

magnets (promotions), 111–112
mailing lists
    direct mail, 89–90, 92–93
    email, 136–137
mailings
    business-to-business, 212–213
    direct mail. *See* direct mail
    mailing lists
        direct mail, 89–90, 92–93
        email, 136–137
malls. *See* shopping centers
manuals (franchises), 51
marketing. *See also* customers, attracting
    advertising, 334
    commandments, 8–10
    competitors, 334
    customers, 8–10, 335–336
    direct mail, 335
    employees, 334
    financial crisis, 308–309
    goals, 7–8
    invoice numbers, 35–36
    marketing plans, 24–26
    myths, 334–336
    orders, 335
    prices, 334
    referrals, 335
    starting businesses, 29–34
    store hours, 335
    strategies, 29–34
    suppliers, 335
    tradeshows, 237–238
    vehicles numbers, 36
    websites, 336
marketing plans, 24–26

media
promotions, 117
radio (publicity), 81–83
reporters (publicity), 80–81
television
direct response, 69–70
infomercials, 70–71
publicity, 81–83
meetings (employees), 285–286
merchant services (credit cards), 27–28
minimum purchases (franchises), 49
mini-stores, 206
mission statements, 23–24
mistakes (businesses), 12–13
MySpace, 134
myths (marketing), 334–336

N

naming businesses, 26–27
negative publicity, 81
networking
associations, 10–11, 329–330
financial crisis, 309–311
strategies, 319–322
non-ad advertising, 62
non-compete agreements (franchises), 50
nonprofits (promotions), 113–114

O

offers (direct mail), 90–91
offices, starting, 18–20
offsetting high prices, 142–143
on-hold messages, 71–72
online. *See* **websites**
opening. *See* **starting**
orders
business-to-business
invoices, 219–220
policies, 219–220
reminders, 217–218
marketing, 335
small orders, 166–167
websites, 131
organizations, 10–11, 329–330
outbound telemarketing, 248–250
outsourcing (financial crisis), 306–307
overstocks, 193–194

P

part-time employees, 184–186
payments
checks (retail stores), 204–205
credit cards
financial crisis, 304–305
merchant services, 27–28
retail stores, 27–28, 204–205
suppliers, 36–37
deferring debt (financial crisis), 304–305
direct mail, 91
retail stores, 204–205
persistence
direct mail, 91
publicity, 78
personality (customer loyalty), 266–267
phone. *See* **telephone**
placement (advertising), 61–62
planning
cultivating ideas, 318–319
financial crisis, 298–299, 311–312, 324–326
researching information, 322–323
policies (business-to-business orders), 219–220
practices (customer service), 284–285
presentations (business-to-business), 213–214
press releases (publicity), 77–79
prices
action plan, 153
adding value, 142–143
branding, 149–150
business-to-business, 215–216, 222
choices, 149
competitors, 140–142
considerations, 140–142
convenience, 142
cost plus, 147
discounts, 196–198
financial crisis, 303–304
high, 149–150
levels, 149
loss leaders, 150–151
lowering, 145–147
marketing, 334
offsetting high prices, 142–143
overview, 140

quality, 149–150, 152
quotes, 151–152
raising, 143–145
strategies, 147–149
suppliers, 148
technology, 141
value, 149–150
windows, 153
problem customers (business-to-business), 224–225
problems (business-to-business), 220–221
products
franchise restrictions, 50
website orders, 131
professional associations, 10–11, 329–330
professionalism
customer loyalty, 266–267
customer service, 288–289
employees, 288–289
salespeople, 156–159
selling, 156–159, 175
promoting business (websites), 129–132
promotions
action plan, 122
anniversaries, 118–119
contests, 115–117
co-ops, 107–108
coupons, 104–105
cross-promotions, 114–115
customers, 186–187, 202–203
delivery, 110–111
discounts, 109–110
events, 107–110
logos, 105–107
magnets, 111–112
media, 117
nonprofits, 113–114
overview, 104
rebates, 104–105
restaurants, 110–111
retail stores, 186–187, 202–203, 206
selling, 168–169
shopping centers, 107–108, 119
strategies, 120–122
unsuccessful, 117

prospects
advertising, 57–58
direct mail, 89–90, 92–93
selling, 172–173
protected territories (franchises), 50
publications (publicity), 78–79, 84
publicity
action plan, 86
advertising comparison, 76–77
articles, 84
negative, 81
overview, 76
persistence, 78
press releases, 77–79
publications, 78–79, 84
radio, 81–83
reporters, 80–81
resources, 78–79
speaking engagements, 83
television, 81–83
strategies/tips, 79–80, 84–86
writing, 84
purchases (franchises), 49
purpose (websites), 125–126

Q

qualifying buyers, 172–173
quality
business-to-business, 215–216
direct mail, 90
prices, 149–150, 152
questions
competitors, 314–317
franchises, 45–48
selling, 161–162
quotes (prices), 151–152

R

radio (publicity), 81–83
raising prices, 143–145
real-world stories (customer service), 291–295
realtors, 21
reasons for failure, 326–329
rebates, 104–105
recesssion. *See* **financial crisis**

reducing costs
  advertising, 72–73
  co-ops, 101–102
  direct mail, 101–102
  financial crisis, 300, 305–306
referrals
  customer loyalty, 270–271
  marketing, 335
rejection (selling), 173–175
relationships, building
  customer service
    action plan, 295
    angry customers, 281–282
    customer satisfaction, 276–290
    employee meetings, 285–286
    employee of the month, 287–288
    employee professionalism, 288–289
    employee rewards, 286–288
    listening, 288–289
    overview, 274–275
    real-world stories, 291–295
    reviewing current practices, 284–285
    store hours, 288
    strategies, 279–280, 282–284
    transaction times, 291
  customers, 166–167, 175
  loyalty
    action plan, 271
    attitude, 266–267
    branding, 267–268
    cards, 268–269
    creating, 264–265
    destroying, 265–266
    doctors, 271
    levels, 261–263
    overview, 260–261
    personality, 266–267
    professionalism, 266–267
    referrals, 270–271
    tracking, 268–269
  retail stores, 187–191
  suppliers, 36–37
  websites, 130
reminders (business-to-business orders), 217–218
remote areas (salespeople), 178
renewal fees (franchises), 49
rent payments (financial crisis), 305–306

renting tradeshow exhibits, 236–237
reporters, 80–81. *See also* **media**
researching information, 322–323
residential sales calls, 170–171
resources, 78–79, 338
response methods (direct mail), 91
response time (business-to-business), 212–213
restaurant promotions, 110–111
restrictions (franchises), 50
retail stores
  action plan, 208
  checks, 204–205
  cleanliness, 206–207
  competitors, 194–196
  consignments, 193–194
  coupons, 203–204
  credit cards, 27–28, 204–205
  customers
    attracting, 186–187, 202–203
    building relationships, 187–191
    impulse buyers, 202
    indecisive, 201
    promotions, 186–187, 202–203
    seminars, 186–187
    seniors, 199–201
    travelers, 204
    unfriendly, 201
  displays, 207
  employees
    finding, 183–184
    hiring, 184–186
    part-time, 184–186
  franchises
    access rights, 50
    action plans, 53
    agreements, 48–50
    buying, 45–48
    choosing, 43–44
    entrepreneurs, 42
    finding, 44–45
    franchisor relationships, 52
    initial fees, 49
    manuals, 51
    minimum purchases, 49
    non-compete agreements, 50
    overview, 42–43
    product restrictions, 50
    protected territories, 50

questions, 45–48
renewal fees, 49
retail stores, 21
risks, 53
royalties, 42, 49
strategies/tips, 45–48
training, 51–52
websites, 44–45
gift cards, 198–199
hardware, 207
locations, 20–23
   CAM fees, 22–23
   franchises, 21
   realtors, 21
   shopping centers, 21–22
   triple net fees, 22–23
mini-stores, 206
overstocks, 193–194
overview, 180–181
payments, 204–205
prices. *See* prices
promotions, 206
sales, 191–193
selection, 199
signs, 207
slow times, 202–203
starting, 20–23
   CAM fees, 22–23
   franchises, 21
   realtors, 21
   shopping centers, 21–22
   triple net fees, 22–23
strategies, 181–182
suppliers, 193–194
telephone directory, 205–206
websites, 136
**reviewing current customer service
   practices, 284–285**
rewards (employees), 286–288
rights (franchises), 50
risks
   franchises, 53
   taking, 319
royalties (franchises), 42, 49

S

sales
   coupons, 203–204
   international, 136

retail stores, 191–193, 203–204
websites, 136
sales managers, 176
salespeople. *See also* **employees;
   selling**
   80-20 rule, 177
   action plan, 178
   business-to-business, 213–214
   commissions, 176–177
   firing, 177
   professionalism, 156–159
   remote areas, 178
   sales managers, 176
   skills, 156–159
   small towns, 178
   Yankee Peddlers, 178
**satisfaction (customer service),
   276–279, 289–290**
selection (retail stores), 199
selling. *See also* **employees;
   salespeople**
   advertising, 168–169
   advisors, 162–163
   assets (financial crisis), 307
   availability, 168–169
   building relationships, 166–167, 175
   business cards, 169–170
   business-to-business, 216–217
   closing, 163–164, 174–175
   clothing, 172
   competitors, 166
   decision makers, 159–160
   following up, 166, 175
   gift certificates, 171
   grooming, 172
   listening, 160–161
   lunches, 164–166
   overview, 156
   professionalism, 156–159, 175
   promotions, 168–169
   prospects, 172–173
   qualifying buyers, 172–173
   questions, 161–162
   rejection, 173–175
   residential sales calls, 170–171
   skills, 156–159
   small orders, 166–167
   strategies, 171
   suspects, 172–173
   waiting, 174

seminars
business-to-business, 222–223
retail stores, 186–187
tradeshow exhibits, 240
seniors, 199–201
service (customer service). *See also*
loyalty
action plan, 295
angry customers, 281–282
customer satisfaction, 276–279, 289–290
employee meetings, 285–286
employee of the month, 287–288
employee professionalism, 288–289
employee rewards, 286–288
listening, 288–289
overview, 274–275
real-world stories, 291–295
reviewing current practices, 284–285
store hours, 288
strategies, 279–280, 282–284
transaction times, 291
setup. *See* **starting**
shopping centers
promotions, 107–108, 119
retail stores, 21–22
signs
advertising, 65–66
retail stores, 207
skills
selling, 156–159
starting businesses, 6–7
slow times (retail stores), 202–203
slowdown. *See* **financial crisis**
small businesses. *See* **businesses**
small office, starting, 18–20
small orders, 166–167
small towns, 178
social networks (websites), 133–135
speaking engagements (publicity), 83
staff. *See* **employees**
starting
businesses
action plan, 13, 39
creative ideas, 3–5
marketing, 29–34
overview, 2, 16
skills, 6–7
timing, 5–6

home businesses, 17–18
retail stores, 20–23
CAM fees, 22–23
franchises, 21
realtors, 21
shopping centers, 21–22
triple net fees, 22–23
small office, 18–20
store hours
customer service, 288
marketing, 335
stores. *See* **businesses**
strategies/tips
advertising, 74
businesses, 12–13
competitors, 314–317
cultivating ideas, 318–319
customer service, 279–280, 282–284
franchises, 45–48
marketing, 29–34
networking, 319–322
prices, 147–149
promotions, 120–122
publicity, 79–80, 84–86
retail stores, 181–182
selling, 171
starting businesses, 3–5
telemarketing, 252–254, 257–258
tradeshow exhibits, 238–240
tradeshows, 231–232, 242–243
websites, 127–128
strip malls. *See* **shopping centers**
suppliers
building relationships, 36–37
credit cards, 36–37
direct mail co-ops, 101–102
finding, 37–38
invoice numbers, 35–36
marketing, 335
prices, 148
retail stores, 193–194
suspects (selling), 172–173

T

taking risks, 319
targeting customers (direct mail), 90,
93–94
teams. *See* **employees**

technology (prices), 141
telemarketing
    action plan, 258
    cold calls, 255
    costs, 256–257
    employees, 251
    emplyees, 250
    inbound, 246–248
    laws, 257
    leads, 254–255
    outbound, 248–250
    overview, 246
    strategies, 252–254, 257–258
    voicemail, 255–256
telephone
    advertising (on-hold messages), 71–72
    telemarketing
        action plan, 258
        cold calls, 255
        costs, 256–257
        employees, 250–251
        inbound, 246–248
        laws, 257
        leads, 254–255
        outbound, 248–250
        overview, 246
        strategies, 252–254, 257–258
        voicemail, 255–256
    telephone directory, 205–206
telephone directory, 205–206
television
    advertising
        direct response, 69–70
        infomercials, 70–71
    publicity, 81–83
territories (franchises), 50
testing advertising, 74
time
    customer service
        store hours, 288
        transaction times, 291
    direct mail
        frequency, 89
        timing, 100–101
    slow times (retail stores), 202–203
    store hours
        customer service, 288
        marketing, 335

timing
    direct mail, 100–101
    starting businesses, 5–6
tips. See strategies/tips
tracking customer loyalty, 268–269
tradeshows
    action plan, 243
    advertising, 237–238
    costs, 232–237
    exhibits
        buying, 236–237
        finding, 236–237
        locations, 235–236
        renting, 236–237
        seminars, 240
        strategies, 238–240
    finding, 229–231
    following up, 241
    marketing, 237–238
    overview, 228–229
    strategies, 231–232, 242–243
training (franchises), 51–52
transaction times (customer service),
    291
travelers (retail stores), 204
triple net fees (retail stores), 22–23
trucks. See vehicles
true stories (customer service),
    291–295
Twitter, 134

U

unfriendly customers, 201
unsuccessful promotions, 117
updating websites, 132–133
urgency (direct mail), 91
utilities (financial crisis), 305–306

V

value (prices), 149–150
vehicles
    advertising, 66, 68–69
    numbers, 36
visitors. See customers
voicemail (telemarketing), 255–256

W

waiting (selling), 174
walls (advertising), 68
wardrobe. *See* **clothing**
websites
   action plan, 137
   advertising, 129–132
   billboards, 67
   blogs, 135–136
   customers
      attracting, 129–132
      building relationships, 130
      charities, 133
   design, 126–127
   email mailing lists, 136–137
   Facebook, 134
   franchises, 44–45
   international sales, 136
   LinkedIn, 135
   marketing, 336
   MySpace, 134
   orders, 131
   overview, 124
   promoting, 129–132
      purpose, 125–126
      resources, 338
      retail stores, 136
      social networks, 133–135
      strategies/tips, 127–128
      Twitter, 134
      updating, 132–133
      YouTube, 134
windows (prices), 153
wish lists, 34–35
words (advertising copy), 60–61
writing
   advertising copy
      headlines, 59–60
      hot words, 60–61
      overview, 58–59
   publicity, 84

Y

Yankee Peddlers, 178
Yellow Pages, 205–206
YouTube, 134